The Wildlife and Countryside Act 1981
The Practitioner's Companion

Barry Denyer-Green LL.M., FRICS,
of Middle Temple, Barrister
Chartered Surveyor

Surveyors Publications
12 Great George Street, London SW1

Published on behalf of
The Royal Institution of Chartered Surveyors
by Surveyors Publications
12 Great George Street, London SW1P 3AD

Printed by Prestige Press (U.K.) Limited, Chesham, Bucks.

ISBN: 0-85406 187 8

PREFACE

Although this 'Practitioners' Companion' has been written for members of the Royal Institution of Chartered Surveyors, I hope that other readers, concerned with agriculture, nature conservation and the countryside, will also find it useful. It consists of an extensive commentary on the Wildlife and Countryside Act 1981, the full text of the Act itself, and appendices containing the Code of Practice for Sites of Special Scientific Importance, model management agreements and the Financial Guidelines for management agreements.

I am very indebted to many knowledgeable people who gave of their time and answered my questions. In particular I thank Alan Vittery of the Nature Conservancy Council, A Morrison, a Director of the Forestry Commission, Ken Jones of ADAS, Ministry of Agriculture, Fisheries and Food, Michael Feist of the Countryside Commission and David Holgate-Pollard of the Department of the Environment. Tom Hooper of Surveyors Publications greatly assisted the task of the author, for which I am grateful. I believe it was an old colleague, Raymond Stedman of Surrey County Council, who suggested I might author this work, I now forgive him! It was an enjoyable and most interesting task.

B.D.G.
February 1983

ACKNOWLEDGEMENTS

Appendix B (SSSI Code of guidance) and Appendix E (Financial guidelines for management agreements) are Crown copyright, and are reproduced with the permission of the Controller of Her Majesty's Stationery Office. Appendix D (Model forms of management agreements) is reproduced with the permission of the Nature Conservancy Council and the Countryside Commission respectively.

CONTENTS

Contents

INTRODUCTION

The Wildlife and Countryside Act is now in force. It consists of three parts. Part I is concerned with the protection of wildlife; it is largely a re-enactment of several earlier statutes with some amendments and additional matters. Part II provides a new code for nature conservation and countryside protection, and Part III makes a number of useful amendments to the laws on public rights of way of particular importance to the countryside.

It is the provisions of Part II that most affect landowners and farmers, and it is here, where the interests of those concerned only with nature conservation and countryside protection are feared to be a threat to people who live and work in the productive sphere of the countryside. The fear is that management judgments may be interfered with, land subjected to conservation blight, and additional controls imposed, which will prevent landowners and farmers from making their own land use decisions. On the other hand, conservationists may argue that it is modern farming practices, sustained by new techniques and public subsidies, that are the real threat to the scientific and recreational importance of the countryside.

The fears of landowners and farmers are largely unfounded in terms of the effectiveness of the legal controls in this Act. The principal tool of both nature conservation and countryside protection is the management agreement. It is voluntarily entered into by owners and occupiers; the incentives are financial payments, and for commonsense solutions shared by all countrymen. These agreements will only be used in those areas of the countryside of exceptional interest or importance.

There are some curious features of the Act which are detailed in the pages that follow. The Code of Guidance on Sites of Special Scientific Importance, and the Financial Guidelines for Management Agreements, set out procedures in relation to those two matters. These documents are not statutory instruments, and apart from their contents which actually coincide with the provisions of the Act itself, they have no more force than the Highway Code. A further point is that whilst the Nature Conservancy Council and local planning authorities may object, in certain circumstances, to the Ministry of Agriculture, Fisheries and Food making a farm capital grant for work harmful to the interests of nature conservation or countryside protection, there is no such right in the Act for these bodies to object to other Ministry grants, or to Forestry Commission grants or felling permissions. These additional grants and felling permissions are partly included in the SSSI Code of Guidance, and partly covered by inter-departmental consultation procedures.

This Act achieved the distinction, when as a Bill proceeding through Parliament, it attracted a record number of amendments. It is to be hoped that the Act will prove less contraversial when in operation, and with commonsense and reasonableness from all parties, will prove a success. Certainly the skills and expertise of chartered surveyors should be in demand.

PART I
PROTECTION OF
WILDLIFE

This Part of the Act provides legal protection for birds, and some animals and plants. It replaces the Protection of Birds Acts 1954-67, and the Conservation of Wild Creatures and Wild Plants Act 1975, with some amendments and additional matters. It prohibits certain methods of killing or taking wild animals; and it restricts the introduction into Great Britain of certain animals and plants.

1.0 PROTECTION OF BIRDS

1.1 Wild Birds May Not be Killed etc.

(Section 1)

This section creates a number of criminal offences in connection with wild birds, their nests and eggs. A wild bird is one which has not been bred in captivity. The criminal offences are subject to certain exceptions, and to certain things that may be done under a licence; these are outlined below. It is an offence to kill, injure or take any wild bird; to take, damage or destroy the nest of any wild bird while that nest is in use or being built; and to take or destroy an egg of any wild bird. It is an offence for any person to have in his possession or control any live or dead wild bird, or any part of one, or anything derived from such a bird, or an egg or part of an egg of a wild bird. Although a wild bird may be in the physical possession of an employee, it might well be within the *control* of the employer who was aware of its existence.

Game Birds

It is, of course, no offence to kill game birds. These are: pheasant, partridge, grouse (or moor game), black (or heath) game, and ptarmigan (section 27). But, certain methods of killing or taking wild birds are prohibited, and these prohibitions (see page 7) also cover game birds.

Special Penalties for Certain Wild Birds

Schedule 1 to the Act contains a list of rare birds which enjoy protection by a special penalty. This is a maximum fine of £1,000 in place of £200 in other cases. Most of the birds in the Schedule (Part I) are protected at all times. The Goldeneye, Pintail, and in Outer Hebrides, Caithness, Sutherland and Wester Ross only, the Greylag Goose, are protected by this special penalty during the close season.

These birds are further protected because it is an offence to intentionally disturb any wild bird in this schedule while it is building a nest, or is in, or near a nest containing eggs or young. It is also an offence to intentionally disturb the dependent young of these birds. A tractor driver who inadvertently disturbs a fieldfare, or, it seems, inevitably disturbs such a bird (which is one of those listed for special protection) in the course of carrying out a lawful activity such as ploughing, commits no offence.

1.2 Wildfowl and other Birds that may be Killed or Taken

The position of game birds has been mentioned. Part I of Schedule 2 to this Act contains a list of wildfowl and other birds that may be killed and taken outside the close season for the bird concerned. The list includes duck, geese, snipe and woodcock; but should be consulted for other species. It is no offence to kill or take these birds, or to injure in the course of attempting to kill during the proper season.

It will remain an offence to kill or take these wild birds on Christmas Day, and in Scotland only, on Sundays. Although, the Secretary of State may make an order, extending the Sunday ban to such parts of England or Wales that he decides (a number of counties are so covered).

The Secretary of State may make an order, defining the close season for any of the listed wild birds. In the absence of any order, the close seasons are:–

1st February to 30th September
Capercaille,
Woodcock (but not in Scotland)
1st February to 11th August
Snipe

21st February to 31st August
Wild duck and wild geese in or over any area below
high-water mark of ordinary spring tides.
1st February to 31st August
all other wild birds in Part I of the Schedule 2,
Woodcock in Scotland,
Wild duck and wild geese elsewhere than below the
high-water mark of ordinary spring tides.

The Secretary of State may also make an order to give
protection to wild birds in Part I of this Schedule during
any period outside the close season, either throughout
Great Britain, or some specified part of it. Such an order
cannot last for longer than 14 days, though successive
orders can be made. The object of this power is to
conserve wildfowl, when, through weather or otherwise,
their numbers are in danger. The Secretary of State may
make a similar order for the wildfowl in Part II of
Schedule 1. Such a ban on shooting will usually be
implemented, following thirteen days of continuous
frost, on the fifteenth such day.

1.3 Areas of Special Protection – Sanctuary Orders

The Secretary of State may make orders for an area of
special protection (section 3). Such an order may protect
wild birds, or any specified wild bird, their nests, eggs and
dependent young at any time, or for a specified time
(during nesting, for example). An order can make it an
offence for any person, who is not authorised, to enter
such an area of special protection. A number of sanctuary
orders have been made in the past: these remain effective.

An order for an area of special protection cannot prevent
those wild birds treated as pests from being killed (see
below), nor can it interfere with any rights of the owner,
lessee or occupier under a licence or agreement.

Before an order is made, the owners and occupiers of the
affected land must receive notice. The Secretary of State
may then make the order when he has the consent of the
owners and occupiers, or they have made no objections
within three months or, if they have objected, the
objections have been withdrawn.

1.4 Circumstances where Birds may be Killed or Taken

The Act specifies a number of circumtances where wild birds may be killed or taken etc., without committing an offence.

Incidental Result of a Lawful Operation

There is one important defence to any prosecution under section 1 or, in the case of areas of special protection, under section 3, where the killing or injuring etc. is the incidental result of doing something lawful: no offence is committed. Crop spraying, ploughing, hedge trimming, even the felling of trees (within the permitted limits), are all lawful: and all may harm wild birds.

Authorised Person

An "authorised person" is a term of some significance. It includes the owner or occupier, or any person authorised by the owner or occupier, of land on which the authorised action takes place; any person authorised by the local authority, the Nature Conservancy Council, a water authority or statutory water undertaker, or a local fisheries committee. Although a person may be authorised by one of these bodies, he may only enter land by consent or under clear statutory authority.

Wild Birds Treated as Pests

Section 2 (2) treats the birds listed in Part II of Schedule 2 as pests. It is not an offence under section 1 or, in areas of special protection, if an "authorised person" kills or takes any of these birds, or destroys the nests or eggs. Such action cannot take place in Scotland on Sundays, or anywhere on Christmas Day.

General Pest Control

An order or requirement of the Ministry of Agriculture, Fisheries and Food under section 98 of the Agriculture Act 1947 must be obeyed even if it means wild birds protected by section 1 or section 3 (areas of special protection) will be killed, injured or taken, or their nests or eggs damaged or destroyed. Such orders or requirements include steps to prevent damage to crops, livestock or foodstuffs caused by pests.

Animal Health

Similarly, an order under section 21 of the Animal Health Act 1981, to destroy wild species including birds in order to prevent the spread of a non-rabies disease among animals is also lawful. But, in complying with any other orders under the Animal Health Act 1981, wild birds listed in Schedule 1 to this Act, their nests and eggs, must not be harmed intentionally. Such orders are wide in scope and enable the Ministry of Agriculture, Fisheries and Food to deal with outbreaks of disease, including rabies and anthrax.

Disabled Birds

It is no offence to take a disabled wild bird to tend and then release. Nor to kill a wild bird which is so disabled that it has no reasonable chance of recovering.

Health, Safety, Disease or Damage

An *authorised* person (see page 6) may kill or injure any wild bird, except those listed in the rare list of Schedule 1, to preserve public health, public or air safety; to prevent the spread of disease; or to prevent serious damage to livestock, crops, growing timber or fisheries.

Licence to Kill or Take etc.

If there are circumstances not covered by the exceptions so far considered, a licence may be obtained from one of several sources to kill or take birds, damage or destroy their nests or eggs. The purposes for which a licence may be obtained are set out in section 16 (1); of these, prevention of serious damage to livestock, foodstuffs for livestock, crops, vegetables, fruit, growing timber or fisheries is important to most farmers and landowners. Application in this case will be to the Ministry of Agriculture, Fisheries and Food.

1.5 Certain Methods of Killing Prohibited

(Section 5)

Articles and Devices

This section prohibits the use of a springe, trap, gin, snare, hook and line, electrical device for killing, stunning or frightening, or any poisonous, poisoned or stupefying substance if any of these are calculated to cause injury to any wild bird. For the purpose of section 5, game birds and birds on the pest list in Schedule 2 are wild birds. There is a good defence if any article of this nature is used for the killing or taking of wild animals that may be lawfully killed or taken in the interests of public health, agriculture, forestry, fisheries or nature conservation, and all reasonable precautions were taken to prevent injury to wild birds.

None of these articles or devices can be used to kill or take any wild bird, nor may any net, baited board, bird-lime (or similar) be used for the purpose.

An authorised person may use a cage-trap or net to take the pest-birds in Part II of Schedule 2; any person may use a wild duck decoy and net which was in use before the Protection of Birds Act 1954; and any person may use a cage-trap or net for game birds taken for the sole purpose of breeding. But a non-hand projected or propelled net is not permitted.

Weapons and Other Aids

The following weapons and aids are prohibited: bow or cross bow; explosive; "automatic or semi-automatic shotgun/with an internal diameter to the barrel at the muzzle of more than 1¾"; target illumination device or device for night shooting; artificial lighting, mirror or dazzle device; gas or smoke; or any chemical wetting agent.

Decoys and Vehicles

Decoys may not be used for the purpose of killing or taking wild birds, nor may a sound recording, or any live bird or animal that is tethered or secured, blinded or maimed or injured. Vehicles may not be used for immediate pursuit of a wild bird it is intended to kill or take.

The Offence

Any offence committed under this section is subject to the special penalty already noted on page 3.

Should be:-
WRONG: AUTOMATIC OR SEMI-AUTOMATIC FIREARM; ANY SHOTGUN WITH AN INTERNAL DIAMETER TO THE BARREL AT THE MUZZLE OF MORE THAN 1¾".

[margin annotation on shotgun line: "any shotgun"]

1.6 **Sale of Wild Birds Prohibited**

(Section 6)

With the exception of the wild birds listed in Part I of Schedule 3 to this Act, it is an offence to offer, sell, advertise or deal in any live wild bird or its eggs. The excepted birds must be ringed and bred in captivity. With the exception of dead feral pigeon and wood pigeon, and the wildfowl and game that are dead between 1st September and 28th February, and listed in Part III of Schedule 3 to this Act, it is an offence for any non-registered person to sell, deal, transport or advertise for sale, any other wild bird. There are other similar offences if any wild bird, not included in Part I of Schedule 3, is shown in a competition.

The special penalty (see page 3) applies if the offence is committed in respect of a wild bird, or egg of a wild bird in the rare list in Schedule 1.

1.7 **Captive Birds**

(Section 7-8)

Birds bred in captivity are not wild birds for the purposes of the earlier provisions of this Act. They, therefore, do not enjoy the same protection against being killed or taken in *section 1*. The measures now described are for the protection of birds bred and kept in captivity.

Registration and Ringing

Section 7 requires that any bird in the list of rare wild birds in Schedule 4 to the Act may only be kept in captivity if registered and ringed. Regulations may be made for this purpose.

Cages and Receptacles

It is an offence to keep a captive bird (wild or otherwise) in any cage or receptacle that is too small to permit the bird to stretch its wings freely (section 8 (1)). This does not apply to poultry, nor if a bird is being transported or held for not more than 72 hours at a show or competition, nor being treated by veterinary surgeon or practitioner.

2.0 PROTECTION OF ANIMALS

(Sections 9-12)

2.1 Offence to Kill, Take or Injure Certain Wild Animals

All wild birds, with specified exceptions, enjoy protection. Not so other animals. Under section 9, only those animals listed in Schedule 5 to this Act are protected. It is an offence to kill, injure or take, with some exceptions, any animal on this list; or to have possession or control of such an animal, dead or alive (section 9 (1)). A few animals are protected under different legislation.

It is also an offence to damage, destroy or obstruct an access to, any structure or place which a Schedule 5 animal uses for shelter or protection, or to disturb such an animal while it is occupying such a structure or place (section 9 (4)). The exceptions to this are considered below.

These two offences do not protect the following Schedule 5 animals:– adder; common frog; viviparous lizard; palmate newt; smooth newt; slow-worm; grass snake; and common toad. But the selling, possessing, dealing, transporting and advertising, for the purpose of sale of all animals in Schedule 5, including these exceptions, is an offence (section 9 (5)).

One important defence is available to a person charged with any of the offences. He is entitled to show that although a wild animal has been killed, injured, taken etc., it was only incidental to some other activity that was perfectly lawful (section 10 (3)). Crop-spraying and other agricultural operations are lawful, and the incidental killing or injuring is not an offence.

2.2 Where No Offence is Committed

Pest Control

The protection in section 9 does not make unlawful any requirement of the Ministry of Agriculture, Fisheries and

Food under section 98 of the Agriculture Act 1947 to take steps to prevent damage to crops, livestock or foodstuffs by pests.

An "authorised person" (see page 6) does not commit an offence by killing or injuring a Schedule 5 animal if this is *immediately* necessary to prevent serious damage to livestock, foodstuffs for livestock, crops, vegetables, fruit, growing timber or any other form of property or to fisheries. Crops may therefore be sprayed, and if this incidently kills any butterflies or any other Schedule 5 animal, no offence is committed (section 10 (4)). It seems that if an "authorised person" foresees that some action ought to be taken to prevent such serious damage, he must first apply for a licence (see below) if Schedule 5 animals are to be killed or injured.

Animal Health

Similarly an order under the Animal Health Act 1981 to destroy wild species, including mammals, to prevent the spread of disease among animals is also lawful (section 10 (1)).

Animals Within Dwelling Houses

It is no offence to damage, destroy or obstruct the access to any structure or nest used by a Schedule 5 animal, or to disturb a Schedule 5 animal occupying such a place, if the structure or nest is within the dwelling house (section 10 (2)). But this exception does not include bats, see below.

Disabled Animals

It is no offence to take a disabled Schedule 5 animal to tend and release it. Nor is it an offence to kill a Schedule 5 animal which is so seriously disabled it has no reasonable chance of recovering (section 10 (3)).

Licence to Kill or Take etc.

As with wild birds, a licence can be obtained for any case not covered above, to kill or take animals in Schedule 5, or to damage or destroy the structures or places where they shelter. The circumstances are set out in section 16 (3). The purposes include the prevention of the spread of disease and the prevention of serious damage to livestock, foodstuffs for livestock, crops, vegetables, fruit, growing timber or any other form of property or to fisheries. Application will be made for these purposes to the Ministry of Agriculture, Fisheries and Food.

2.3 **Bats**

Bats enjoy particular protection. It is an offence to kill, take or disturb bats in the non-living area parts of a dwelling-house, (i.e. in the loft) or in any other place, without first notifying the Nature Conservancy Council. The Council must be allowed reasonable time to give advice (section 10 (5)).

2.4 **Certain methods of killing or taking prohibited**

(Section 11 and Schedule 6)

This section makes it an offence to use any self-locking snare calculated to cause injury to any wild animal; to use a self-locking snare, a bow, cross-bow, or any explosive to kill or take any wild animal; or to use a live animal or bird as a decoy to kill or take any wild animal (section 11(1)).

The section then makes reference to a list of certain wild animals in Schedule 6. The list includes the badger, wild cat, hedgehog and red squirrel, among others, some of the animals being in Schedule 5 (animals protected under section 9 – see above), and some are not in that Schedule at all. It is an offence to use certain devices, such as traps or snares which may injure any Schedule 6 wild animal. It is also an offence to use these or a number of other devices listed in section 11 (2) for the purpose of killing or taking any Schedule 6 wild animal. If traps, snares, electric stunning devices or poison or stupefying substances are being used to kill or take animals in the interests of public health, agriculture, forestry, fisheries or nature conservation, and reasonable precautions are being taken to avoid injury to Schedule 6 animals, no offence is committed. This will usually provide a good defence to the actions of most farmers or foresters.

If a person sets a snare which could cause injury to any animal living wild, he will commit an offence if he does not inspect it a least once every day (section 11 (3)).

2.5 **Amendments to earlier statutes concerned with the protection of mammals**

(Section 12 and Schedule 7)
A number of detailed amendments are made as follows:

Ground Game Act 1880

This Act gives the occupier of land an inseparable right to kill hares and rabbits. It is now amended to allow the occupier, or one other person, and with the written authority of the person entitled to the ground game, to shoot at night.

Dogs (Protection of Livestock) Act 1953

It is now an offence under this Act to allow a dog to be at large (not on a lead or under close control) in a field or enclosure in which there are sheep. This does not apply to the dogs of the occupier or to police, guide, sheep or working gun dogs or a pack of hounds. This should assist the farmer who experiences a lot of sheep-worrying; he can inform culprits of this offence.

Deer Act 1963

This Act establishes a close season for deer; it restricts the methods of killing deer; and it provides exceptions enabling deer to be killed to prevent damage to crops etc. The Act is now amended with restrictions on the use of shotguns and a prohibition on the shooting of deer at night.

Conservation of Seals Act 1970

Licences may now be issued under this Act to cull seals which are damaging important natural habitats. This takes into account the new law on SSSIs and marine nature reserves.

Badgers Act 1973

This prohibited the killing or taking of badgers, but excepted the owner of the land, who was killing badgers to protect crops or livestock. Although an owner or other authorised person may still kill badgers to prevent serious damage to land, crops or livestock, he must now obtain a licence from the Ministry of Agriculture,

Fisheries or Food, except in cases of urgent necessity. The NCC also issue licences to kill or take badgers for scientific or research reasons.

3.0 PROTECTION OF PLANTS

(Section 13)

Schedule 8 wild plants

Schedule 8 to the Act contains a list of rare wild plants that are protected. They may not be intentionally picked, uprooted, or destroyed by any person, including the landowner. There are also offences of selling, dealing, transporting or advertising Schedule 8 plants.

If the damage to any such plant is incidental to some lawful operation, that is a defence to any prosecution. Therefore, the person using a combine harvester, or a hedge-trimmer, that destroys a protected Schedule 8 plant will not be committing an offence. A dilemma has arisen in Yorkshire, the only habitat of one of the Schedule 8 plants, the thistle broomrape. It is a parasite to the creeping thistle which must be destroyed by farmers under the Weeds Act 1959. However no offence will be committed if thistle broomrape is incidentally destroyed in lawfully destroying the creeping thistle.

Other wild plants

Any other wild plant, that is not in Schedule 8, and is growing wild and of a kind which ordinarily grows in Great Britain in a wild state, may not be intentionally uprooted by any person. This does not include the owner or occupier of the land or persons authorised by the owner or occupier.

4.0 PREVENTING THE ESCAPE OF NEW SPECIES OF ANIMALS OR PLANTS

(Section 14)

Animals

Any person responsible for the management of a safari park, private zoo or collection of animals should be aware that this section makes it an offence to release, or allow to escape into the wild any animal which is not ordinarily resident and is not otherwise a regular visitor to Great Britain in the wild state. The same offence covers a list of animals in Part I of Schedule 9 to the Act. Lions obviously fall into the first category, and the Schedule itself includes such animals as coypu, mink, and the familiar grey squirrel.

Plants

It is also an offence to plant or cause to grow in the wild the following plants: giant hogweed, giant kelp, japanese knotweed and japanese seaweed (Part II of Schedule 9). These are plants which are known to be damaging to the existing ecological balance in our waterways.

Reasonable Precautions to be taken

In respect of the escape of animals, and perhaps these plants, it can always happen that an escape results from an accident or the act of some other person. It is a good defence to any charge that the accused person took all reasonable steps and exercised all due diligence to avoid the escape. This must mean proper supervision and systems of security and inspection.

5.0 THE IMPORT AND EXPORT OF ENDANGERED SPECIES

(Section 15 and Schedule 10)

These provisions are of slight interest, unless a person is concerned with the management of a private zoo or collection of animals. They make a number of amendments to the Endangered Species (Import and Export) Act 1976. These include provisions for licences for the import or export of endangered species; a restriction on the import of certain species; and, a prohibition against sales of certain animals and plants. The lists of animals and plants to which there is a restriction on sale are found in Parts II and III of Schedule 10 to the 1981 Act.

6.0 OFFENCES ANĎ PROSECUTIONS

(Sections 17 – 21)

A number of rather technical matters concerning criminal offences and their prosecution are covered by these sections. In outline, it is an`offence to make a false statement to obtain a licence or registration, where such is required; and it is an offence to attempt to commit any of the offences in this Part of the Act.

Section 19 confers a number of powers on the police to stop and search, or to make arrests, in connection with offences under this Act.

Although prosecutions will usually be brought by the police, the local authority also has power to institute proceedings (see section 25 (2)). However, a criminal prosecution can be brought by any person (unless the statute itself prevents this) a possibility which landowners, or indeed conservationists, may wish to consider.

7.0 POWERS AND FUNCTIONS

(Sections 22 - 25)

7.1 Secretary of State's power to vary Schedules

Under section 22, the Secretary of State may make orders to vary the Schedules to the Act that list birds, animals and plants. In particular he may add or remove, either generally, or for a particular area, birds in Schedules 1 to 4. He may also vary the animals and plants, species which may not be introduced into Great Britain, listed in Schedule 9.

His power to vary Schedules 5 and 8 is noted below.

7.2 Function of the Nature Conservancy Council

Section 24 requires the NCC to review, every five years, the list of protected animals in Schedule 5, and protected plants in Schedule 8, and to advise the Secretary of State whether any animal or plant should be added to or removed from these Schedules. The NCC must, in giving any advice, provide a statement of reasons. The Secretary of State may then add to these Schedules any animal or plant which in his opinion is in danger of extinction, or is likely to become so endangered unless conservation measures are taken. He may remove from the list any animal or plant which is no longer in such danger (section 22 (3)). This could mean that if the otter population increased to satisfactory numbers, the otter hunts could seek the removal of otters from Schedule 5.

7.3 Function of local authorities

Not only may local authorities prosecute for any offences under this Part of the Act, but they have a duty to bring to the attention of the public and of school children the effect of the offences, and of orders, under this Act (section 25). Presumably by notices, leaflets etc.

PART II
NATURE
CONSERVATION
AND
COUNTRYSIDE
PROTECTION

It is this Part of the Act which will be of most interest to landowners and their advisers. It contains important changes to the status and effectiveness of sites of special scientific interest — SSSIs. It makes provision for the protection of limestone pavements, and for the creation of marine nature reserves.

There are new provisions for management agreements with landowners for the purposes of nature conservation and the conservation or enhancement of the natural beauty or amenity of the countryside. These agreements may contain financial payments. In National Parks, there is a possibility of restricting certain agricultural operations on moor or heathland.

It must be said at the outset that nature conservation and the protection of the countryside are still very much a matter for landowners and farmers. Activities which many people consider harmful to the interests of conservation, such as wetland drainage, hedge removal, woodland clearance, or afforestation of uplands, are not as such prohibited by this Act. In much of the countryside the Act is irrelevant. Only in the exceptional areas (SSSIs, National Parks and some other special areas) will the Act have application and even here its effectiveness may be limited by the lack of financial resources available to the appropriate bodies, and the fact that landowners are free, in many cases, to reject restrictions proposed by the conservation bodies.

Management agreements, entered into voluntarily by landowners, and containing restrictions on agricultural or forestry operations, are the basic safeguards of nature conservation and countryside protection in this Act. If this Act is to be a success, and management agreements are to be concluded between the parties involved, then a good deal of negotiation will be called for to achieve the terms of these agreements that will be acceptable to both landowners and the conservation and other bodies concerned.

1.0 AREAS OF SPECIAL SCIENTIFIC INTEREST (SSSIs)
(Section 28)

1.1 What is an area of special scientific interest?

Usually referred to as an SSSI (a site of special scientific importance), it is an area of land of special interest by reason of any of its flora, fauna, or geological or physiographical features. There are about 4000 SSSIs in Great Britain covering 6% of the land surface, ranging from a high humidity gorge in Merionnydd to Beachy Head in Sussex. The Nature Conservancy Council (NCC) is responsible for the selection of SSSIs in accordance with published criteria ("The selection of SSSIs"). There is a Code of Guidance on SSSIs which explains the procedures in this Act and additional arrangements to ensure the protection of these areas (see Appendix B). It has been approved by Parliament, but it has no statutory force itself and can be likened to the Highway Code. In many respects the Code goes further than the requirements of the Act. The circumstances where that is so are described in this commentary.

So far as landowners are concerned, the principal features of section 28 are threefold. Firstly, that landowners should now be formally notified of the existence and interest of a SSSI covering their land, and of *potentially damaging operations* to the SSSI. Secondly, landowners are prohibited from carrying out the *potentially damaging operations* without first giving notice to the NCC, so enabling the NCC to consider, and consult about how best to further nature conservation. And finally, in those cases where the NCC object to the carrying out of any of the *potentially damaging operations*, the NCC may, and in certain cases, must, offer the landowner a management agreement which could contain financial recompense in exchange for restrictions to safeguard the interests of the SSSI.

1.2 Notification of SSSI status

SSSIs existing before 30th November 1981:

Notification to owners and occupiers

These will have been notified in the past to the local planning authorities concerned under section 23 of the National Parks and Access to the Countryside Act 1949. Although that provision is now superseded by section 28 of the 1981 Act, the notifications and status of existing SSSIs remain effective. It is required for the first time that landowners should be informed of the existence of the SSSI status of their land (S.28(1)). All owners and occupiers (and there are some 30,000) must be notified of any SSSI that existed before 30th November 1981. The notification must state the flora, fauna, or geological or physiographical features which make the area of special scientific interest, and must specify the operations which are likely to damage those features. (See paragraphs 4 - 5 of the Code - Appendix B).

New SSSIs to be notified after 30th November 1981

Preliminary notice of intention

Before the NCC formally notify an area as a SSSI or an extension to an existing SSSI, it must give preliminary notice of its intention to the local planning authorities, owners and occupiers and the Secretary of State (section 28 (2)).

The preliminary notice of intention must:–

a)   describe the location of the site;

b)   make reference to a map;

c)   state the flora, fauna, or geological or physiographical features which make the area of special scientific interest;

d)   specify the *potentially damaging operations* likely to harm the special features; and

e)   specify a time (at least three months), and arrangements, for the making of representations and objections.

1.3 Potentially damaging operations

In the case of both existing and new SSSIs the NCC are required to prepare one list of *potentially damaging operations* for each SSSI. As an SSSI may affect land in several ownerships, and different types of land, a list common to the whole site will go to each owner and occupier, and may therefore include operations of no relevance to a particular piece of land or owner. The inclusion of an activity as a *potentially damaging operation*, that may not be prohibited in respect of part of a site, is one unfortunate feature of the notification process which may cause unnecessary concern to some landowners.

Unfortunately, the Act has made no provision if the NCC omit a *potentially damaging operation* from the notification, or do not anticipate a particular harm. It cannot later add to the notified list of *potentially damaging operations*. If some new feature of scientific interest emerges, the NCC would then be justified in renotifying the site, and including further *potentially damaging operations*. Otherwise it may only resort to advising the Secretary of State to make a Nature Conservation Order under section 29 (see below) in extreme cases.

Persons notified

The Act does not define "owners and occupiers". The NCC are taking a wide view of "occupier" and will give notice to all tenants, licensees, commoners and crofters who have rights in the land. In the case of commoners and crofters, an appropriate representative committee will be informed in place of each individual.

The Code (paragraph 6) also provides that the Ministry of Agriculture, Fisheries and Food (Agriculture Department in Scotland), Forestry Commission, Water and similar authorities will be informed. These bodies will make their views known to the NCC, formally, as the views of the Secretary of State whose representations and objections the NCC must consider. MAFF, for example, may advise that the SSSI area is larger than necessary to protect the special interests, and will adversely affect agricultural interests too seriously.

Objections to SSSI status

In the case of new SSSIs first notified after 30 November 1981, the NCC "shall consider any representation or objection duly made" (section 28 (2)). Owners and occupiers have no right to make representations or objections where their land was within a SSSI before this date. This means that whereas an objection can be made concerning the list of potentially damaging operations in respect of new SSSIs, that is not possible in the case of the large number of existing SSSIs now for the first time being formally notified to landowners.

Although the NCC may take the view that notification of an area as a SSSI is a statement of scientific fact. It is clear from the words of the Act just quoted that it must act in a quasi-judicial capacity and give full and proper consideration to, for example, the contrary scientific evidence that a landowner may put forward in his objection. The NCC may have to give reasons for the rejection of a representation or objection. It would seem that this process is subject to the rules of natural justice because the consequences of SSSI notification could affect the interests of landowners. Even though the effect of notification is not necessarily to prohibit the *potentially damaging operations*, there may be delay (see below) before a proposed activity can be carried out, and that delay, and the uncertainty it causes, may be deleterious both to landownership and land value. This will doubtless be called conservation blight.

It is not always the case that the boundary of a SSSI follows convenient physical features, it may follow a contour line rather than field boundaries. It would be appropriate for a landowner to represent that a SSSI boundary should not inconveniently cross the corners of fields, etc.

In the case of new SSSIs first notified after 30 November 1981, can the potentially damaging operations be carried out between notice of intention and formal notification?

During this period – whilst objections and representations are being considered, and consultations are undertaken – the area is not a formally notified SSSI or extension to a SSSI. The Code (paragraph 7) directs that owners and occupiers should not, in advance of the NCC's final decision carrying out any of the *potentially damaging operations*. This goes beyond the requirements of section 28, which only puts restrictions on *potentially damaging operations* once an area is finally notified.

It could well be that the special scientific interest of an area becomes more vulnerable if brought to the attention of landowners through the SSSI process: there must always be the temptation for someone, who is unsure and fears he will lose financially, to destroy the special interests.

1.4 Formalities of Final Notification

Following the NCC's consideration of any representations or objections, and the conclusion of consultations with owners, occupiers and the other interested bodies, the area must then be formally notified as a SSSI (section 28 (1)).

Persons notified

As with the preliminary notice of intention, the NCC must formally notify the local planning authority, owners and occupiers, and the Secretary of State.

Form of notification

This will:–

a) describe the location of the site;

b) make reference to a map;

c) state the special scientific features;

d) specify the *potentially damaging operations*; and

e) if appropriate, the reasons for the NCC's conclusions.

These requirements may differ, from those in the preliminary notice of intention, to take into account the conclusions of the NCC following its consideration of objections and representations.

Registration as a local land charge

Each SSSI must be registered as a local land charge by the NCC (section 28(11)). This constitutes notice to any purchaser of the land.

Untraced owners or occupiers

If no owner or occupier can be found, a notification can be fixed to an object on the land (section 28 (3)).

1.5 **What are the consequences of SSSI notification?**

These are briefly summarised:

a) it is an offence for the owner or occupier to carry out any of the *potentially damaging operations* (for exceptions see page 25) specified in the original notification unless written notice of the proposed work is given to the NCC and:–

   (i) the NCC give consent; or
   (ii) the work is done in accordance with a management agreement; or
   (iii) three months have elapsed from the notice (see further below).

(b) before giving planning permission for any development affecting a SSSI, the local planning authority must consult the NCC (see D.O.E. Circular 108/77 – "Nature Conservation and Planning")

(c) the public do not have any right of access just because an area is a SSSI; they are confined to any public footpaths or bridleways although, if the area is open country, and this can include woodland, rivers and other waters, the local planning authority may offer to make an access agreement, or make a compulsory access order, under Part V of the National Parks and Access to the Countryside Act 1949, and sections 16-21 of the Countryside Act 1968.

(d) the NCC may offer to make a management agreement with the owner, under section 15 of the Countryside Act 1968; or the owner may seek such an agreement (see further below)

(e) there may be a capital transfer tax concesssion where land is, in the opinion of the Treasury, of outstanding scientific interest (see section 34, Finance Act 1975 and "Capital taxation and the National Heritage" – H.M. Treasurey); there are also capital gains tax concessions for sales to approved bodies.

1.6 **What must an owner do if he proposes carrying out any operations listed in the SSSI notification?**

Remember, it is an offence to carry out any of the operations listed in the SSSI notification without reasonable excuse, consent of the NCC, or until three months have elapsed from giving notice of intention to do the work. A model notice is at Appendix A.

The proposal needs planning permission

If a proposal requires planning permission, e.g. to erect buildings or carry out engineering operations, and that planning permission is granted following an application to the local planning authority, then the owner or occupier has a reasonable excuse to carry out the notified operations without reference to the NCC: it is no offence. The reason for this is that the local planning authority will have consulted the NCC about the planning application.

The proposal is development but permission is granted by the General Development Order.

The General Development Order grants planning permission for a number of classes of development, e.g. erection of agricultural or forestry buildings, within limits. In this case the owner or occupier must serve notice of his proposal on the NCC (see below).

Emergency operations

It is a reasonable excuse to carry out any notified operation which is an emergency and the NCC is informed as soon as reasonable practicable after the event (section 28 (8)). For example, felling a dangerous tree, where felling is notified as a *potentially damaging operation*.

The land is already subject to a SSSI or NNR management agreement

The land included in a SSSI may already be the subject of a SSSI management agreement with the NCC under section 15 of the Countryside Act 1968; or, if it is coincidentally a National Nature Reserve, a NNR management agreement under section 16 of the National Parks and Access to the Countryside Act 1949. If the terms of such a management agreement permit work to be carried out, it will be no offence to carry out any operation in accordance with those terms. A management agreement may itself require that the NCC be informed before certain work is done.

In all other cases, the owner or occupier must send written notice of his proposals, its nature and location to the NCC (addresses at Appendix C). If the NCC grant consent to the operations proposed, the work may proceed. If the owner or occupier who sent notice of a proposal to carry out a notified operation, hears nothing from the NCC within three months of his notice, he may also proceed with the work. It would seem advisable to send these written notices by recorded delivery.

1.7 How does the NCC deal with a notice of intention to carry out notified operations?

The Code of Guidance (see Appendix B) sets out the steps the NCC should take upon receiving a notice from an owner or occupier that a notified potentially damaging operation is proposed. The NCC is expected to respond within one month of the notice. It can grant consent to the work; the notified operation may then be carried out. Alternatively, it may explain to the owner or occupier that the work should not be carried out at all, or it should be modified in some way. The further action that the NCC may take is as follows:

1.8 The NCC may offer a SSSI or (NNR) management agreement

The NCC may offer to enter into a management agreement. This will contain terms to protect the SSSI; it may provide that work be carried out, and whether the NCC or the owner, occupier or lessee is to pay the cost, or how it is to be shared. The agreement may also include an obligation on the NCC to make financial payments to the owner and or occupier. A specimen SSSI agreement is at Appendix D. The financial provisions are explained on page 51 below, together with the right to refer disputed terms of an agreement to arbitration.

The owner or occupier offered a management agreement

is fully entitled to refuse to sign such an agreement. He may wait until three months have elapsed since he first gave notice of his intention to carry out notified operations; he is then free to proceed with those operations.

1.9 The NCC may object to a farm capital grant

Farm capital grants are made under section 29 of the Agriculture Act 1970. The present grant is known as the Investment Grant; it is detailed in the Agriculture and Horticulture Grant Scheme 1980 and described in the Ministry of Agriculture, Fisheries and Food (MAFF) Explanatory Leaflet AHS2.

There is also the Development Grant from the E.E.C., detailed in the Agriculture and Horticulture Development Scheme 1980, and described in MAFF Explanatory Leaflet AHS 5.

If an owner or occupier has applied to the Ministry for an Investment Grant in respect of work on land within a SSSI, MAFF must consider the conservation of those features that give the land its special scientific interest in deciding whether to approve the grant (section 32 (1)). The NCC may object to the making of an Investment Grant if the proposed work will destroy or damage (or in cases where the work has already been done, has destroyed or damaged) the special features of the SSSI. If, as a result of NCC objection, MAFF refuse a grant, the NCC will, as described below, be obliged to offer a management agreement to the owner or occupier concerned.

There is no right in the Act to enable the NCC to formally object to the making of a Development Grant; neither, if MAFF refuse to make a Development Grant on conservation grounds, is there any obligation on the NCC to offer a management agreement. But as the NCC will always be informed of proposed damaging operations to a SSSI, and will state its views in any consultation process, it is understood that whenever a Development Grant is refused on conservation grounds, the NCC will offer a management agreement.

The SSSI Code of Guidance speaks of farm capital grants. This is a generic term, and does of course now mean the Investment Grant. It is unfortunate that common terminology cannot be used in publications intended for the general public use.

In cases where the NCC makes an objection to an Investment Grant, paragraph 17 of the Code of Guidance (see Appendix B) requires the Ministry of Agriculture's Agricultural Development and Advisory Service (ADAS) to give advice and seek modifications of the proposed work which will be acceptable to both the grant applicant and the NCC. If no modifications can be agreed, and the NCC maintain its objection, the NCC will provide a detailed statement of its conservation case, and ADAS will prepare a feasibility of the agricultural proposals.

The NCC may wish to sustain its objection to the making of the grant, on the grounds set out in its detailed statement, because it believes the proposed activities will damage the special flora or fauna interests. It must so inform the applicant and ADAS within three months of the original notice of intention sent to it by the owner or occupier in which the proposed notifiable operations were stated.

It is important to realise that under the Agriculture and Horticulture Grant Scheme 1980, whilst prior approval is not required for eligible work for an Investment Grant in the normal case, there is a special procedure where the land concerned is in a National Nature Reserve or a SSSI. This is set out in Appendix 7 of the MAFF Explanatory Leaflet for Investment Grants - AHS 2 (1982). The grant applicant must also comply with the requirements of the Wildlife and Countryside Act 1981 if his proposals are notifiable operations (see above).

The MAFF leaflet says that the grant applicant must consult with the NCC *before* starting work, and is required to sign a declaration when claiming grant that he has done so. The SSSI Code of Guidance (paragraph 17 (d)) warns that the grant may be refused by the Minister if work is carried out before the grant application is decided. The MAFF Leaflet says that if the work is undertaken before the Minister's decision (where it is otherwise lawful to do so), the grant will be at risk as the Minister's decision will be based on the situation prior to the work commencing.

The MAFF Leaflet still being issued in early 1983 was seriously at variance with the SSSI protection procedure in the 1981 Act. Under the SSSI protection procedures, it will be recalled that notifiable potentially damaging operations cannot be carried out unless, agreed in writing by the NCC, or under the terms of a management agreement, or three months have elapsed since the owner or occupier gave written notice of intention to the NCC specifying the proposed work. The MAFF Leaflet says in Appendix 7 that the work may go ahead if the NCC do not reply to the landowner's consultation request within one month, or the NCC give no reasons for its objections within two months. The MAFF Leaflet should make it clear that the provisions of the Wildlife and Countryside Act 1981 must also be complied with. It is understood that MAFF intend to re-issue this Leaflet to take into account the provisions of the Act and Code of Guidance.

If the grant application is approved, the applicant may then carry out the work if three months have elapsed since he gave notice of his intention to carry out the notified operations to the NCC or earlier if the NCC give its consent.

If the grant application is refused by the Ministry on *nature conservation grounds*, the applicant and the NCC will be informed and the NCC must, within three months of the grant refusal, offer to the applicant a SSSI (or NNR) management agreement; this agreement may impose restrictions to conserve the special interests of the SSSI and contain financial payments to the applicant (see above). The applicant is not obliged to enter into such an agreement, and he is entitled to carry out his proposals as soon as three months have elapsed from his original notice to the NCC. It is suggested by this author that an owner should defer any earlier offers of a management agreement until his grant application is determined.

1.10 The NCC may offer to lease or purchase the land

If the NCC objects to the carrying out of the potentially damaging operations following written notice by an owner or occupier, it may offer to lease or purchase the land concerned. The NCC can only use compulsory powers of acquisition if it is unable to conclude a management agreement, and it considers the land should be acquired *in the national interest* as a national nature reserve (section 17 of the National Parks and Access to the Countryside Act 1949).

1.11 SSSIs and Forestry Operations

Forestry operations, such as planting or felling, may be notified to an owner or occupier of land in a SSSI, as potentially damaging operations. It will then be necessary for the person concerned to serve written notice to the NCC, if he proposes carrying out any notified potentially damaging operations, as described above at page 24.

Whereas the Act enables the NCC to formally object to the making of a farm capital grant for work that has damaged, or may damage, the special interests of a site, there is no equivalent right to the NCC in cases where a landowner applies under the Forestry Grant Scheme for a planting grant, or is given felling permission, by a felling licence, or under an approved plan of operations in respect of work that is a notified potentially damaging operation. This omission in the Act is met by paragraph 18 of the Code of Guidance.

The Code provides that if a person applies for a forestry grant (this must mean an application to join the Forestry Grant Scheme – Form FGS1) or a felling permission for work that is a notified potentially damaging operation, the Forestry Commission will consult with the NCC, and with the applicant. If no agreement about the proposals can be reached, and the NCC persists in its objection to the work, the Forestry Commission will consult with the Minister responsible for forestry (Ministry of Agriculture, Fisheries and Food, in England; appropriate Secretaries of State, in Scotland and Wales). Following the advice of the Minister the Forestry Commission will decide whether the grant or felling permission is to be refused on *nature conservation grounds*.

As the Act of 1981 does not provide for the Forestry Commission refusing a grant or felling permission, and the Code of Guidance is not a document with any legislative effect, the legality of the Commission making such a refusal on nature conservation grounds is doubtful. It is suggested that the Commission can only refuse a grant or felling permission on grounds that are valid for the purposes of the Forestry Grant Scheme or under the arrangements for felling permissions.

If the Forestry Commission do refuse a grant or felling permission on nature conservation grounds, the Code provides that the NCC will *normally* offer the applicant a management agreement within three months of the decision. It would be unfortunate if the NCC did not in *all cases* offer such an agreement. The agreement may contain restrictions and financial provisions; the applicant is not obliged to sign, and once three months have elapsed from his original notice to the NCC, he is free to proceed with his proposals, except where the work remains unlawful in the absence of a felling permission.

1.12 **What about the meaning of a potentially damaging operation?**
One problem could well occur in the future. An owner has received a notification that some or all of his land is a SSSI and a list of potentially damaging operations harmful to the SSSI. If the owner is proposing to carry out an activity which is only doubtfully such a notified operation; or, his proposed activity is not itself a notified operation but some incidental result of his proposal will cause harm of the type prohibited, what is he to do?

The Code of Guidance recommends that an owner should always consult the NCC (paragraphs 22-24), but there seems no procedure for resolving any difference as to whether a proposal is in fact a notified operation.

2.0 **SPECIAL PROTECTION FOR CERTAIN AREAS OF SPECIAL SCIENTIFIC INTEREST**
(Section 29)

2.1 **Secretary of State has power to make a Nature Conservation Order**

If land is of special interest by reason of its flora, fauna, or geological or physiographical features, the Secretary of State make a Nature Conservation Order for the following purposes:

(a) to ensure the survival in Great Britain of any kind of animal or plant; or

(b) to comply with an international obligation; or

(c) where the land is of national importance, to ensure the conservation of any of its flora, fauna, or geological or physiographical features.

Although it would not seem essential for the land to have been already notified as a SSSI that is almost certainly to have been the case.

Because Nature Conservation Orders come into effect immediately, they could be used for the urgent protection of an important area pending the formal notification as a SSSI.

Nature Conservation Orders are intended for those areas of exceptional interest, nationally and sometimes internationally. It has been suggested that upto forty such areas may initially be considered.

The first order was made in October 1982 in respect of Baddesley Common, Hampshire, an area its new owner wanted to reclaim for farming. The order prohibits ploughing, seeding, use of fertilisers and pesticides, discharge of waste, drainage and soil disturbance, removal of trees or plants and the introduction of new species. Baddesley Common is said to be one of the few remaining ungrazed valley bogs in the lowlands of England outside the New Forest.

2.2 The consequences of a Nature Conservation Order

Potentially damaging operations

The order will specify operations which the Secretary of State considers will be likely to damage or destroy the special interests of the land. It is then an offence for the owner, occupier or *any other person* (only owners or occupiers are made liable in SSSIs) to carry out any specified operation unless written notice is given to the NCC and:–

a) the NCC give consent, or,

b)   the work is done in accordance with a management agreement; or

c)   three months have elapsed from the notice of intention *(but this period can be extended)*

It should be noted, that the period of three months, from the landowner's notice of intention to carry out specified potentially damaging operations, and during which it would be an offence to do such work, can be extended in the case of Nature Conservation Orders. This period cannot be extended under ordinary SSSI protection.

As with SSSIs, no offence is committed if a specified potentially damaging operation is carried out with planning permission granted following an application, or is done in an emergency and particulars are reported to the NCC as soon as practicable (section 29 (9)).

The NCC may object to a farm capital grant

The arrangements for dealing with the right of the NCC to object to a farm capital grant, and its obligation to offer a management agreement, are just the same as those in respect of SSSIs (see page 27).

Conservation options

The NCC may offer to make a management agreement (as in a SSSI), to purchase the land, or in proper cases, to use powers of compulsory purchase. If any of these responses are made to a landowner's notice of intention to carry out specified potentially damaging operations, the three month period, during which it is an offence to carry out such operations, is then extended.

Compensation

The owner or lessee may be entitled to compensation.

Restoration

If an offence has been committed, a court may order the restoration of the land.

These matters are more fully considered below.

2.3 How is a Nature Conservation Order made?

Notice

A Nature Conservation Order will usually be made following a request by the NCC to the Secretary of State. A notice, that an Order has been made, must be published in a local newspaper, and served on every owner and occupier of the affected land (see Schedule 11). If an owner or occupier cannot be traced, the notice may be affixed to the land. The notice will state the effect of a Nature Conservation Order, where it may be inspected, and how representations or objections to it may be made. At least 28 days must be allowed for making representations or objections. An order takes effect immediately on being made.

Representations and objections

Whilst any person may make a representation or objection, the owner or occupier should scrutinize the Order carefully paying particular attention to the prohibited operations. If the prohibited operations are going to interfere with his use of the land, he should prepare and send a letter listing the prohibitions to which he objects, and *in each case,* giving a full justification for his objection. If representations or objections are not withdrawn, the Secretary of State will appoint an inspector to hold a public local inquiry, or otherwise to hear the objector. The objector should ensure that the NCC representative is present, and that he obtains beforehand the NCC case for a Nature Conservation Order.

The Secretary of State's decision

Upon receiving his inspector's report, the Secretary of State may decide whether the Order is to remain in effect, be amended or be revoked. If he makes no decision within nine months, the Order ceases to have effect. Notice is again served on all owners and occupiers.

2.4 What must an owner do if he proposes carrying out any operation prohibited by a Nature Conservation Order?

Because land in a Nature Conservation Order will also invariably be a notified SSSI, the advice already given on page 24 above in relation to SSSIs will apply. In particular, written notice must be sent to the NCC before prohibited operations are carried out (it seems advisable to use recorded delivery). This is unnecessary if planning permission has been granted upon application to the local planning authority. Although the local authority are required to consult the NCC about any application affecting a SSSI, it seems that objections made by the NCC will be only one matter the local planning authority will consider in making a decision on *planning merits*. The effectiveness of a Nature Conservation Order can therefore be lost if development is allowed under a grant of planning permission following an application.

2.5 The powers of the NCC in a Nature Conservation Order area

If an area, covered by a Nature Conservation Order, is also a SSSI, the NCC can deal with any notice of intention to carry out prohibited operations as described on page 26 above (e.g. offer a management agreement, object to a farm capital grant, offer to lease or buy the land, or grant consent to the work).

Management agreements

In the case of a Nature Conservation Order, the three month period following the owner or occupier's notice to do prohibited operations, and during which no such work can be done, can be extended. If the NCC offer a management agreement containing provisions for financial payments during the initial three month period, and that agreement is not concluded within that period, none of the prohibited operations may be carried out during an extended period of twelve months from the original Notice of intention to do work.

If a management agreement is signed by the parties during the extended period of twelve months, the prohibited operations may then only be carried out, if permitted at all, in accordance with the terms of the agreement.

However, if a management agreement is rejected by the owner or occupier, or the NCC withdraws its offer of an agreement, the period during which the prohibited operations may not be carried out continues until a date twelve months from the original notice to do work, or to a date three months from the rejection or withdrawal, whichever is the later date. This gives the NCC time to consider compulsory purchase (see below) (section 29 (6)).

An owner or occupier of land covered by a Nature Conservation Order is under some pressure to conclude a management agreement (it must include financial payments) if he wishes to avoid the possibility of compulsory purchase.

Purchase by the NCC

During the initial three month period, the NCC may offer to purchase the legal interest in the land held by the person who gave notice of intention to do prohibited works. If that is the case, the three month period is extended to twelve months as with an offer of a management agreement (section 29 (6)).

The NCC must then either agree terms for the purchase of the land within the extended twelve months, or it should make an order for the compulsory acquisition of the land. The NCC can only use powers of compulsory purchase if it is unable to conclude a reasonable management agreement under section 16 of the National Parks and Access to the Countryside Act 1949.

If the NCC do decide to make a compulsory purchase order, the prohibition against carrying out the operations that are regarded as damaging remains in force until the date the NCC obtain possession of the land under the compulsory purchase order, or if the order is withdrawn, the date of withdrawal or, if the Secretary of State decides not to confirm the order, the date of his decision.

2.6 **Compensation and Nature Conservation Orders**

(Section 30)

An owner of an interest in land affected by a Nature Conservation Order may obtain compensation in the following circumstances:

Depreciation in value of farmland

When a Nature Conservation Order is finally made or confirmed, an owner of an interest in the affected land is entitled to claim compensation from the NCC for the depreciation in value of land due to the Order. Only land which is part of an agriculture unit is eligible. The rules for the assessment of compensation in section 5 of the Land Compensation Act 1961 apply, and appeal is to the Lands Tribunal (section 30(2)(4)(5) and (6)). Compensation must be claimed within six months of the Secretary of State's notice of the order or his confirmation.

Expenses, loss or damage due to an extended period of prohibition

Where a Nature Conservation Order has been made, and the owner or occupier has given notice of intention to carry out prohibited operations, the period during which he may not proceed with those operations can be extended, as described above, to twelve months or longer. The owner of any interest in the land (not just farm land), can then claim compensation for any expenditure which is rendered abortive or for any loss or damage due to that extended period of prohibition (section 30 (3)). For example, if the effect of the extended period, during which he cannot carry out the prohibited operations, means that the owner loses profit on a crop, or the sale of timber, he can be compensated. Compensation must be claimed within six months of the expiration of the extended period.

Compensation claims

The Wildlife and Countryside (Claim for Compensation under section 30) Regulations 1982 (SI 1346) provide the time limits mentioned above, and stipulate that claims must be addressed to the offices of the NCC.

Under a management agreement

If a management agreement is concluded between the

NCC and the owner or occupier, that agreement must contain compensation terms if the land is in a Nature Conservation Order. Management agreements are described in Appendix D; the financial provisions are discussed at page 51 below.

2.7 Nature Conservation Orders and restoration

(Section 31)

If an owner or occupier carries out any of the prohibited operations contrary to the 1981 Act, he may be prosecuted. And, if he has destroyed or damaged any of the features of special interest, the court can make a restoration order requiring the land to be restored to its previous condition. There is a substantial penalty of £1,000 maximum and up to £100 per day if a restoration order is not complied with.

2.8 Conclusions

Unless an owner desires to rid himself of land covered by a Nature Conservation Order, it would seem in his interest to conclude a management agreement with the NCC containing the most satisfactory financial terms obtainable. For further advice – see the Code of Guidance, paragraphs 34-41 (Appendix B).

3.0 LIMESTONE PAVEMENT ORDERS

(Section 34)

There are about 5,000 acres of limestone pavements in Great Britain. They are said to be features of great beauty and botanical and geological interest. This section gives power to the Secretary of State or the county planning authority to make an order for the protection of these pavements. The NCC and the Countryside Commission will notify the local planning authority of the existence of these features. The making of an order allows for an inquiry into any objections (schedule 11).

It will be an offence to remove or disturb any limestone in land covered by a limestone pavement order unless planning permission is first obatined following an application to the local planning authority. Section 34 gives protection to limestone pavements in perpetuity, and without any compensation. There are no exclusions for the benefit of agriculture.

4.0 NATIONAL NATURE RESERVES

(Section 35)

This section simply gives statutory recognition to the term "National" in relation to nature reserves considered by the NCC to be of national importance. Any such reserve managed under an agreement with the NCC, or, owned and managed by the NCC, or owned and managed by a body such as a local authority, may be declared by the NCC as a national nature reserve (NNR). If a local authority applies to the NCC to have any nature reserve declared a national nature reserve, the NCC may then make byelaws for the protection of the reserve. NNRs will now usually be notified as a SSSI because this will give the area the protection afforded by section 28, as well as the advantages of the NNR protection in the National Parks and Access to the Countryside Act 1949. Under the 1949 Act, byelaws can be made for the protection of a NNR, and, if a management agreement is refused by the owner or occupier, the NCC may then exercise powers of compulsory purchase.

Section 72 of the 1981 Act amends The Countryside Act 1968: SSSI management agreements can now be made in respect of NNRs.

5.0 MARINE NATURE RESERVES

(Sections 36-37)

MNRs are a new concept. The NCC may advise the Secretary of State to designate any area of sea or tidal water, and the land so covered, as a MNR for the purpose of conserving marine flora or fauna or geological or physiographical features of special interest, or for suitable conditions for the study and research of those interests.

A MNR may extend from the seaward limit of territorial water up to the highwater mark. It may also include the tidal parts of rivers and estuaries. Although such areas are prima facie vested in the Crown, other persons may have established rights by custom or otherwise. The NCC may mark the extent of a MNR by buoys or suitable markers.

The main object of MNR status is to enable the NCC to make byelaws for the proper protection of the special interests. These may restrict the entry into the area of persons or vessels, acts damaging to animals or plants, and the deposit of rubbish. The byelaws cannot restrict non-pleasure boats, and can only restrict pleasure boats during particular times of the year to particular parts of the MNR. It would seem that section 37 authorises byelaws which may interfere with the public right to fish in tidal waters.

6.0 NATURE CONSERVANCY COUNCIL MAY MAKE GRANTS AND LOANS

(Section 38)

This section gives the NCC a general power (with the Secretary of State's consent) to give financial assistance by grants or loans to any person furthering nature conservation or its understanding.

Although funds are likely to be limited, this could be a source of financial assistance to the landowner or local authority incurring expenditure on nature conservation or in providing facilities to enable the public to visit areas of conservation interest.

7.0 COUNTRYSIDE MANAGEMENT AGREEMENTS
(Section 39)

This section enables a local planning authority (in a National Park, the county planning authority) to make a management agreement with any person with an interest in land. The purpose of such an agreement is the conservation or enhancement of the natural beauty or amenity of land in the countryside or the promotion of public enjoyment of such land.

There are no powers to compel owners to make management agreements. But they may be persuaded to do so because of the financial inducements contained in the agreement, or because the Ministry of Agriculture, Fisheries and Food has refused to make a grant under the farm capital grants scheme (see below), or because of their own genuine interest and concern about the countryside. The power of the local planning authority to object to a farm capital grant, and its consequential obligation to offer a management agreement is likely to be the most usual initiative for these agreements.

7.1 Duration of Management Agreements

The management agreement may last for an agreed period of time, or it may be agreed that it shall continue without any such limitation (section 39 (1)). It is suggested that an owner should not tie up his land for too long a period, as it is always difficult to anticipate future events (need to sell, death, change in farm produce prices etc.) If a management agreement is made for a twenty year period, the owner should seek a break-clause at, say, five year intervals.

7.2 Contents of Management Agreements

A management agreement may contain the following matters (section 39 (2)):

a) restrictions on the use of certain methods of cultivation, e.g. no ploughing of downland;

b) restrictions on the use of land for agricultural purposes, e.g. areas of woodland shall not be cleared for conversion to agricultural land;

c) restrictions on the exercise of rights over the land, e.g. no shooting;

d) obligations on the owner or occupier to carry out certain works or agricultural or forestry operations, e.g. planting of broad-leaved trees;

e) permission for the local planning authority to enter to carry out works to fulfil any of their functions under the National Parks and Access to the Countryside Act 1949 or the Countryside Act 1968, e.g.

provision of camping and picnic sites (but an owner should consider the financial implications and compensation before agreeing to such a term);

f) any other incidental and consequential provisions, particularly for financial payments by the local planning authority to the owner or vice-versa.

A draft of an hypothetical management agreement, with comments is found at Appendix D.

The financial provisions of management agreements are separately considered at page 51 below.

7.3 Who is bound by a Management Agreement?

Only a person with an interest in land, i.e. as a freeholder or lessee, will be a party to a management agreement. The person who signs binds himself and those deriving title under or from him. If, therefore, an owner-occupier signs, he is bound, any tenant or lessee to whom he grants a lease *after the date of the agreement* is bound, and so is any person who purchases the land. But if the land is already the subject of a tenancy, the landlord cannot sign a management agreement which will bind any existing tenant, nor can a tenant sign to bind his landlord, or any future tenant under a new tenancy (section 39 (3)).

It could well be that an agricultural tenant is offered a management agreement because an application by him for a farm capital grant has been refused following an objection by the local planning authority. The landlord should also be involved, and insist upon a complementary agreement containing financial compensation to reflect any deleterious effect on rental values which might be induced by management agreement restrictions.

A tenant for life is authorised by this section to sign a management agreement binding on the land (section 39 (4)).

7.4 The enforcement of Management Agreements

A management agreement is a deed; it contains undertakings by either party which are called covenants. A breach of covenant by one party enables the other to bring an action for damages and or for an injunction to restrain that breach. The Financial Guidelines for management agreements (see Appendix E) suggest at paragraph 43 that an agreement should contain provisions enabling the local planning authority to recover any compensation already paid in the case of lump sum payments, or to cease further payments in the case of annual payments, if the agreement is breached by deliberate action of the owner or occupier. It also suggests at paragraph 44 that if an agreement is breached by a third party (e.g. a statutory undertaker); the agreement should contain provisions which would allow the local planning authority to exercise a discretion to stop paying any further compensation, and to recover from the owner a proportion of any capital sum already paid which is attributable to the unexpired terms of the agreement.

7.5 Modifying the terms of a Management Agreement

A management agreement can only be modified in a manner provided by its terms (if any) or by a further agreement in substitution for the first. Unlike planning agreements under section 52 of the Town and Country Planning Act 1971, which are enforceable as if they were restrictive covenants, a management agreement cannot be modified by the Lands Tribunal in the way it has power to modify planning agreements.

7.6 Related and other powers of local planning authorities

Attention is drawn to other powers of local planning authorities which may be relevant in the context of management agreements.

Planning agreements

These are made between a local planning authority and a person with an interest in land for the purpose of restricting or regulating the development or use of land (section 52 of the Town and Country Planning Act 1971). There is precedent for their use in countryside protection. The landowner should expect some planning advantage as an inducement.

Access agreements

These agreements, made between owner and a local planning authority, are to enable the public to have access for open-air recreation to *open country* (Part V of the National Parks and Access to the Countryside Act 1949 and sections 16-21 of the Countryside Act 1968). The definition of open country includes mountain, moor, heath, down, cliff, foreshore, woodlands and any river or canal, or water through which a river or canal flows. Owners may receive financial payments under an access agreement, bye-laws may be made, and wardens employed by the local planning authority to supervise and regulate the public.

8.0 AGRICULTURE AND THE COUNTRYSIDE
(Section 41)

8.1 General Duties

Section 11 of the Countryside Act 1968 places a duty on every Minister, government department and public body to "have regard to the desirability of conserving the natural beauty and amenity of the countryside", when exercising their powers under any enactment. Section 37 of the same Act (as amended by the 1981 Act) places a further duty on every Minister, the Countryside Commission, the NCC and local authorities "to have due regard to the needs of agriculture and forestry and to the economic and social interests of rural areas" when exercising their functions under the Acts of 1968 and 1981.

Although these are legislative expressions of intention to satisfy lobby pressure, they can have only slight legal consequence. Attention must turn to more specific matters.

8.2 Ministry of Agriculture to supply free advice

The Ministry must give free advice (section 41 (1)) to:

a) farmers, on the conservation and enhancement of the natural beauty and amenity of the countryside;

b) farmers, on the diversification into other enterprises of benefit to the rural economy; and

c) government departments and other bodies concerned with diversification into other enterprises.

8.3 Farm capital grants and the countryside

If an owner or occupier of land applies to the Ministry of Agriculture, Fisheries and Food for a farm capital grant towards work on land in a National Park or in *an area specified* under section 41 (3) of this Act, the Ministry must consider the countryside as well as the purpose of the farm capital grant scheme. In considering the countryside, it must exercise its functions to further the conservation and enhancement of the natural beauty and amenity of the countryside and the promotion of its enjoyment by the public.

8.4 The local planning authority may object to a farm capital grant

Where an application is made for a farm capital grant for work on land in a National Park, or in *an area specified* under section 41 (3), the local planning authority can object to the making of the grant on the ground that the activities proposed will have an adverse effect on the natural beauty or amenity of the countryside or its enjoyment by the public. A local planning authority has no right to object to any other type of grant than the farm capital grant at present known as the investment grant.

If an objection is made, the Ministry will not make a grant until it has considered the objections, and, in England, consulted the Secretary of State.

8.5 The local planning authority must offer a Management Agreement

Following an objection by the local planning authority, the Ministry may decide to refuse a farm capital grant on *countryside conservation grounds*. The local planning authority *must*, within three months of the Ministry's decision, offer to make a management agreement with the person who applied for the grant. The offer must include a draft agreement which imposes restrictions on the activities for which the farm capital grant was refused, and terms for financial payments to be made to the applicant. The financial terms are considered below at page 51.

The applicant is not obliged to enter into a management agreement. Indeed, until he signs such an agreement, he is still free to carry out the work to which the local planning authority object, though he will lose his farm capital grant.

8.6 Financial terms may be arbitrated

If the applicant dislikes the financial terms of the draft management agreement, he may require, within one month of receiving the offer, that those terms be determined by arbitration (section 50 (2)). If the arbitrator determines amounts higher than those offered by the local planning authority, it must amend the terms of its draft agreement to give effect to the arbitrators award.

8.7 Summary

The arrangements just described can be summarised:

applicant applies for farm capital grant for work in a National Park or *specified area*;

MAFF invite comments from LPA;

LPA may object on countryside conservation grounds;

MAFF consider objections, and may consult DOE;

MAFF either make grant or refuse it;

If MAFF refuse on countryside conservation grounds, LPA must offer management agreement within three months;

Applicant can request arbitration within one month;

Arbitrator makes his award, and LPA amend if higher than amounts in draft.

All this seems to add up to some very considerable delay.

9.0 FORESTRY AND THE COUNTRYSIDE

It should be noted that the interests of forestry are not specifically affected by this Act in relation to the protection of the countryside. Unlike section 41 (3), which enables local planning authorities to object to the making of a farm capital grant, there is no equivalent power to enable objections to be made to forestry grants or felling permissions, in the National Parks or *specified areas*.

In relation to SSSIs, the Act also omitted any reference to the right of the NCC to object to forestry grants or felling permissions, but that omission was met by the inclusion of the Forestry Commission within the scope of the Code of Guidance. In the case of countryside protection, the national park and local planning authorities can only rely on the usual consultation procedures with the Forestry Commission.

10.0 NATIONAL PARKS

(Sections 42-46)

10.1 Ploughing up or conversion of moor or heath land

Section 42 replaces section 14 of the Countryside Act 1968. It provides that the Minister of Agriculture, Fisheries and Food and the Secretary of State for the Environment may together make an order to protect moor or heath land in the area of a National Park.

If an order is made, it will then be an offence, subject as discussed below, if any person ploughs up or converts into agricultural land any land covered by the order and which has not been agricultural land within the preceding 20 years. The order may also prohibit certain specified agricultural or forestry operations which may affect the character or appearance of the moor or heath (i.e. drainage or afforestation).

Owner or occupier is proposing to plough or convert moor or heath land

Any person intending to carry out ploughing or any other activity prohibited by the order must give written notice to the county planning authority with full details.

Powers of the county planning authority

The authority, when informed of a proposal to plough up etc., must in turn inform the Minister of Agriculture, the Secretary of State, the Nature Conservancy Council and the Countryside Commission.

The authority may give its consent to the proposed operation, which may then proceed. If it makes no decision either way within three months of the owner or occupier's original notice, the work may also proceed. But if the authority refuse consent during the initial three month period, this merely has the effect of prohibiting the ploughing up or conversion for twelve months from the original notice. Thereafter, the owner or occupier can carry out the operations he proposed in his written notice.

The purpose of the twelve month delay is to enable the county planning authority to offer the owner or occupier a management agreement under section 39 of this Act (see page 40). A management agreement can then contain restrictions on operations and the use of land together with provisions for payments which the owner or occupier may be prepared to accept. It must be emphasised that there is no compulsion to sign a management agreement, and a person may simply wait out the twelve month delay period in the face of a county planning authority refusal of consent.

Officers of the Department of Environment, Ministry of Agriculture, Fisheries and Food, and the county planning authority are authorised to enter private land in conection with this section. Twenty-four hours notice should be given unless a possible offence is being investigated (section 51).

10.2 Maps of moor or heath land in a National Park

Section 43 places a duty on every county planning authority whose area covers a National Park to make a map (probably on a 1:25,000 scale), of the Park showing areas of moor or heath which are important to conserve for their natural beauty. This map must be made before 30th November 1983, and then annually reviewed.

The map is to be printed and made available for sale to the public.

Clearly the information on the map can then be of value in considering whether an order should be made under section 42 to protect moor or heath land from being ploughed up etc., or in deciding whether the owner should be offered a management agreement under section 39.

10.3 Grants and loans to landowners in National Parks

A county planning authority has power to make a grant or loan to any person who incurs expenditure on the conservation and enhancement of the natural beauty of a National Park, or the promotion of its enjoyment by the public. Conditions for financial assistance of this nature may be attached (section 44).

The authority is not obliged to give this financial assistance, but a landowner might hope to be helped, e.g. in an uneconomic tree planting scheme, or to provide facilities for visitors.

10.4 Varying the boundaries of a National Park

A National Park is designated under, and in accordance with a consultation procedure in the National Parks and Access to the Countryside Act 1949. Section 45 of the 1981 Act now enables the Countryside Commission to vary the boundaries of a National Park by a variation order. Formerly only the Secretary of State had this power. There is an elaborate consultation procedure and the variation order still needs the confirmation of the Secretary of State.

10.5 Membership of National Park authorities

Section 46 makes provision for the membership of a joint planning board, special planning board or National Park committee, in an area of a National Park. In particular it provides for the number, method of appointment and duration of office of the members who are to be appointed by the district councils. It will be recalled that district councils do not (with minor exceptions) have planning functions in a National Park. These are exercised by the county planning authority, or a joint or special planning board.

11.0 MISCELLANEOUS COUNTRYSIDE MATTERS

(Sections 47-49)

11.1 Countryside Commission

Section 47 and Schedule 13 reconstitute the Countryside Commission as a body funded by a grant-in-aid basis. It is now an independent body rather than an arm of the Department of the Environment. It has been argued that with its civil service personnel, who probably seek advancement in the main-stream government departments, the Commission has been unable to pursue policies and strategies that are seen to be separate and independently valid from those of the government. It will now recruit its own staff.

11.2 Duties of water authorities in respect of nature conservation and the countryside

Section 48 amends section 22 of the Water Act 1973, and imposes a duty on water authorities and the appropriate Ministers when exercising their functions under the Water Act 1973 and the Land Drainage Act 1976.

The duty is to further the conservation and enhancement of natural beauty and the conservation of flora, fauna and geological or physiographical features of special interest.

The Minister of Agriculture took this duty into account when deciding the drainage of Halvergate Marshes in the Norfolk Broads in November 1982. He made a decision which balanced the interests of agriculture and conservation in relation to the drainage scheme.

11.3 Power to appoint wardens

Wardens can be appointed under the National Parks and Access to the Countryside Act 1949 and the Countryside Act 1968. But appointments were limited to land belonging to the local planning authority and in a

National Park or an area of outstanding natural beauty; or land covered by an access agreement or order; or common land in a National Park.

Section 49 of the 1981 Act extends the power to appoint wardens to supervise and assist the public to any land in a National Park or in the countryside if the public have access to the land and the owner of the land consents. See also section 62 for a power to appoint wardens for public rights of way.

12.0 FINANCIAL GUIDELINES FOR MANAGEMENT AGREEMENTS

These Guidelines were issued as a Circular (4/83) on the 28th January 1983. They are reproduced in full as Appendix E to this Companion.

The guidance is the form of a number of general points relevant to the conclusion of a management agreement. It includes the appropriate steps towards reaching an agreement, the assessment and arrangements for financial payments, and provisions for arbitration. It does not set out actual levels of payment. Throughout the Guidelines runs an underlying assumption that an owner or occupier should be compensated for actual loss of income or, in appropriate cases, depreciation in the market value of the affected land. In practice there will be considerable negotiation; but the object appears to be that an owner or occupier should neither lose nor gain financially out of a management agreement.

12.1 The Scope of the Financial Guidelines

Reference has already been made to the circumstances where management agreements *must* be offered by the NCC or local planning authorities (see pages 26 and 45). Management agreements may also be voluntarily offered; in particular the NCC will offer an agreement whenever a grant applicant is refused *any* grant by MAFF, and normally if a grant or felling permission is refused by the Forestry Commission. It has already been noted that there is no right for the NCC and local planning authorities to object to the making of grants other than the farm capital grant, consequently if these other grants are refused on conservation grounds, there is no obligation to offer an agreement under this Act (see page 45)

Section 50 of the 1981 Act provides that payments in management agreements to owners and occupiers, must be in accordance with these Financial Guidelines. The payments are to recompense landowners for their voluntary agreement for agreed restrictions on operations which would damage the conservation value of the land. When the NCC or a local planning authority is offering an owner or occupier a management agreement, the Guidelines refer to the authority as the offeror, and the owner or occupier as the offeree.

12.2 Landlords and Tenants

If an authority offers a tenant a management agreement, it may contain restrictions which will have implications for the tenancy agreement (in particular the tenancy obligations in respect of good husbandry). Accordingly, the tenant is required to give a written assurance that his landlord has been fully informed (paragraph 7).

The Guidelines suggest that where the principal management agreement is with the tenant, the landlord should be encouraged to join as a party, or to make a complementary agreement with the inducement of nominal compensation. Indeed if a tenant of agricultural land did not get his landlord to agree to the management agreement restrictions, the landlord may be able to serve a notice to remedy in respect of matters the tenant has agreed as restrictions on his operations in the management agreement (paragraph 8).

12.3 First Steps towards a Management Agreement

The Guidelines advise that the owner or occupier should not make a contract or commitment with a third party, after the date he gives notice of his intention to carry out the operations, if this may increase the compensation burden (paragraph 11).

A short term agreement is recommended, containing a

nominal sum of compensation, as an interim arrangement pending the conclusion of negotiations for the final management agreement (paragraph 12). The owner or occupier would agree not to carry out the *damaging operations* during a fixed period (between 6 and 12 months).

12.4 Methods of Payment

Owners and occupiers should be able to choose either a lump sum payment or annual payments for the final agreement. Tenants would only be offered annual payments (paragraph 13). Landlords are envisaged as being entitled to a nominal sum.

Calculation of lump sum payments

The Guidelines recommend that a single lump sum for a management agreement over a 20 year period (or longer) will be calculated as follows (paragraph 15):

"The amount should be equal to the difference between the restricted and unrestricted value of the owner or owner-occupier's interest, calculated having regard to the rule for assessment in respect of the compulsory acquisition of an interest in land, as set out in Section 5 of the Land Compensation Act 1961 . . . ."

Annex B to the Guidelines indicates the details the owner or owner-occupier should give to the authority.

If the value of the affected land is say £2000 per acre, and the same land subject to the restrictions on agricultural or other operations is worth £1,500 per acre, the lump sum payment will be at the rate of £500 per acre. But as the restrictions are only voluntarily accepted by the owner or owner-occupier, negotiations will be a significant part of the process. Payments for restrictions on forestry operations are considered separately below at 12.5.

Calculation of annual payments

In the case of owner or owner-occupiers choosing this method for an agreement over a 20-year period (or a term as agreed) "the payments should reflect net profits forgone because of the agreement" (paragraph 16). This will be nominal in the case of landlords.

Annual payments to tenants are available so long as the tenant remains in occupation.

The information to be supplied by the person opting for annual payments is detailed at Annex C to the Financial Guidelines. Certain information about crops, livestock and labour in respect of the whole farm is required. Particular information is then requested about the area which is to be subject of the restrictions under a management agreement. As the offer of an agreement may have arisen because the owner or occupier gave notice of an intention to carry out potentially grant-aided work or improvements to the area, details of the proposed improvement must be given.

The annual financial effect of the intended improvement can then be worked out by completing Parts 2 to 4 of the form at Annex C. Parts 2 and 3 of this form assume that any annual loss will flow only from a restriction on the carrying out of the intended improvement which initiated the management agreement offer. It is important to the authority offering the agreement to include restrictions to fully protect the area, and these may well go further than a restriction only on the intended improvement. If this is so, the owner or occupier must provide information about the full effect of his losses flowing from all restrictions. The form does not clearly allow for this.

The Guidelines give an option of either an individual assessment of annual payments *or* 'standard' payments. *Standard annual payments* would be offered as a tariff for well defined categories of land and restrictions on farming operations. The tariff would be agreed with consultative bodies of farmers and landowners, and revised every five years. With annual payments, the agreement would provide for adjustments at five year intervals, and make provision for arbitration (see paragraphs 41-42). In the case of an agreement with a landlord, it is envisaged that rents would continue to be reviewed on the basis that the tenant was not restricted in his farming operations.

12.5 Forestry Operations

Annex A to the Guidelines makes provision for the special

problems of determining payments for restrictions on forestry operations. These restrictions could be an outright prohibition of planting or felling, or a modification of management practices.

Lump sum payments are to be calculated in one of two ways at the option of the owner or occupier. The first method is an individual assessment of net revenue forgone based on a comparison of discounted streams of expenditure and income over the appropriate period. The second method is based on the depreciation in value of the land or woodlands assessed under the rules in section 5 of the Land Compensation Act 1961.

Annual payments, where required, can be calculated from the lump sum as determined by the first of the two methods above. In all cases the authority will be advised by the Forestry Commission whether a grant would have been payable, and this will be taken into account in assessing loss.

12.6 Grants and the calculation of payments

Paragraph 23 of the Guidelines says that in calculating management agreement payments, it must be assumed that a farm capital grant would have been payable but for the agreed restrictions. As profits from a grant-aided improvement will usually be higher than from an improvement not grant-aided, the financial payments must consequently be higher to make good the extra loss.

Some exceptions to this general rule are noted at paragraphs 24-26. The difficulty in these cases is that if the payments are calculated at lower levels on the assumption of no grant, they may be insufficient incentive to induce conclusion of an agreement.

There are special arrangements with regard to the calculation of the farm capital grant investment limits, and of the relevant rate of grant.

12.7 Phasing-in payments

Because the forgone development restricted by a management agreement may have taken some period of time to fully implement, and generate maximum intended revenue, paragraph 28 envisages that payments should take this into account and be consequently smaller in the earlier years.

12.8 Professional fees and other costs

The reasonable fees of professional advisers should be paid by the authority (paragraph 29).

The management agreement may also provide that abortive expenditure reasonably incurred within the previous twelve months can be reimbursed, as well as any other loss or damage directly attributable to the agreement.

12.9 Formal Offer and Arbitration

The owner of occupier should receive a draft agreement within 3 months of a refusal by MAFF, on conservation grounds, of a farm capital grant (paragraphs 21-21).

The formal offer of a management agreement, which will follow a period of negotiations, must include a statement that the owner or occupier has a right to dispute the amounts offered within one month. (See section 50 (3) of the 1981 Act.)

An arbitrator will be appointed by the parties; if they cannot agree, the Secretary of State will appoint one.

Where a management agreement is required by the Act to be offered to an owner or occupier, and the arbitrator determines that the payments should be higher than offered, the authority offering the agreement must amend the terms accordingly (section 50(3)).

In those cases where a management agreement is being offered voluntarily by the authority, the authority may choose to give effect to the arbitrator's award, or to withdraw the offer. The arbitrator can award the costs against either party (paragraph 37). This point should be carefully watched.

The agreement will usually be effective from a date 3 months after the owner or occupier first informed the appropriate authority of his proposed operations. Payments are made as from that date, and interest should be payable. Annual payments will be backdated to this date, and thereafter will be payable on the dates specified in the agreement.

12.10 Breach of a management agreement

Deliberate breach by the owner or occupier

The Guidelines envisage that an agreement would contain terms to deal with a breach of this nature. In the case of annual payments, no further payments would be made. In the case of a lump sum payment, a proportion of the original lump sum would be repayable having regard to the period of the agreement and the number of years unexpired.

Action by a third party or natural or accidental causes

If, through the action of a third party, or through natural or accidental causes, the object of the management agreement can no longer be achieved, the terms should enable the agreement to be terminated. Annual payments would then cease after the next payment due, and a proportion of any lump sum would, at the discretion of the authority, be repayable having regard to the period of the agreement and the number of years unexpired.

12.11 Financial payments and Capital Taxation

Where land is of outstanding scenic, historic or scientific interest, it may be given conditional exemption from capital transfer tax. It can also be designated if a maintenance fund is set up to provide for its upkeep and the provision of public access.

In these cases, the owner is required to give undertakings which may be similar in effect to the restrictions in a management agreement. The Guidelines suggest (paragraph 48) that a management agreement should contain a term that requires the owner to inform the authority if any such exemption or designation is granted. In this event the agreement would then be terminated and the payments thereunder would cease to be repayable as discussed above at 12.10. Differences between the capital taxation undertakings and the management agreement restrictions would be met, if necessary, by a new agreement.

An owner cannot therefore doubly benefit from the fiscal reliefs and from the financial payments under a management agreement.

PART III
PUBLIC RIGHTS
OF WAY

This Part of the Act makes a number of amendments to the law of public rights of way that are of particular concern to the management of the countryside.

Because the arrangements for the preparation and revision of definitive maps and statements of public rights of way, contained in the National Parks and Access to the Countryside Act 1949, have proved unsatisfactory, sections 53 to 58 of the 1981 Act contain a new code now in force.

There are further provisions covering bulls on land crossed by public rights of way, regulation of traffic on footpaths, bridleways and byways, and restrictions on the ploughing of public rights of way.

1.0 MAPS OF PUBLIC RIGHTS OF WAY

(Sections 53-58)

Under the National Parks and Access to the Countryside Act 1949, the county councils had a duty to survey and record public footpaths, public bridleways and roads used as public footpaths and bridleways. A *draft* map (indicating routes) and statement (describing each route) was first prepared; then a *provisional* map and statement incorporating objections accepted by the county council; and finally, after unresolved objections were determined in the Crown Court, a *definitive* map and written statement were prepared and published. Persons who believed that a right of way was omitted or excluded from a *draft* map and statement could appeal to the Secretary of State. Definitive maps and statements were then required to be reviewed at least every five years. This elaborate procedure is now to be replaced as follows.

1.1 Modification and review of the definitive map and statement

The county council for the area will now be required to modify, by an order, the existing definitive map and statement (or if none exists, one to be prepared) when any one of certain defined events occur. The initial modifications must be made as soon as reasonably practicable after this section comes into force. Thereafter the map and statement must be kept under continuous review with further modifications being effected as and when one of the defined events take place.

1.2 Events which require modification of the map and statement

Section 53(3) defines the following events, the occurrence of which then requires the definitive map to be modified by an order.

a) The lawful stopping up, diversion, widening or extension of any public highway required to be recorded on the maps (e.g. there are powers in the Highways Act 1980, sections 118-120, to divert or extinguish public footpaths and bridleways);

b) A public highway ceases to be of the type recorded on the map and statement (e.g. a footpath has become a bridleway);

c) A new public footpath or bridleway is created (by a dedication agreement of the landowner – a public path agreement; or following compulsory powers used by a local authority – a public path order, sections 25-26 of the Highways Act 1980);

d) A footpath or bridleway has been used by the public for 20 years without interruption, and it is then presumed to be dedicated as a public footpath or bridleway (section 31, Highways Act 1980);

e) The county council has accepted evidence that a right of way exists which is not on the map and statement; or one is shown there, but is not a public right of way; or one is misdescribed on the map and statement.

1.3 Modification that may be requested

Any person may request that an order be made in respect of (d) or (e) above.

A request must be accompanied by documentary evidence (see Schedule 14 to the 1981 Act). A landowner could therefore request that a path or bridleway shown in the map and statement be deleted as it is not a public footpath or bridleway. Conversely, members of the public could request that a footpath or bridleway be added to the map and statement after 20 years of uninterrupted public use.

If the county council refuse the request, the applicant may appeal to the Secretary of State.

1.4 Procedure for making a modification order

In the case of a modification to give effect to any matter within (d) and (e) (see above), Schedule 15 to the Act lays down a procedure. Briefly, this procedure requires that intended orders must be given publicity, objections and representations may be made, and affected owners and occupiers informed. If there are no objections or representations, or if any made are withdrawn, the county council may then confirm the order (if the order itself needs amendment at this stage, the Secretary of State must confirm it). If objections and representations are made, and not withdrawn, the Secretary of State will appoint an inspector to hold a public local inquiry or private hearing. The inspector will then make a report to the Secretary of State, following which the Secretary of State may confirm the order, with or without any amendments.

1.5 Reclassification of roads used as public footpaths and bridleways

(Section 54)

This section abandons the old classification of a road used as "a public path". The National Parks and Access to the Countryside Act 1949 recognises "a road used as a public path" as a highway mainly used as a public footpath or bridleway but over which greater public rights of way were alleged to exist, e.g., unsurfaced "green roads" not normally used by vehicular traffic, but over which such traffic had legal rights.

Any road used as a public footpath or bridleway will now be described as a *byway* if public rights of way for vehicular traffic also exist. If there are no rights for vehicular traffic over a road, it will be described as a *bridleway*; and if a road is shown not to include bridleway rights, it will be described as a *footpath*. One great advantage of the new descriptions will be to deter the use of "green roads" by motor cyclists except where such a road is clearly shown to include vehicular rights.

1.6 No further old-style surveys or reviews

Section 55 requires that no further surveys or reviews of public rights of way need be carried out under the old arrangements of the National Parks and Access to the Countryside Act 1949.

However, if a county council has not yet completed an original survey, it is still required to prepare a map and written statement of byways, bridleways and footpaths to serve as the definitive map and written statement.

1.7 What is the legal consequence of a right of way appearing in the definitive map and statement?

This is answered by section 56. If the map indicates a public footpath, that is conclusive evidence that there is, at least, a public footpath. But it does not preclude the possibility that a greater public right may exist.

If the map indicates a public bridleway or a road used as a public path, then again, that is conclusive evidence of a public bridleway, but does not preclude the possibility that a greater public right may exist. A public bridleway means that the public have rights to proceed on foot, on horse-back, to lead a horse, or (under section 30 of the Countryside Act 1968) a right to ride a bicycle provided cyclists give way to pedestrians and persons on horseback.

The indication on the map of a byway means that the public has rights for vehicular and all other kinds of traffic. The written statement that accompanies each map is conclusive as to the position and width of the appropriate right of way.

The legal consequences outlined above pertain to a "relevant date". This date will be specified in each *written statement* or *modification order*.

1.8 Rights of way maps and statements to be available for public inspection

Section 57 requires each county council to put a copy of the definitive map and written statement in each district of its area so that members of the public may inspect free of charge at all reasonable hours. If any modification orders have been made, these must be similarly available.

2.0 BULLS ON LAND CROSSED BY PUBLIC RIGHT OF WAY

(Section 59)

This section makes it a criminal offence to keep a bull at large in a field or enclosure crossed by a public right of way, (fine up to £200 for a summary offence). Until now this only applied in Scotland and in certain counties; it is now an offence nationwide. No offence is committed in keeping any bull at large in open hill areas as these will not be fields or enclosures.

Presumably a tethered bull is not 'at large', so that even if its tether breaks, no offence would be committed until the occupier becomes aware that the bull is 'at large'.

Young bulls excepted

The offence does not include a bull of any breed under the age of ten months; such a bull may therefore be kept in a field with a public right of way. The most useful method of ageing cattle is by observing the number and condition of a beast's teeth!

Bulls of non-dairy breed excepted

The section provides that no offence is committed if a bull which is not of *'a recognised dairy breed'*, is run at large *with cows or heifers* in a field through which a public right of way passes.

A recognised dairy breed includes the following breeds: Ayrshire, British Friesian, British Holstein, Dairy Shorthorn, Guernsey, Jersey and Kerry. The Secretary of State may vary this list. Bulls of the other dual purpose breeds, and of the beef breeds, are therefore permitted in the circumstances outlined above.

Because of the difficulties of breed recognition etc, on the part of walkers and the local constabulary, successful prosecutions are going to be few under this section.

3.0 REGULATION OF FOOT PASSENGERS AND OTHERS

(Section 60)

The Road Traffic Regulation Act 1967 is extended to cover public footpaths, bridleways and byways, and traffic now includes foot passengers and persons driving, riding or leading horses or other animals of draught or burden. This means that traffic regulation orders can now be made in respect of such traffic.

The most likely use of this power is to make a temporary order prohibiting horses and other animals from using a bridleway or byways for up to three months. Let us hope that we do not get a one-way system for the North Downs Way!

4.0 PLOUGHING OF PUBLIC FOOTPATHS AND BRIDLEWAYS

(Section 61)

Although a public footpath or bridleway which follows the headlands or side of a field or enclosure may not be ploughed, a footpath or bridleway which crosses agricultural land may be ploughed if that is the convenient way of ploughing the land (section 134 of the Highways Act 1980).

The Wildlife and Countryside Act 1981 makes the following changes to this legal right to plough a footpath or bridleway.

Written notice of intention to plough not required

The requirement of a written notice to the highway authority of an intention to plough is now abolished.

Reinstatement of the surface

The occupier is now required to reinstate the surface of

the footpath or bridleway as soon as may be after completing the ploughing, and, in any event within two weeks of the date when ploughing commenced. If exceptional weather conditions prevent this, the re-instatement must be completed as soon as is reasonably practicable.

Criminal Offence
If a footpath or bridleway along the side or headland of a field is ploughed, or an unmetalled track such as a byway (green road) is ploughed, it is an offence with a fine up to £200 on summary conviction. Proceedings may be brought by the parish or district council as well as by the highway authority.

Restoration by the local authority
Under section 134 of the Highways Act 1980, the highway authority (and in cases where the district council maintains the footpath or bridleway, the district council) has power to restore the surface of a footpath or bridleway which has been unlawfully ploughed, or which has not been restored by the occupier after a lawful ploughing. These authorities can also recover the expenses of restoration from the occupier.

This power is now extended to include other highways as well as footpaths and bridleways (section 61 (8)). This means that the highway authority can restore a byway (this should assist the preservation of green roads).

Temporary diversion following ploughing
The power of the local highway authority to make a temporary diversion order (up to three months) because, following a ploughing, it is in the interests of good farming not to restore the footpath or bridleway immediately, is unchanged (see section 135 of the Highways Act 1980).

5.0 WARDENS FOR PUBLIC RIGHTS OF WAY
(Section 62)

This section permits a local authority to appoint wardens to advise and assist the public in connection with the use of footpaths, bridleways or byways in the countryside. This could be useful to landowners suffering from large numbers of pedestrians and horseriders, and where the public rights of way are not easily identified.

6.0 SIGNPOSTING PUBLIC RIGHTS OF WAY

(Section 65)

Under section 27 of the Countryside Act 1968, a highway authority may, after consulting the owner or occupier of land, erect signposts along public footpaths or bridleways. They are also required, in the same section, to erect signs at every point where a public footpath or bridleway leaves a metalled road (unless this is agreed with the parish council to be unnecessary).

The 1981 Act now extends section 27 of the Countryside Act 1968 to include byways. A byway was defined on page 61 above; it is a public highway for all traffic though used mainly as a footpath or bridleway (i.e. a green road).

7.0 PROCEDURE FOR CREATION, STOPPING UP OR DIVERSION OF PUBLIC FOOTPATHS AND BRIDLEWAYS
(Section 63 and Schedule 16)

Public footpaths and bridleways may be stopped up or diverted (and new footpaths and bridleways created) to enable development to be carried out for which planning permission has been granted – see section 210 of the Town and Country Planning Act 1971. The 1981 Act makes a number of detailed modifications to the procedures which are outlined below.

Public footpaths and bridleways may also be stopped up or diverted, on certain grounds,under sections 119-120 of the Highways Act. The 1981 Act similarly modifies some of the procedures.

7.1 Notices and Publicity

The requirement that an order to stop up, divert or create

a footpath or bridleway must be advertised in the London Gazette is now dropped. When an order is made by a local authority, it must notify certain persons, and give the order publicity, to enable people to make representations and objections to the Secretary of State. Groups, such as the Commons, Open Spaces and Footpaths Preservation Society and the Ramblers Association, will be notified direct. Notice of the order must also be posted at each end of the path, at council offices in the locality and other appropriate places (parish notice boards?).

The notices must be given or displayed at least 28 days before the period mentioned in the notices for making representations and objections has expired. When served on owners, occupiers and local authorities, they must include a copy of the order, and when posted at each end of the path in question, they must include a plan.

7.2 The Inspector may decide

When objections and representations are made to a stopping up or diversion order, and an inspector has made a report following a public inquiry or hearing, it is the Secretary of State that has hitherto made the final decision whether to confirm the order. The 1981 Act now permits the Secretary of State to direct that the inspector can make the decision except in certain specified classes of use. The decision of the inspector will have the same legal effect as if it was the decision of the Secretary of State.

7.3 Grounds for a diversion order

Under section 119 of the Highway Act 1980, a footpath or bridleway can only be diverted if the local authority is satisfied that the diversion is necessary for securing the efficient use of the land or it will provide a shorter or more commodious path or way.

The 1981 Act has removed these two grounds. Section 119 of the Highways Act 1980 now simply requires that the local authority should make an order for the diversion of a footpath or bridleway, if it is expedient to do so "in the interests of the owner, lessee or of the public".

This change should certainly help landowners if they can show the local authority that a right of way should be diverted for reasons, other than the efficient use of land. The meaning of 'efficient use of land' was strained in *Roberton* v. *Secretary of State* ([1976] 1 All E.R. 689) to permit the diversion of a footpath near Chequers which posed an assassination risk to the Prime Minister.

Wildlife and Countryside Act 1981

CHAPTER 69

ARRANGEMENT OF SECTIONS

PART I

WILDLIFE

Protection of birds

Wildlife and Countryside Act 1981

1981 CHAPTER 69

An Act to repeal and re-enact with amendments the Protection of Birds Acts 1954 to 1967 and the Conservation of Wild Creatures and Wild Plants Act 1975; to prohibit certain methods of killing or taking wild animals; to amend the law relating to protection of certain mammals; to restrict the introduction of certain animals and plants; to amend the Endangered Species (Import and Export) Act 1976; to amend the law relating to nature conservation, the countryside and National Parks and to make provision with respect to the Countryside Commission; to amend the law relating to public rights of way; and for connected purposes.
[30th October 1981]

B E IT ENACTED by the Queen's most Excellent Majesty, by and with the advice and consent of the Lords Spiritual and Temporal, and Commons, in this present Parliament assembled, and by the authority of the same, as follows:—

PART I

WILDLIFE

Protection of birds

1.—(1) Subject to the provisions of this Part, if any person intentionally—

(*a*) kills, injures or takes any wild bird ;

(*b*) takes, damages or destroys the nest of any wild bird while that nest is in use or being built ; or

(*c*) takes or destroys an egg of any wild bird,

he shall be guilty of an offence.

Protection of wild birds, their nests and eggs.

(2) Subject to the provisions of this Part, if any person has in his possession or control—

(a) any live or dead wild bird or any part of, or anything derived from, such a bird ; or

(b) an egg of a wild bird or any part of such an egg,

he shall be guilty of an offence.

(3) A person shall not be guilty of an offence under subsection (2) if he shows that—

(a) the bird or egg had not been killed or taken, or had been killed or taken otherwise than in contravention of the relevant provisions ; or

(b) the bird, egg or other thing in his possession or control had been sold (whether to him or any other person) otherwise than in contravention of those provisions ;

and in this subsection " the relevant provisions " means the provisions of this Part and of orders made under it and, in the case of a bird or other thing falling within subsection (2)(a), the provisions of the Protection of Birds Acts 1954 to 1967 and of orders made under those Acts.

(4) Any person convicted of an offence under subsection (1) or (2) in respect of—

(a) a bird included in Schedule 1 or any part of, or anything derived from, such a bird ;

(b) the nest of such a bird ; or

(c) an egg of such a bird or any part of such an egg,

shall be liable to a special penalty.

(5) Subject to the provisions of this Part, if any person intentionally—

(a) disturbs any wild bird included in Schedule 1 while it is building a nest or is in, on or near a nest containing eggs or young ; or

(b) disturbs dependent young of such a bird,

he shall be guilty of an offence and liable to a special penalty.

(6) In this section " wild bird " does not include any bird which is shown to have been bred in captivity.

(7) Any reference in this Part to any bird included in Schedule 1 is a reference to any bird included in Part I and, during the close season for the bird in question, any bird included in Part II of that Schedule.

Exceptions to s. 1.

2.—(1) Subject to the provisions of this section, a person shall not be guilty of an offence under section 1 by reason of the killing or taking of a bird included in Part I of Schedule 2 outside the close season for that bird, or the injuring of such a bird outside that season in the course of an attempt to kill it.

(2) Subject to the provisions of this section, an authorised person shall not be guilty of an offence under section 1 by reason of—

  (a) the killing or taking of a bird included in Part II of Schedule 2, or the injuring of such a bird in the course of an attempt to kill it ;

  (b) the taking, damaging or destruction of a nest of such a bird ; or

  (c) the taking or destruction of an egg of such a bird.

(3) Subsections (1) and (2) shall not apply in Scotland on Sundays or on Christmas Day ; and subsection (1) shall not apply on Sundays in any area of England and Wales which the Secretary of State may by order prescribe for the purposes of that subsection.

(4) In this section and section 1 " close season " means—

  (a) in the case of capercaillie and (except in Scotland) woodcock, the period in any year commencing with 1st February and ending with 30th September;

  (b) in the case of snipe, the period in any year commencing with 1st February and ending with 11th August ;

  (c) in the case of wild duck and wild geese in or over any area below high-water mark of ordinary spring tides, the period in any year commencing with 21st February and ending with 31st August ;

  (d) in any other case, subject to the provisions of this Part, the period in any year commencing with 1st February and ending with 31st August.

(5) The Secretary of State may by order made with respect to the whole or any specified part of Great Britain vary the close season for any wild bird specified in the order.

(6) If it appears to the Secretary of State expedient that any wild birds included in Part II of Schedule 1 or Part I of Schedule 2 should be protected during any period outside the close season for those birds, he may by order made with respect to the whole or any specified part of Great Britain declare any period (which shall not in the case of any order exceed fourteen days) as a period of special protection for those birds ; and this section and section 1 shall have effect as if any period of special protection declared under this subsection for any birds formed part of the close season for those birds.

(7) Before making an order under subsection (6) the Secretary of State shall consult a person appearing to him to be a representative of persons interested in the shooting of birds of the kind proposed to be protected by the order.

3.—(1) The Secretary of State may by order make provision with respect to any area specified in the order providing for all or any of the following matters, that is to say—

(a) that any person who, within that area or any part of it specified in the order, at any time or during any period so specified, intentionally—

(i) kills, injures or takes any wild bird or any wild bird so specified ;

(ii) takes, damages or destroys the nest of such a bird while that nest is in use or being built ;

(iii) takes or destroys an egg of such a bird ;

(iv) disturbs such a bird while it is building a nest or is in, on or near a nest containing eggs or young ; or

(v) disturbs dependent young of such a bird,

shall be guilty of an offence under this section ;

(b) that any person who, except as may be provided in the order, enters into that area or any part of it specified in the order at any time or during any period so specified shall be guilty of an offence under this section ;

(c) that where any offence under this Part, or any such offence under this Part as may be specified in the order, is committed within that area, the offender shall be liable to a special penalty.

(2) An authorised person shall not by virtue of any such order be guilty of an offence by reason of—

(a) the killing or taking of a bird included in Part II of Schedule 2, or the injuring of such a bird in the course of an attempt to kill it ;

(b) the taking, damaging or destruction of the nest of such a bird ;

(c) the taking or destruction of an egg of such a bird ; or

(d) the disturbance of such a bird or dependent young of such a bird.

(3) The making of any order under this section with respect to any area shall not affect the exercise by any person of any right vested in him, whether as owner, lessee or occupier of any land in that area or by virtue of a licence or agreement.

(4) Before making any order under this section the Secretary of State shall give particulars of the intended order either by notice in writing to every owner and every occupier of any land included in the area with respect to which the order is to be made or, where the giving of such a notice is in his opinion impracticable, by advertisement in a newspaper circulating in the district in which that area is situated.

(5) The Secretary of State shall not make an order under this section unless—

(a) all the owners and occupiers aforesaid have consented thereto ;

(b) no objections thereto have been made by any of those owners or occupiers before the expiration of a period of three months from the date of the giving of the notice or the publication of the advertisement ; or

(c) any such objections so made have been withdrawn.

4.—(1) Nothing in section 1 or in any order made under Exceptions to section 3 shall make unlawful— ss. 1 and 3.

(a) anything done in pursuance of a requirement by the Minister of Agriculture, Fisheries and Food or the Secretary of State under section 98 of the Agriculture 1947 c. 48. Act 1947, or by the Secretary of State under section 39 of the Agriculture (Scotland) Act 1948 ; 1948 c. 45.

(b) anything done under, or in pursuance of an order made under, section 21 or 22 of the Animal Health Act 1981 ; 1981 c. 22. or

(c) except in the case of a wild bird included in Schedule 1 or the nest or egg of such a bird, anything done under, or in pursuance of an order made under, any other provision of the said Act of 1981.

(2) Notwithstanding anything in the provisions of section 1 or any order made under section 3, a person shall not be guilty of an offence by reason of—

(a) the taking of any wild bird if he shows that the bird had been disabled otherwise than by his unlawful act and was taken solely for the purpose of tending it and releasing it when no longer disabled ;

(b) the killing of any wild bird if he shows that the bird had been so seriously disabled otherwise than by his unlawful act that there was no reasonable chance of its recovering ; or

(c) any act made unlawful by those provisions if he shows that the act was the incidental result of a lawful operation and could not reasonably have been avoided.

(3) Notwithstanding anything in the provisions of section 1 or any order made under section 3, an authorised person shall not be guilty of an offence by reason of the killing or injuring of any wild bird, other than a bird included in Schedule 1, if he shows that his action was necessary for the purpose of—

(a) preserving public health or public or air safety ;

(*b*) preventing the spread of disease ; or

(*c*) preventing serious damage to livestock, foodstuffs for livestock, crops, vegetables, fruit, growing timber, or fisheries.

Prohibition of certain methods of killing or taking wild birds.

5.—(1) Subject to the provisions of this Part, if any person—

(*a*) sets in position any of the following articles, being an article which is of such a nature and is so placed as to be calculated to cause bodily injury to any wild bird coming into contact therewith, that is to say, any springe, trap, gin, snare, hook and line, any electrical device for killing, stunning or frightening or any poisonous, poisoned or stupefying substance ;

(*b*) uses for the purpose of killing or taking any wild bird any such article as aforesaid, whether or not of such a nature and so placed as aforesaid, or any net, baited board, bird-lime or substance of a like nature to bird-lime ;

(*c*) uses for the purpose of killing or taking any wild bird—

    (i) any bow or crossbow ;

    (ii) any explosive other than ammunition for a firearm ;

    (iii) any automatic or semi-automatic weapon ;

    (iv) any shot-gun of which the barrel has an internal diameter at the muzzle of more than one and three-quarter inches ;

    (v) any device for illuminating a target or any sighting device for night shooting ;

    (vi) any form of artificial lighting or any mirror or other dazzling device ;

    (vii) any gas or smoke not falling within paragraphs (*a*) and (*b*) ; or

    (viii) any chemical wetting agent ;

(*d*) uses as a decoy, for the purpose of killing or taking any wild bird, any sound recording or any live bird or other animal whatever which is tethered, or which is secured by means of braces or other similar appliances, or which is blind, maimed or injured ; or

(*e*) uses any mechanically propelled vehicle in immediate pursuit of a wild bird for the purpose of killing or taking that bird,

he shall be guilty of an offence and be liable to a special penalty.

(2) Subject to subsection (3), the Secretary of State may by order, either generally or in relation to any kind of wild bird specified in the order, amend subsection (1) by adding any method of killing or taking wild birds or by omitting any such method which is mentioned in that subsection.

(3) The power conferred by subsection (2) shall not be exer-
ciseable, except for the purpose of complying with an international obligation, in relation to any method of killing or taking
wild birds which involves the use of a firearm.

(4) In any proceedings under subsection (1)(*a*) it shall be a
defence to show that the article was set in position for the
purpose of killing or taking, in the interests of public health,
agriculture, forestry, fisheries or nature conservation, any wild
animals which could be lawfully killed or taken by those means
and that he took all reasonable precautions to prevent injury
thereby to wild birds.

(5) Nothing in subsection (1) shall make unlawful—

(*a*) the use of a cage-trap or net by an authorised person for
the purpose of taking a bird included in Part II of
Schedule 2 ;

(*b*) the use of nets for the purpose of taking wild duck in a
duck decoy which is shown to have been in use imme
diately before the passing of the Protection of Birds Act 1954 c. 30.
1954 ; or

(*c*) the use of a cage-trap or net for the purpose of taking
any game bird if it is shown that the taking of the bird
is solely for the purpose of breeding ;

but nothing in this subsection shall make lawful the use of any
net for taking birds in flight or the use for taking birds on the
ground of any net which is projected or propelled otherwise
than by hand.

6.—(1) Subject to the provisions of this Part, if any person— Sale etc. of
live or dead
(*a*) sells, offers or exposes for sale, or has in his possession wild birds,
or transports for the purpose of sale, any live wild eggs etc.
bird other than a bird included in Part I of Schedule 3,
or an egg of a wild bird or any part of such an egg ;
or

(*b*) publishes or causes to be published any advertisement
likely to be understood as conveying that he buys or
sells, or intends to buy or sell, any of those things,

he shall be guilty of an offence.

(2) Subject to the provisions of this Part, if any person who
is not for the time being registered in accordance with regulations made by the Secretary of State—

(*a*) sells, offers or exposes for sale, or has in his possession
or transports for the purpose of sale, any dead wild
bird other than a bird included in Part II or III of
Schedule 3, or any part of, or anything derived from,
such a wild bird ; or

(*b*) publishes or causes to be published any advertisement likely to be understood as conveying that he buys or sells, or intends to buy or sell, any of those things,

he shall be guilty of an offence.

(3) Subject to the provisions of this Part, if any person shows or causes or permits to be shown for the purposes of any competition or in any premises in which a competition is being held—

(*a*) any live wild bird other than a bird included in Part I of Schedule 3 ; or

(*b*) any live bird one of whose parents was such a wild bird,

he shall be guilty of an offence.

(4) Any person convicted of an offence under this section in respect of—

(*a*) a bird included in Schedule 1 or any part of, or anything derived from, such a bird ; or

(*b*) an egg of such bird or any part of such an egg,

shall be liable to a special penalty.

(5) Any reference in this section to any bird included in Part I of Schedule 3 is a reference to any bird included in that Part which was bred in captivity and has been ringed or marked in accordance with regulations made by the Secretary of State ; and regulations so made may make different provision for different birds or different provisions of this section.

(6) Any reference in this section to any bird included in Part II or III of Schedule 3 is a reference to any bird included in Part II and, during the period commencing with 1st September in any year and ending with 28th February of the following year, any bird included in Part III of that Schedule.

(7) The power of the Secretary of State to make regulations under subsection (2) shall include power—

(*a*) to impose requirements as to the carrying out by a person registered in accordance with the regulations of any act which, apart from the registration, would constitute an offence under this section ; and

(*b*) to provide that any contravention of the regulations shall constitute such an offence.

(8) Regulations under subsection (2) shall secure that no person shall become or remain registered—

(*a*) within five years of his having been convicted of an offence under this Part for which a special penalty is provided ; or

(b) within three years of his having been convicted of any PART I
other offence under this Part so far as it relates to the
protection of birds or other animals or any offence
involving their ill-treatment,

no account being taken for this purpose of a conviction which
has become spent by virtue of the Rehabilitation of Offenders 1974 c. 53.
Act 1974.

(9) Any person authorised in writing by the Secretary of State
may, at any reasonable time and (if required to do so) upon
producing evidence that he is authorised, enter and inspect any
premises where a registered person keeps any wild birds for the
purpose of acertaining whether an offence under this section is
being, or has been, committed on those premises.

(10) Any person who intentionally obstructs a person acting in
the exercise of the power conferred by subsection (9) shall be
guilty of an offence.

7.—(1) If any person keeps or has in his possession or under Registration
his control any bird included in Schedule 4 which has not been etc. of certain
registered and ringed or marked in accordance with regulations captive birds.
made by the Secretary of State, he shall be guilty of an offence
and be liable to a special penalty.

(2) The power of the Secretary of State to make regulations
under subsection (1) shall include power—

(a) to impose requirements which must be satisfied in
relation to a bird included in Schedule 4 before it
can be registered in accordance with the regulations ;
and

(b) to make different provision for different birds or
different descriptions of birds.

(3) If any person keeps or has in his possession or under his
control any bird included in Schedule 4—

(a) within five years of his having been convicted of an
offence under this Part for which a special penalty is
provided ; or

(b) within three years of his having been convicted of any
other offence under this Part so far as it relates to
the protection of birds or other animals or any offence
involving their ill-treatment,

he shall be guilty of an offence.

(4) If any person knowingly disposes of or offers to dispose
of any bird included in Schedule 4 to any person—

(a) within five years of that person's having been convicted
of such an offence as is mentioned in paragraph (a) of
subsection (3) ; or

PART I

(*b*) within three years of that person's having been con victed of such an offence as is mentioned in paragraph (*b*) of that subsection,

he shall be guilty of an offence.

(5) No account shall be taken for the purposes of subsections (3) and (4) of any conviction which has become spent for the purpose of the Rehabilitation of Offenders Act 1974.

1974 c. 53.

(6) Any person authorised in writing by the Secretary of State may, at any reasonable time and (if required to do so) upon producing evidence that he is authorised, enter and inspect any premises where any birds included in Schedule 4 are kept for the purpose of ascertaining whether an offence under this section is being, or has been, committed on those premises.

(7) Any person who intentionally obstructs a person acting in the exercise of the power conferred by subsection (6) shall be guilty of an offence.

Protection of captive birds.

8.—(1) If any person keeps or confines any bird whatever in any cage or other receptacle which is not sufficient in height, length or breadth to permit the bird to stretch its wings freely, he shall be guilty of an offence and be liable to a special penalty.

(2) Subsection (1) does not apply to poultry, or to the keeping or confining of any bird—

(*a*) while that bird is in the course of conveyance, by whatever means ;

(*b*) while that bird is being shown for the purposes of any public exhibition or competition if the time during which the bird is kept or confined for those purposes does not in the aggregate exceed 72 hours ; or

(*c*) while that bird is undergoing examination or treatment by a veterinary surgeon or veterinary practitioner.

(3) Every person who—

(*a*) promotes, arranges, conducts, assists in, receives money for, or takes part in, any event whatever at or in the course of which captive birds are liberated by hand or by any other means whatever for the purpose of being shot immediately after their liberation ; or

(*b*) being the owner or occupier of any land, permits that land to be used for the purposes of such an event,

shall be guilty of an offence and be liable to a special penalty.

Protection of other animals

9.—(1) Subject to the provisions of this Part, if any person Protection of intentionally kills, injures or takes any wild animal included certain wild in Schedule 5, he shall be guilty of an offence. animals.

(2) Subject to the provisions of this Part, if any person has in his possession or control any live or dead wild animal included in Schedule 5 or any part of, or anything derived from, such an animal, he shall be guilty of an offence.

(3) A person shall not be guilty of an offence under subsection (2) if he shows that—

(a) the animal had not been killed or taken, or had been killed or taken otherwise than in contravention of the relevant provisions ; or

(b) the animal or other thing in his possession or control had been sold (whether to him or any other person) otherwise than in contravention of those provisions ;

and in this subsection " the relevant provisions " means the provisions of this Part and of the Conservation of Wild Creatures 1975 c. 48. and Wild Plants Act 1975.

(4) Subject to the provisions of this Part, if any person intentionally—

(a) damages or destroys, or obstructs access to, any structure or place which any wild animal included in Schedule 5 uses for shelter or protection ; or

(b) disturbs any such animal while it is occupying a structure or place which it uses for that purpose,

he shall be guilty of an offence.

(5) Subject to the provisions of this Part, if any person—

(a) sells, offers or exposes for sale, or has in his possession or transports for the purpose of sale, any live or dead wild animal included in Schedule 5, or any part of, or anything derived from, such an animal ; or

(b) publishes or causes to be published any advertisement likely to be understood as conveying that he buys or sells, or intends to buy or sell, any of those things,

he shall be guilty of an offence.

(6) In any proceedings for an offence under subsection (1), (2) or (5)(a), the animal in question shall be presumed to have been a wild animal unless the contrary is shown.

PART I
Exceptions to
s. 9.

1947 c. 48.
1948 c. 45.

1981 c. 22.

10.—(1) Nothing in section 9 shall make unlawful—

    (*a*) anything done in pursuance of a requirement by the Minister of Agriculture, Fisheries and Food or the Secretary of State under section 98 of the Agriculture Act 1947, or by the Secretary of State under section 39 of the Agriculture (Scotland) Act 1948 ; or

    (*b*) anything done under, or in pursuance of an order made under, the Animal Health Act 1981.

(2) Nothing in subsection (4) of section 9 shall make unlawful anything done within a dwelling-house.

(3) Notwithstanding anything in section 9, a person shall not be guilty of an offence by reason of—

    (*a*) the taking of any such animal if he shows that the animal had been disabled otherwise than by his unlawful act and was taken solely for the purpose of tending it and releasing it when no longer disabled ;

    (*b*) the killing of any such animal if he shows that the animal had been so seriously disabled otherwise than by his unlawful act that there was no reasonable chance of its recovering ; or

    (*c*) any act made unlawful by that section if he shows that the act was the incidental result of a lawful operation and could not reasonably have been avoided.

(4) Notwithstanding anything in section 9, an authorised person shall not be guilty of an offence by reason of the killing or injuring of a wild animal included in Schedule 5 if he shows that his action was necessary for the purpose of preventing serious damage to livestock, foodstuffs for livestock, crops, vegetables, fruit, growing timber or any other form of property or to fisheries.

(5) A person shall not be entitled to rely on the defence provided by subsection (2) or (3)(*c*) as respects anything done in relation to a bat otherwise than in the living area of a dwelling house unless he had notified the Nature Conservancy Council of the proposed action or operation and allowed them a reasonable time to advise him as to whether it should be carried out and, if so, the method to be used.

(6) An authorised person shall not be entitled to rely on the defence provided by subsection (4) as respects any action taken at any time if it had become apparent, before that time, that that action would prove necessary for the purpose mentioned in that subsection and either—

    (*a*) a licence under section 16 authorising that action had not been applied for as soon as reasonably practicable after that fact had become apparent ; or

    (*b*) an application for such a licence had been determined.

11.—(1) Subject to the provisions of this Part, if any person— PART I

   (a) sets in position any self-locking snare which is of such Prohibition a nature and so placed as to be calculated to cause of certain bodily injury to any wild animal coming into contact methods of therewith; killing or taking wild

   (b) uses for the purpose of killing or taking any wild animals. animal any self-locking snare, whether or not of such a nature or so placed as aforesaid, any bow or cross-bow or any explosive other than ammunition for a firearm; or

   (c) uses as a decoy, for the purpose of killing or taking any wild animal, any live mammal or bird whatever,

he shall be guilty of an offence.

(2) Subject to the provisions of this Part, if any person—

   (a) sets in position any of the following articles, being an article which is of such a nature and so placed as to be calculated to cause bodily injury to any wild animal included in Schedule 6 which comes into contact therewith, that is to say, any trap or snare, any electrical device for killing or stunning or any poisonous, poisoned or stupefying substance;

   (b) uses for the purpose of killing or taking any such wild animal any such article as aforesaid, whether or not of such a nature and so placed as aforesaid, or any net;

   (c) uses for the purpose of killing or taking any such wild animal—

      (i) any automatic or semi-automatic weapon;

      (ii) any device for illuminating a target or sighting device for night shooting;

      (iii) any form of artificial light or any mirror or other dazzling device; or

      (iv) any gas or smoke not falling within paragraphs (a) and (b);

   (d) uses as a decoy, for the purpose of killing or taking any such wild animal, any sound recording; or

   (e) uses any mechanically propelled vehicle in immediate pursuit of any such wild animal for the purpose of driving, killing or taking that animal,

he shall be guilty of an offence.

(3) Subject to the provisions of this Part, if any person—

   (a) sets in position any snare which is of such a nature and so placed as to be calculated to cause bodily injury to any wild animal coming into contact therewith; and (*b*) while the snare remains in position fails, without reasonable excuse, to inspect it, or cause it to be inspected, at least once every day,

he shall be guilty of an offence.

(4) The Secretary of State may, for the purpose of complying with an international obligation, by order, either generally or in relation to any kind of wild animal specified in the order, amend subsection (1) or (2) by adding any method of killing or taking wild animals or by omitting any such method as is mentioned in that subsection.

(5) In any proceedings for an offence under subsection (1)(*b*) or (*c*) or (2)(*b*), (*c*), (*d*) or (*e*), the animal in question shall be presumed to have been a wild animal unless the contrary is shown.

(6) In any proceedings for an offence under subsection (2)(*a*) it shall be a defence to show that the article was set in position by the accused for the purpose of killing or taking, in the interests of public health, agriculture, forestry, fisheries or nature conservation, any wild animals which could be lawfully killed or taken by those means and that he took all reasonable precautions to prevent injury thereby to any wild animals included in Schedule 6.

Protection of certain mammals.   **12.** Schedule 7, which amends the law relating to the protection of certain mammals, shall have effect.

Protection of plants

Protection of wild plants.   **13.**—(1) Subject to the provisions of this Part, if any person—

(*a*) intentionally picks, uproots or destroys any wild plant included in Schedule 8 ; or

(*b*) not being an authorised person, intentionally uproots any wild plant not included in that Schedule,

he shall be guilty of an offence.

(2) Subject to the provisions of this Part, if any person—

(*a*) sells, offers or exposes for sale, or has in his possession or transports for the purpose of sale, any live or dead wild plant included in Schedule 8, or any part of, or anything derived from, such a plant ; or

(*b*) publishes or causes to be published any advertisement likely to be understood as conveying that he buys or sells, or intends to buy or sell, any of those things,

he shall be guilty of an offence.

(3) Notwithstanding anything in subsection (1), a person shall not be guilty of an offence by reason of any act made unlawful by that subsection if he shows that the act was an incidental result of a lawful operation and could not reasonably have been avoided.

PART I

(4) In any proceedings for an offence under subsection (2)(*a*), the plant in question shall be presumed to have been a wild plant unless the contrary is shown.

Miscellaneous

14.—(1) Subject to the provisions of this Part, if any person releases or allows to escape into the wild any animal which—

Introduction of new species etc.

    (*a*) is of a kind which is not ordinarily resident in and is not a regular visitor to Great Britain in a wild state ; or

    (*b*) is included in Part I of Schedule 9,

he shall be guilty of an offence.

(2) Subject to the provisions of this Part, if any person plants or otherwise causes to grow in the wild any plant which is included in Part II of Schedule 9, he shall be guilty of an offence.

(3) Subject to subsection (4), it shall be a defence to a charge of committing an offence under subsection (1) or (2) to prove that the accused took all reasonable steps and exercised all due diligence to avoid committing the offence.

(4) Where the defence provided by subsection (3) involves an allegation that the commission of the offence was due to the act or default of another person, the person charged shall not, without leave of the court, be entitled to rely on the defence unless, within a period ending seven clear days before the hearing, he has served on the prosecutor a notice giving such information identifying or assisting in the identification of the other person as was then in his possession.

(5) Any person authorised in writing by the Secretary of State may, at any reasonable time and (if required to do so) upon producing evidence that he is authorised, enter any land for the purpose of ascertaining whether an offence under subsection (1) or (2) is being, or has been, committed on that land ; but nothing in this subsection shall authorise any person to enter a dwelling.

(6) Any person who intentionally obstructs a person acting in the exercise of the power conferred by subsection (5) shall be guilty of an offence.

PART I
Endangered
species
(import and
export).
1976 c. 72.

15.—(1) The Endangered Species (Import and Export) Act 1976 shall have effect subject to the amendments provided for in Schedule 10 ; and in that Schedule " the 1976 Act " means that Act.

(2) The functions of the Nature Conservancy Council shall include power to advise or assist—

(a) any constable ;

(b) any officer commissioned or other person appointed or authorised by the Commissioners of Customs and Excise to exercise any function conferred on the Commissioners by the said Act of 1976 ; or

(c) any person duly authorised by the Secretary of State under section 7(3) of that Act,

in, or in connection with, the enforcement of that Act or any order made under it.

Supplemental

Power to
grant licences.

16.—(1) Sections 1, 5, 6(3), 7 and 8 and orders under section 3 do not apply to anything done—

(a) for scientific or educational purposes ;

(b) for the purpose of ringing or marking, or examining any ring or mark on, wild birds ;

(c) for the purpose of conserving wild birds ;

(d) for the purpose of protecting any collection of wild birds ;

(e) for the purposes of falconry or aviculture ;

(f) for the purposes of any public exhibition or competition ;

(g) for the purposes of taxidermy ;

(h) for the purpose of photography ;

(i) for the purposes of preserving public health or public or air safety ;

(j) for the purpose of preventing the spread of disease ; or

(k) for the purposes of preventing serious damage to livestock, foodstuffs for livestock, crops, vegetables, fruit, growing timber or fisheries,

if it is done under and in accordance with the terms of a licence granted by the appropriate authority.

(2) Section 1 and orders under section 3 do not apply to anything done for the purpose of providing food for human consumption in relation to—

(a) a gannet on the island of Sula Sgeir ; or

(*b*) a gull's egg or, at any time before 15th April in any year, a lapwing's egg,

if it is done under and in accordance with the terms of a licence granted by the appropriate authority.

(3) Sections 9(1), (2) and (4), 11(1) and (2) and 13(1) do not apply to anything done—

(*a*) for scientific or educational purposes ;

(*b*) for the purpose of ringing or marking, or examining any ring or mark on, wild animals ;

(*c*) for the purpose of conserving wild animals or wild plants or introducing them to particular areas ;

(*d*) for the purpose of protecting any zoological or botanical collection ;

(*e*) for the purpose of photography ;

(*f*) for the purpose of preserving public health or public safety ;

(*g*) for the purpose of preventing the spread of disease ; or

(*h*) for the purpose of preventing serious damage to livestock, foodstuffs for livestock, crops, vegetables, fruit, growing timber or any other form of property or to fisheries,

if it is done under and in accordance with the terms of a licence granted by the appropriate authority.

(4) The following provisions, namely—

(*a*) section 6(1) and (2) ;

(*b*) sections 9(5) and 13(2) ; and

(*c*) section 14,

do not apply to anything done under and in accordance with the terms of a licence granted by the appropriate authority.

(5) Subject to subsection (6), a licence under the foregoing provisions of this section—

(*a*) may be, to any degree, general or specific ;

(*b*) may be granted either to persons of a class or to a particular person ;

(*c*) may be subject to compliance with any specified conditions ;

(*d*) may be modified or revoked at any time by the appropriate authority ; and

(*e*) subject to paragraph (*d*), shall be valid for the period stated in the licence ;

and the appropriate authority may charge therefor such reasonable sum (if any) as they may determine.

(6) A licence under subsection (1), (2) or (3) which authorises any person to kill wild birds or wild animals—

  (a) shall specify the area within which, and the methods by which the wild birds or wild animals may be killed; and

  (b) subject to subsection (5)(d), shall be valid for the period, not exceeding two years, stated in the licence.

(7) It shall be a defence in proceedings for an offence under section 8(b) of the Protection of Animals Act 1911 or section 7(b) of the Protection of Animals (Scotland) Act 1912 (which restrict the placing on land of poison and poisonous substances) to show that—

1911 c. 27.
1912 c. 14.

  (a) the act alleged to constitute the offence was done under and in accordance with the terms of a licence issued under subsection (1) or (3); and

  (b) any conditions specified in the. licence were complied with.

(8) For the purposes of a licence granted under the foregoing provisions of this section, the definition of a class of persons may be framed by reference to any circumstances whatever including, in particular, their being authorised by any other person.

(9) In this section " the appropriate authority " means—

  (a) in the case of a licence under paragraph (a), (b) or (c) of subsection (1), either the Secretary of State after consultation with whichever one of the advisory bodies he considers is best able to advise him as to whether the licence should be granted, or the Nature Conservancy Council;

  (b) in the case of a licence under any of paragraphs (d) to (g) of subsection (1), subsection (2) or paragraph (a) or (b) of subsection (4), the Secretary of State after such consultation as aforesaid;

  (c) in the case of a licence under paragraph (h) of subsection (1) or any of paragraphs (a) to (e) of subsection (3), the Nature Conservancy Council;

  (d) in the case of a licence under paragraph (i), (j) or (k) of subsection (1) or paragraph (f), (g) or (h) of subsection (3) or a licence under paragraph (c) of subsection (4) which authorises anything to be done in relation to fish or shellfish, the agriculture Minister; and

  (e) in the case of any other licence under paragraph (c) of subsection (4), the Secretary of State.

(10) The agriculture Minister—

  (a) shall from time to time consult with the Nature Conservancy Council as to the exercise of his functions under this section ; and

  (b) shall not grant a licence of any description unless he has been advised by the Council as to the circumstances in which, in their opinion, licences of that description should be granted.

17. A person who, for the purposes of obtaining, whether for himself or another, a registration in accordance with regulations made under section 6(2) or 7(1) or the grant of a licence under section 16—

  (a) makes a statement or representation, or furnishes a document or information, which he knows to be false in a material particular ; or

  (b) recklessly makes a statement or representation, or furnishes a document or information, which is false in a material particular,

shall be guilty of an offence.

18.—(1) Any person who attempts to commit an offence under the foregoing provisions of this Part shall be guilty of an offence and shall be punishable in like manner as for the said offence.

(2) Any person who for the purposes of committing an offence under the foregoing provisions of this Part, has in his possession anything capable of being used for committing the offence shall be guilty of an offence and shall be punishable in like manner as for the said offence.

19.—(1) If a constable suspects with reasonable cause that any person is committing or has committed an offence under this Part, the constable may without warrant—

  (a) stop and search that person if the constable suspects with reasonable cause that evidence of the commission of the offence is to be found on that person ;

  (b) search or examine any thing which that person may then be using or have in his possession if the constable suspects with reasonable cause that evidence of the commission of the offence is to be found on that thing ;

  (c) arrest that person if he fails to give his name and address to the constable's satisfaction ;

(*d*) seize and detain for the purposes of proceedings under this Part any thing which may be evidence of the commission of the offence or may be liable to be forfeited under section 21.

(2) If a constable suspects with reasonable cause that any person is committing an offence under this Part, he may, for the purpose of exercising the powers conferred by subsection (1), enter any land other than a dwelling-house.

(3) If a justice of the peace is satisfied by information on oath that there are reasonable grounds for suspecting that—

(*a*) an offence under section 1, 3, 5, 7 or 8 in respect of which this Part or any order made under it provides for a special penalty ; or

(*b*) an offence under section 6, 9, 11(1) or (2), 13 or 14,

has been committed and that evidence of the offence may be found on any premises, he may grant a warrant to any constable (with or without other persons) to enter upon and search those premises for the purpose of obtaining that evidence.

In the application of this subsection to Scotland, the reference to a justice of the peace includes a reference to the sheriff.

Summary prosecutions.

20.—(1) This section applies to—

(*a*) any offence under section 1(1) or 3(1) involving the killing or taking of any wild bird or the taking of an egg of such a bird ;

(*b*) any offence under section 9(1) involving the killing or taking of any wild animal ; and

(*c*) any offence under section 13(1) involving the picking uprooting or destruction of any wild plant.

(2) Summary proceedings for an offence to which this section applies may be brought within a period of six months from the date on which evidence sufficient in the opinion of the prosecutor to warrant the proceedings came to his knowledge ; but no such proceedings shall be brought by virtue of this section more than two years after the commission of the offence.

(3) For the purpose of this section a certificate signed by or on behalf of the prosecutor and stating the date on which such evidence as aforesaid came to his knowledge shall be conclusive evidence of that fact ; and a certificate stating that matter and purporting to be so signed shall be deemed to be so signed unless the contrary is proved.

21.—(1) Subject to subsection (5), a person guilty of an offence under section 1, 3, 5, 6, 7 or 8 shall be liable on summary conviction—

    (a) in a case where this Part or any order made under it provides that he shall be liable to a special penalty, to a fine not exceeding £1,000 ;

    (b) in any other case, to a fine not exceeding £200.

PART I
Penalties, forfeitures etc.

(2) Subject to subsection (5), a person guilty of an offence under section 9 or 11(1) or (2) shall be liable on summary conviction to a fine not exceeding £1,000.

(3) Subject to subsection (5), a person guilty of an offence under section 11(3), 13 or 17 shall be liable on summary conviction to a fine not exceeding £500.

(4) A person guilty of an offence under section 14 shall be liable—

    (a) on summary conviction, to a fine not exceeding the statutory maximum ;

    (b) on conviction on indictment, to a fine.

(5) Where an offence to which subsection (1), (2) or (3) applies was committed in respect of more than one bird, nest, egg, other animal, plant or other thing, the maximum fine which may be imposed under that subsection shall be determined as if the person convicted had been convicted of a separate offence in respect of each bird, nest, egg, animal, plant or thing.

(6) The court by which any person is convicted of an offence under this Part—

    (a) shall order the forfeiture of any bird, nest, egg, other animal, plant or other thing in respect of which the offence was committed ; and

    (b) may order the forfeiture of any vehicle, animal, weapon or other thing which was used to commit the offence and, in the case of an offence under section 14, any animal or plant which is of the same kind as that in respect of which the offence was committed and was found in his possession.

(7) Any offence under this Part shall, for the purpose of conferring jurisdiction, be deemed to have been committed in any place where the offender is found or to which he is first brought after the commission of the offence.

22.—(1) The Secretary of State may by order, either generally or with respect to particular provisions of this Part, particular areas of Great Britain or particular times of the year, add any bird to, or remove any bird from, any of or any Part of Schedules 1 to 4.

Power to vary Schedules.

(2) An order under subsection (1) adding any bird to Part II of Schedule 1 or Part I of Schedule 2 may prescribe a close season in the case of that bird for the purposes of sections 1 and 2 ; and any close season so prescribed shall commence on a date not later than 21st February and end on a date not earlier than 31st August.

(3) The Secretary of State may, on a representation made to him by the Nature Conservancy Council, by order, either generally or with respect to particular provisions of this Part, particular areas of Great Britain or particular times of the year—

(a) add to Schedule 5 or Schedule 8 any animal or plant which, in his opinion, is in danger of extinction in Great Britain or is likely to become so endangered unless conservation measures are taken ; and

(b) remove from Schedule 5 or Schedule 8 any animal or plant which, in his opinion, is no longer so endangered or likely to become so endangered.

(4) The Secretary of State may, for the purpose of complying with an international obligation, by order, either generally or with respect to particular provisions of this Part or particular times of the year—

(a) add any animals to, or remove any animals from, Schedule 5 or Schedule 6 ; and

(b) add any plants to, or remove any plants from, Schedule 8.

(5) The Secretary of State may by order, either generally or with respect to particular areas of Great Britain—

(a) add any animals to, or remove any animals from, Part I of Schedule 9 ; and

(b) add any plants to, or remove any plants from, Part II of that Schedule.

Advisory bodies and their functions.

23.—(1) The Secretary of State may—

(a) establish any body or bodies, consisting in each case of such members as he may from time to time appoint ;

(b) assign to any body or bodies the duty referred to in subsection (4).

(2) Without prejudice to his power under subsection (1), the Secretary of State shall, as soon as practicable after the commencement date,—

(a) establish at least one body under paragraph (a) of subsection (1) ; or

(b) assign to at least one body, under paragraph (b) of that subsection, the duty referred to in subsection (4).

(3) A reference in this Part to an advisory body is a reference to a body which is established under subsection (1) or to which the duty there referred to is assigned under that subsection.

(4) It shall be the duty of an advisory body to advise the Secretary of State on any question which he may refer to it or on which it considers it should offer its advice—

  (a) in connection with the administration of this Part; or
  (b) otherwise in connection with the protection of birds or other animals or plants.

(5) In so far as it does not have power to do so apart from this subsection, an advisory body may publish reports relating to the performance by it of its duty under subsection (4).

(6) Before appointing a person to be a member of an advisory body established under subsection (1)(a), the Secretary of State shall consult such persons or bodies as he thinks fit.

(7) The Secretary of State may, out of moneys provided by Parliament and to such an extent as may be approved by the Treasury, defray or contribute towards the expenses of an advisory body established under subsection (1)(a).

24.—(1) The Nature Conservancy Council may at any time Functions of and shall five years after the passing of this Act and every Nature five years thereafter, review Schedules 5 and 8 and advise the Conservancy Secretary of State whether, in their opinion,— Council.

  (a) any animal should be added to, or removed from, Schedule 5;
  (b) any plant should be added to, or removed from, Schedule 8.

(2) Advice may be given under subsection (1) either generally or with respect to particular provisions of this Part, particular areas of Great Britain or particular times of the year; and any advice so given shall be accompanied by a statement of the reasons which led the Council to give that advice.

(3) The Council shall include any advice so given and the statement accompanying it in the annual report submitted by them to the Secretary of State under paragraph 17 of Schedule 3 to the Nature Conservancy Council Act 1973. 1973 c. 54.

(4) The functions of the Council shall include power to advise or assist—

  (a) any constable;
  (b) any proper officer of a local authority; or
  (c) any person duly authorised by the Secretary of State under section 6(9), 7(6) or 14(5),

in, or in connection with, the enforcement of the provisions of this Part or any order or regulations made under it.

PART 1
Functions of
local
authorities.

25.—(1) Every local authority shall take such steps as they consider expedient for bringing to the attention of the public and of schoolchildren in particular the effect of—

(a) the provisions of this Part ; and

(b) any order made under this Part affecting the whole or any part of their area.

(2) A local authority in England and Wales may institute proceedings for any offence under this Part or any order made under it which is committed within their area.

Regulations,
orders,
notices etc.

26.—(1) Any power to make regulations or orders under this Part shall be exercisable by statutory instrument.

(2) A statutory instrument containing regulations under this Part, or an order under a provision of this Part other than sections 2(6), 3, 5 and 11, shall be subject to annulment in pursuance of a resolution of either House of Parliament.

(3) No order under section 5 or 11 shall be made unless a draft of the order has been laid before and approved by a resolution of each House of Parliament.

(4) Before making any order under this Part, the Secretary of State—

(a) except in the case of an order under section 2(6), shall give to any local authority affected and, except in the case of an order under section 3, any other person affected, by such means as he may think appropriate, an opportunity to submit objections or representations with respect to the subject matter of the order ;

(b) except in the case of an order under section 22(3), shall consult with whichever one of the advisory bodies he considers is best able to advise him as to whether the order should be made ; and

(c) may, if he thinks fit, cause a public inquiry to be held.

(5) Notice of the making of an order under this Part shall be published by the Secretary of State—

(a) if the order relates in whole or in part to England and Wales, in the London Gazette ; and

(b) if the order relates in whole or in part to Scotland, in the Edinburgh Gazette.

(6) The Secretary of State shall give consideration to any proposals for the making by him of an order under this Part with respect to any area which may be submitted to him by a local authority whose area includes that area.

27.—(1) In this Part, unless the context otherwise requires—

" advertisement " includes a catalogue, a circular and a price list;

" advisory body " has the meaning given by section 23 ;

" agriculture Minister " means the Minister of Agriculture, Fisheries and Food or the Secretary of State ;

" authorised person " means—

(a) the owner or occupier, or any person authorised by the owner or occupier, of the land on which the action authorised is taken ;

(b) any person authorised in writing by the local authority for the area within which the action authorised is taken ;

(c) as respects anything done in relation to wild birds, any person authorised in writing by any of the following bodies, that is to say, the Nature Conservancy Council, a water authority or any other statutory water undertakers, a district board for a fishery district within the meaning of the Salmon Fisheries 1862 c. 97. (Scotland) Act 1862 or a local fisheries committee constituted under the Sea Fisheries Regulation Act 1966 c. 38. 1966 ;

so, however, that the authorisation of any person for the purposes of this definition shall not confer any right of entry upon any land ;

" automatic weapon " and " semi-automatic weapon " do not include any weapon the magazine of which is incapable of holding more than two rounds ;

" aviculture " means the breeding and rearing of birds in captivity ;

" destroy ", in relation to an egg, includes doing anything to the egg which is calculated to prevent it from hatching, and " destruction " shall be construed accordingly ;

" domestic duck " means any domestic form of duck ;

" domestic goose " means any domestic form of goose ;

" firearm " has the same meaning as in the Firearms Act 1968 c. 27. 1968 ;

" game bird " means any pheasant, partridge, grouse (or moor game), black (or heath) game or ptarmigan ;

" livestock " includes any animal which is kept—

(a) for the provision of food, wool, skins or fur ;

(b) for the purpose of its use in the carrying on of any agricultural activity ; or

(c) for the provision or improvement of shooting or fishing ;

" local authority " means—

>(a) in relation to England and Wales, a county, district or London borough council and the Greater London Council ;

>(b) in relation to Scotland, a regional, islands or district council ;

" occupier ", in relation to any land other than the foreshore, includes any person having any right of hunting, shooting, fishing or taking game or fish ;

" pick ", in relation to a plant, means gather or pluck any part of the plant without uprooting it ;

" poultry " means domestic fowls, geese, ducks, guinea-fowls, pigeons and quails, and turkeys ;

" sale " includes hire, barter and exchange and cognate expressions shall be construed accordingly ;

" uproot ", in relation to a plant, means dig up or otherwise remove the plant from the land on which it is growing ;

" vehicle " includes aircraft, hovercraft and boat ;

" water authority ", in relation to Scotland, has the same meaning as in the Water (Scotland) Act 1980 ;

1980 c. 45.

" wild animal " means any animal (other than a bird) which is or (before it was killed or taken) was living wild ;

" wild bird " means any bird of a kind which is ordinarily resident in or is a visitor to Great Britain in a wild state but does not include poultry or, except in sections 5 and 16, any game bird ;

" wild plant " means any plant which is or (before it was picked, uprooted or destroyed) was growing wild and is of a kind which ordinarily grows in Great Britain in a wild state.

(2) A bird shall not be treated as bred in captivity for the purposes of this Part unless its parents were lawfully in captivity when the egg was laid.

(3) Any reference in this Part to an animal of any kind includes, unless the context otherwise requires, a reference to an egg, larva, pupa, or other immature stage of an animal of that kind.

(4) This Part shall apply to the Isles of Scilly as if the Isles were a county and as if the Council of the Isles were a county council.

(5) This Part extends to the territorial waters adjacent to Great Britain, and for the purposes of this Part any part of Great Britain which is bounded by territorial waters shall be taken to include the territorial waters adjacent to that part.

PART II

NATURE CONSERVATION, COUNTRYSIDE AND NATIONAL PARKS

Nature conservation

28.—(1) Where the Nature Conservancy Council are of the Areas of opinion that any area of land is of special interest by reason of special scientific any of its flora, fauna, or geological or physiographical features, interest. it shall be the duty of the Council to notify that fact—

(*a*) to the local planning authority in whose area the land is situated ;

(*b*) to every owner and occupier of any of that land ; and

(*c*) to the Secretary of State.

(2) Before giving a notification under subsection (1), the Council shall give notice to the persons mentioned in that subsection—

(*a*) setting out the proposed notification ; and

(*b*) specifying the time (not being less than three months from the date of the giving of the notice) within which and the manner in which, representations or objections with respect thereto may be made,

and shall consider any representation or objections duly made.

(3) If, after reasonable inquiry has been made, the Council are satisfied that it is not practicable to ascertain the name or address of an owner or occupier of any land a notification or notice required to be served on him may be served by addressing it to him by the description " owner " or " occupier " of the land (describing it) and by affixing it to some conspicuous object or objects on the land.

(4) A notification under subsection (1)(*b*) shall specify—

(*a*) the flora, fauna, or geological or physiographical features by reason of which the land is of special interest ; and

(*b*) any operations appearing to the Council to be likely to damage that flora or fauna or those features.

(5) The owner or occupier of any land which has been notified under subsection (1)(*b*) shall not carry out, or cause or permit to be carried out, on that land any operation specified in the notification unless—

(*a*) one of them has, after the commencement date, given the Council written notice of a proposal to carry out the operation specifying its nature and the land on which it is proposed to carry it out ; and

(*b*) one of the conditions specified in subsection (6) is fulfilled.

(6) The said conditions are—

(a) that the operation is carried out with the Council's written consent;

(b) that the operation is carried out in accordance with the terms of an agreement under section 16 of the 1949 Act or section 15 of the 1968 Act; and

(c) that three months have expired from the giving of the notice under subsection (5).

(7) A person who, without reasonable excuse, contravenes subsection (5) shall be liable on summary conviction to a fine not exceeding £500.

(8) It is a reasonable excuse in any event for a person to carry out an operation if—

(a) the operation was authorised by a planning permission granted on an application under Part III of the Town and Country Planning Act 1971 or Part III of the Town and Country Planning (Scotland) Act 1972; or

1971 c. 78.
1972 c. 52.

(b) the operation was an emergency operation particulars of which (including details of the emergency) were notified to the Council as soon as practicable after the commencement of the operation.

(9) The Council shall have power to enforce the provisions of this section; but nothing in this subsection shall be construed as authorising the Council to institute proceedings in Scotland for an offence.

(10) Proceedings in England and Wales for an offence under subsection (7) shall not, without the consent of the Director of Public Prosecutions, be taken by a person other than the Council.

(11) A notification under subsection (1)(b) of land in England and Wales shall be a local land charge.

(12) A notification under subsection (1)(b) of land in Scotland shall be registered either—

(a) in a case where the land is registered in that Register, in the Land Register of Scotland; or

(b) in any other case, in the appropriate Division of the General Register of Sasines.

(13) Section 23 of the 1949 Act (which is superseded by this section) shall cease to have effect; but any notification given under that section shall have effect as if given under subsection (1)(a).

(14) Subsection (2) shall not apply in relation to a notification of any land under subsection (1)(b) where a notification of that land under the said section 23 has effect as if given under subsection (1)(a).

29.—(1) Where it appears to the Secretary of State expedient to do so—

PART II
Special
protection for
certain areas of
special
scientific
interest.

> (a) in the case of any land to which this paragraph applies, for the purpose of securing the survival in Great Britain of any kind of animal or plant or of complying with an international obligation; or
>
> (b) in the case of any land to which this paragraph applies, for the purpose of conserving any of its flora, fauna, or geological or physiographical features,

he may, after consultation with the Nature Conservancy Council, by order apply subsection (3) to that land ; and the provisions of Schedule 11 shall have effect as to the making, confirmation and coming into operation of orders under this section.

An order made under this section may be amended or revoked by a subsequent order so made.

(2) Paragraphs (a) and (b) of subsection (1) apply to any land which in the opinion of the Secretary of State is—

> (a) of special interest ; and
>
> (b) in the case of paragraph (b) of that subsection, of national importance,

by reason of any of its flora, fauna, or geological or physiographical features.

(3) Subject to subsection (4), no person shall carry out on any land to which this subsection applies any operation which—

> (a) appears to the Secretary of State to be likely to destroy or damage the flora, fauna, or geological or physiographical features by reason of which the land is land to which paragraph (a) or, as the case may be, paragraph (b) of subsection (1) applies ; and
>
> (b) is specified in the order applying this subsection to the land.

(4) Subsection (3) shall not apply in relation to any operation carried out, or caused or permitted to be carried out, by the owner or occupier of the land if—

> (a) one of them has, after the commencement date, given the Council notice of a proposal to carry out the operation, specifying its nature and the land on which it is proposed to carry it out ; and
>
> (b) one of the conditions specified in subsection (5) is fulfilled.

(5) The said conditions are—

> (a) that the operation is carried out with the Council's written consent ;

PART II

(b) that the operation is carried out in accordance with the terms of an agreement under section 16 of the 1949 Act or section 15 of the 1968 Act ; and

(c) subject to subsections (6) and (7), that three months have expired from the giving of the notice under subsection (4).

(6) If before the expiration of the period mentioned in paragraph (c) of subsection (5) the Council offer to enter into an agreement for the acquisition of the interest of the person who gave the notice under subsection (4) or an agreement under section 16 of the 1949 Act or section 15 of the 1968 Act providing for the making by them of payments to that person, that paragraph shall have effect as if for the said period there were substituted—

(a) where the agreement is entered into before the expiration of twelve months from the giving of the notice, the period expiring on the day on which it is entered into ;

(b) in any other case, twelve months from the giving of the notice or three months from rejection or withdrawal of the offer to enter into the agreement, whichever period last expires.

(7) If before the expiration of the period mentioned in paragraph (c) of subsection (5), or that paragraph as it has effect by virtue of subsection (6), an order is made for the compulsory acquisition by the Council of the interest of the person who gave the notice under subsection (4), that paragraph shall have effect as if for the said period there were substituted the period expiring—

(a) in the case of an order which is confirmed, on the day on which the Council enter on the land ;

(b) in any other case, on the day on which the order is withdrawn or the Secretary of State decides not to confirm it.

(8) A person who, without reasonable excuse, contravenes subsection (3) shall be liable—

(a) on summary conviction, to a fine not exceeding the statutory maximum ;

(b) on conviction on indictment, to a fine.

(9) It is a reasonable excuse in any event for a person to carry out an operation if—

(a) the operation was authorised by a planning permission granted on an application under Part III of the Town and Country Planning Act 1971 or Part III of the Town and Country Planning (Scotland) Act 1972 ; or

(b) the operation was an emergency operation particulars of which (including details of the emergency) were noti-

1971 c. 78.
1972 c. 52.

fied to the Council as soon as practicable after the commencement of the operation.

(10) An order made under this section in relation to land in Scotland shall be registered either—

    (a) in a case where the land affected by the order is registered in that Register, in the Land Register of Scotland ; or

    (b) in any other case, in the appropriate Division of the General Register of Sasines.

(11) A report submitted by the Council to the Secretary of State under paragraph 17 of Schedule 3 to the Nature Conservancy Council Act 1973 for any year shall set out particulars of any areas of land as respects which orders under this section have come into operation during that year. 1973 c. 54.

30.—(1) Subsection (2) applies where an order is made under section 29 and subsection (3) applies where— Compensation where order is made under s. 29.

    (a) notice of a proposal to carry out an operation is duly given to the Nature Conservancy Council under subsection (4) of that section ; and

    (b) paragraph (c) of subsection (5) of that section has effect as modified by subsection (6) or (7) of that section.

(2) The Council shall pay compensation to any person having at the time of the making of the order an interest in land comprised in an agricultural unit comprising land to which the order relates who, on a claim made to the Council within the time and in the manner prescribed by regulations under this section, shows that the value of his interest is less than what it would have been if the order had not been made ; and the amount of the compensation shall be equal to the difference between the two values.

(3) The Council shall pay compensation to any person having at the time of the giving of the notice an interest in land to which the notice relates who, on a claim made to the Council within the time and in the manner prescribed by regulations under this section, shows that—

    (a) he has reasonably incurred expenditure which has been rendered abortive, or expenditure in carrying out work which has been rendered abortive, by reason of paragraph (c) of subsection (5) of section 29 having effect as modified by subsection (6) or (7) of that section ; or

    (b) he has incurred loss or damage which is directly attributable to that paragraph having effect as so modified ;

but nothing in this subsection shall entitle any such person to compensation in respect of any reduction in the value of his interest in the land.

(4) For the purposes of subsection (2)—

(*a*) an interest in land shall be valued as at the time when the order is made ;

(*b*) where a person, by reason of his having more than one interest in land, makes more than one claim under that subsection in respect of the same order, his various interests shall be valued together ;

1973 c. 26.

1973 c. 56.

(*c*) section 10 of the Land Compensation Act 1973 (mortgages, trusts for sale and settlements) or section 10 of the Land Compensation (Scotland) Act 1973 (restricted interests in land) shall apply in relation to compensation under that subsection as it applies in relation to compensation under Part I of that Act.

1961 c. 33.

1963 c. 51.

(5) For the purposes of assessing any compensation payable under subsection (2), the rules set out in section 5 of the Land Compensation Act 1961 or section 12 of the Land Compensation (Scotland) Act 1963 shall, so far as applicable and subject to any necessary modifications, have effect as they have effect for the purpose of assessing compensation for the compulsory acquisition of an interest in land.

(6) No claim shall be made under subsection (2) in respect of any order under section 29 unless the Secretary of State has given notice under paragraph 6(1) or (2) of Schedule 11 of his decision in respect of the order ; and, without prejudice to subsection (4)(*a*), that decision will be taken into account in assessing the compensation payable in respect of the order.

(7) Compensation under this section shall carry interest, at the rate for the time being prescribed under section 32 of the Land Compensation Act 1961 or section 40 of the Land Compensation (Scotland) Act 1963, from the date of the claim until payment.

(8) Except in so far as may be provided by regulations under this section, any question of disputed compensation under this section shall be referred to and determined by the Lands Tribunal or the Lands Tribunal for Scotland.

(9) In relation to the determination of any such question, the provisions of sections 2 and 4 of the Land Compensation Act 1961 or sections 9 and 11 of the Land Compensation (Scotland) Act 1963 (procedure and costs) shall apply, subject to any necessary modifications and to the provisions of any regulations under this section.

(10) Regulations under this section shall be made by the Secretary of State and shall be made by statutory instrument subject to annulment in pursuance of a resolution of either House of Parliament.

(11) In this section " agricultural unit " means land which is PART II
occupied as a unit for agricultural purposes, including any dwelling-house or other building occupied by the same person for the
purpose of farming the land.

31.—(1) Where the operation in respect of which a person Restoration
is convicted of an offence under section 29 has destroyed or where order
damaged any of the flora, fauna, or geological or physiographi- under s. 29 is
cal features by reason of which the land on which it was carried contravened.
out is of special interest, the court by which he is convicted,
in addition to dealing with him in any other way, may make
an order requiring him to carry out, within such period as may
be specified in the order, such operations for the purpose of
restoring the land to its former condition as may be so specified.

(2) An order under this section made on conviction on indictment shall be treated for the purposes of sections 30 and 42(1)
and (2) of the Criminal Appeal Act 1968 (effect of appeals on 1968 c. 19.
orders for the restitution of property) as an order for the restitution of property ; and where by reason of the quashing by the
Court of Appeal of a person's conviction any such order does
not take effect, and on appeal to the House of Lords the conviction is restored by that House, the House may make any order
under this section which could be made on his conviction by the
court which convicted him.

(3) In the case of an order under this section made by a
magistrates' court the period specified in the order shall not
begin to run—
   (a) in any case until the expiration of the period for the
       time being prescribed by law for the giving of notice
       of appeal against a decision of a magistrates' court ;
   (b) where notice of appeal is given within the period so
       prescribed, until determination of the appeal.

(4) At any time before an order under this section has been
complied with or fully complied with, the court by which it was
made may, on the application of the person against whom it
was made, discharge or vary the order if it appears to the court
that a change in circumstances has made compliance or full
compliance with the order impracticable or unnecessary.

(5) If, within the period specified in an order under this section,
the person against whom it was made fails, without reasonable
excuse, to comply with it, he shall be liable on summary conviction—
   (a) to a fine not exceeding £1,000 ; and
   (b) in the case of a continuing offence, to a further fine not
       exceeding £100 for each day during which the offence
       continues after conviction.

(6) If, within the period specified in an order under this section, any operations specified in the order have not been carried out, the Nature Conservancy Council may enter the land and carry out those operations and recover from the person against whom the order was made any expenses reasonably incurred by them in doing so.

(7) In the application of this section to Scotland—

(a) subsections (2) and (3) shall not apply ; and

(b) for the purposes of any appeal or review, an order under this section is a sentence.

Duties of agriculture Ministers with respect to areas of special scientific interest.

1970 c. 40.

32.—(1) Where an application for a grant under a scheme made under section 29 of the Agriculture Act 1970 (farm capital grants) is made as respects expenditure incurred or to be incurred for the purpose of activities on land notified under section 28(1) or land to which section 29(3) applies, the appropriate Minister—

(a) shall, so far as may be consistent with the purposes of the scheme and section 29 of the said Act of 1970, so exercise his functions thereunder as to further the conservation of the flora, fauna, or geological or physiographical features by reason of which the land is of special interest ; and

(b) where the Nature Conservancy Council have objected to the making of the grant on the ground that the activities in question have destroyed or damaged or will destroy or damage that flora or fauna or those features, shall not make the grant except after considering the objection and, in the case of land in England, after consulting with the Secretary of State.

(2) Where, in consequence of an objection by the Council, an application for a grant as respects expenditure to be incurred is refused on the ground that the activities in question will have such an effect as is mentioned in subsection (1)(b), the Council shall, within three months of their receiving notice of the appropriate Minister's decision, offer to enter into, in the terms of a draft submitted to the applicant, an agreement under section 16 of the 1949 Act or section 15 of the 1968 Act—

(a) imposing restrictions as respects those activities ; and

(b) providing for the making by them of payments to the applicant.

(3) In this section " the appropriate Minister " has the same meaning as in section 29 of the said Act of 1970.

33.—(1) The Ministers shall from time to time, after consultation with the Nature Conservancy Council and such persons appearing to them to represent other interests concerned as they consider appropriate—

> (a) prepare codes containing such recommendations, advice and information as they consider proper for the guidance of—
>
> > (i) persons exercising functions under sections 28 to 32 ; and
> >
> > (ii) persons affected or likely to be affected by the exercise of any of those functions ; and
>
> (b) revise any such code by revoking, varying, amending or adding to the provisions of the code in such manner as the Ministers think fit.

(2) A code prepared in pursuance of subsection (1) and any alterations proposed to be made on a revision of such a code shall be laid before both Houses of Parliament forthwith after being prepared ; and the code or revised code, as the case may be, shall not be issued until the code or the proposed alterations have been approved by both Houses.

(3) Subject to subsection (2), the Ministers shall cause every code prepared or revised in pursuance of subsection (1) to be printed, and may cause copies of it to be put on sale to the public at such price as the Ministers may determine.

34.—(1) Where the Nature Conservancy Council or the Commission are of the opinion that any land in the countryside which comprises a limestone pavement is of special interest by reason of its flora, fauna or geological or physiographical features, it shall be the duty of the Council or the Commission to notify that fact to the local planning authority in whose area the land is situated.

(2) Where it appears to the Secretary of State or the relevant authority that the character or appearance of any land notified under subsection (1) would be likely to be adversely affected by the removal of the limestone or by its disturbance in any way whatever, the Secretary of State or that authority may make an order (in this section referred to as a " limestone pavement order ") designating the land and prohibiting the removal or disturbance of limestone on or in it ; and the provisions of Schedule 11 shall have effect as to the making, confirmation and coming into operation of limestone pavement orders.

(3) The relevant authority may, after consultation with the Council and the Commission, amend or revoke a limestone pavement order made by the authority ; and the Secretary of State may, after such consultation as aforesaid, amend or revoke

108 *Wildlife and Countryside Act 1981*

PART II   any such order made by him or that authority but, in the case
of an order made by that authority, only after consultation with
that authority.

(4) If any person without reasonable excuse removes or
disturbs limestone on or in any land designated by a limestone
pavement order he shall be liable —

(a) on summary conviction, to a fine not exceeding the
statutory maximum ;

(b) on conviction on indictment, to a fine.

(5) It is a reasonable excuse in any event for a person to
remove or disturb limestone or cause or permit its removal or
disturbance, if the removal or disturbance was authorised by a
planning permission granted on an application under Part III
1971 c. 78.   of the Town and Country Planning Act 1971 or Part III of the
1972 c. 52.   Town and Country Planning (Scotland) Act 1972.

(6) In this section—

" the Commission " means the Countryside Commission in
relation to England and Wales and the Countryside
Commission for Scotland in relation to Scotland ;

" limestone pavement " means an area of limestone which
lies wholly or partly exposed on the surface of the
ground and has been fissured by natural erosion ;

" the relevant authority " means the county planning authority in relation to England and Wales and the authority
exercising district planning functions in relation to
Scotland.

National
nature
reserves.

    35.—(1) Where the Nature Conservancy Council are satisfied
that any land which—

(a) is being managed as a nature reserve under an agreement entered into with the Council ;

(b) is held by the Council and is being managed by them
as a nature reserve ; or

(c) is held by an approved body and is being managed
by that body as a nature reserve,

is of national importance, they may declare that land to be a
national nature reserve.

(2) A declaration by the Council that any land is a national
nature reserve shall be conclusive of the matters declared ; and
subsections (4) and (5) of section 19 of the 1949 Act shall
apply in relation to any such declaration as they apply in
relation to a declaration under that section.

(3) On the application of the approved body concerned, the
Council may, as respects any land which is declared to be a
national nature reserve under subsection (1)(c), make byelaws
for the protection of the reserve.

(4) Subsections (2) and (3) of section 20 and section 106 of   PART II
the 1949 Act shall apply in relation to byelaws under this section
as they apply in relation to byelaws under the said section 20.

(5) In this section—

" approved body " means a body approved by the Council
for the purposes of this section ;

" nature reserve " has the same meaning as in Part III of
the 1949 Act.

36.—(1) Where, in the case of any land covered (continuously Marine
or intermittently) by tidal waters or parts of the sea in or nature
adjacent to Great Britain up to the seaward limits of territorial reserves.
waters, it appears to the Secretary of State expedient, on an
application made by the Nature Conservancy Council, that the
land and waters covering it should be managed by the Council
for the purpose of—

(a) conserving marine flora or fauna or geological or physiographical features of special interest in the area ; or

(b) providing, under suitable conditions and control, special
opportunities for the study of, and research into,
matters relating to marine flora and fauna and the
physical conditions in which they live, or for the study
of geological and physiographical features of special
interest in the area,

he may by order designate the area comprising that land and
those waters as a marine nature reserve ; and the Council shall
manage any area so designated for either or both of those
purposes.

(2) An application for an order under this section shall be
accompanied by—

(a) a copy of the byelaws which, if an order is made, the
Council propose making under section 37 for the protection of the area specified in the application ; and

(b) a copy of any byelaws made or proposed to be made
for the protection of that area by a relevant authority ;

and an order made on the application shall authorise the making under that section of such of the byelaws proposed to be
made by the Council as may be set out in the order with or
without modifications.

(3) Byelaws the making of which is so authorised—

(a) shall not require the Secretary of State's consent under
subsection (1) of section 37 ; and

(b) notwithstanding anything in the provisions applied by
subsection (4) of that section, shall take effect on their
being made.

PART II

(4) The provisions of Schedule 12 shall have effect as to the making, validity and date of coming into operation of orders under this section ; and an order made under this section may be amended or revoked by a subsequent order so made.

(5) The powers exercisable by the Council for the purpose of managing an area designated as a marine nature reserve under this section shall include power to install markers indicating the existence and extent of the reserve.

(6) Nothing in this section or in byelaws made under section 37 shall interfere with the exercise of any functions of a relevant authority, any functions conferred by or under an enactment (whenever passed) or any right of any person (whenever vested).

(7) In this section—

"enactment" includes an enactment contained in a local Act ;

"local authority" means—

> (a) in relation to England and Wales, a county council, a district council, the Greater London Council or a London borough council ;

> (b) in relation to Scotland, a regional council, an islands council or a district council ;

"relevant authority" means a local authority, a water authority or any other statutory water undertakers, an internal drainage board, a navigation authority, a harbour authority, a pilotage authority, a lighthouse authority, a conservancy authority, a river purification board, a district board for a fishery district within the meaning of the Salmon Fisheries (Scotland) Act 1862, or a local fisheries committee constituted under the Sea Fisheries Regulation Act 1966.

1862 c. 97.

1966 c. 38.

Byelaws for protection of marine nature reserves.

37.—(1) The Nature Conservancy Council may, with the consent of the Secretary of State make byelaws for the protection of any area designated as a marine nature reserve under section 36.

(2) Without prejudice to the generality of subsection (1), byelaws made under this section as respects a marine nature reserve—

> (a) may provide for prohibiting or restricting, either absolutely or subject to any exceptions—

>> (i) the entry into, or movement within, the reserve of persons and vessels ;

>> (ii) the killing, taking, destruction, molestation or disturbance of animals or plants of any description

in the reserve, or the doing of anything therein which will interfere with the sea bed or damage or disturb any object in the reserve ; or

(iii) the depositing of rubbish in the reserve ;

(*b*) may provide for the issue, on such terms and subject to such conditions as may be specified in the byelaws, of permits authorising entry into the reserve or the doing of anything which would otherwise be unlawful under the byelaws ; and

(*c*) may be so made as to apply either generally or with respect to particular parts of the reserve or particular times of the year.

(3) Nothing in byelaws made under this section shall—

(*a*) prohibit or restrict the exercise of any right of passage by a vessel other than a pleasure boat ; or

(*b*) prohibit, except with respect to particular parts of the reserve at particular times of the year, the exercise of any such right by a pleasure boat.

(4) Nothing in byelaws so made shall make unlawful—

(*a*) anything done for the purpose of securing the safety of any vessel, or of preventing damage to any vessel or cargo, or of saving life ;

(*b*) the discharge of any substance from a vessel ; or

(*c*) anything done more than 30 metres below the sea bed.

(5) Sections 236 to 238 of the Local Government Act 1972 1972 c. 70. or sections 202 to 204 of the Local Government (Scotland) Act 1973 c. 65. 1973 (which relate to the procedure for making byelaws, authorise byelaws to impose fines not exceeding the amount there specified and provide for the proof of byelaws in legal proceedings) shall apply to byelaws under this section as if the Council were a local authority within the meaning of the said Act of 1972 or the said Act of 1973, so however that in relation to such byelaws the said sections shall apply subject to such modifications (including modifications increasing the maximum fines which the byelaws may impose) as may be prescribed by regulations made by the Secretary of State.

Regulations under this subsection shall be made by statutory instrument which shall be subject to annulment in pursuance of a resolution of either House of Parliament.

(6) In relation to byelaws under this section the confirming authority for the purposes of the said section 236 or the said section 202 shall be the Secretary of State.

(7) The Secretary of State may, after consultation with the Council, direct them—

(a) to revoke any byelaws previously made under this section ; or

(b) to make any such amendments of any byelaws so made as may be specified in the direction.

(8) The Council shall have power to enforce byelaws made under this section ; but nothing in this subsection shall be construed as authorising the Council to institute proceedings in Scotland for an offence.

(9) Proceedings in England and Wales for an offence under byelaws made under this section shall not, without the consent of the Director of Public Prosecutions, be taken by a person other than the Council.

(10) In this section " vessel " includes a hovercraft and any aircraft capable of landing on water and " pleasure boat " shall be construed accordingly.

(11) References in this section to animals or plants of any description include references to eggs, seeds, spores, larvae or other immature stages of animals or plants of that description.

Grants and loans by Nature Conservancy Council.

38.—(1) The Nature Conservancy Council may, with the consent of, or in accordance with a general authorisation given by, the Secretary of State, give financial assistance by way of grant or loan, or partly in the one way and partly in the other, to any person in respect of expenditure incurred or to be incurred by him in doing anything which, in their opinion, is conducive to nature conservation or fostering the understanding of nature conservation.

(2) No consent or general authorisation shall be given by the Secretary of State under subsection (1) without the approval of the Treasury.

(3) On making a grant or loan under this section the Council may impose such conditions as they think fit including (in the case of a grant) conditions for repayment in specified circumstances.

(4) The Council shall so exercise their powers under subsection (3) as to ensure that any person receiving a grant or loan under this section in respect of premises to which the public are to be admitted, whether on payment or otherwise, shall, in the means of access both to and within the premises, and in the parking facilities and sanitary conveniences to be

available (if any), make provision, so far as it is in the circum- PART II
stances both practicable and reasonable, for the needs of members of the public visiting the premises who are disabled.

(5) The exercise of the Council's powers under this section
shall be subject to any direction given to the Council by the
Secretary of State.

(6) Section 3 of the Nature Conservancy Council Act 1973 1973 c. 54.
(which is superseded by this section) shall cease to have effect.

Countryside

39.—(1) A relevant authority may, for the purpose of con- Management
serving or enhancing the natural beauty or amenity of any land agreements
which is both in the countryside and within their area or pro- with owners
moting its enjoyment by the public, make an agreement (in this of land.
section referred to as a "management agreement") with any
person having an interest in the land with respect to the management of the land during a specified term or without limitation
of the duration of the agreement.

(2) Without prejudice to the generality of subsection (1), a
management agreement—

(a) may impose on the person having an interest in the land
restrictions as respects the method of cultivating the
land, its use for agricultural purposes or the exercise
of rights over the land and may impose obligations on
that person to carry out works or agricultural or
forestry operations or do other things on the land ;

(b) may confer on the relevant authority power to carry
out works for the purpose of performing their functions
under the 1949 Act and the 1968 Act ; and

(c) may contain such incidental and consequential provisions (including provisions for the making of payments by either party to the other) as appear to the
relevant authority to be necessary or expedient for the
purposes of the agreement.

(3) The provisions of a management agreement with any
person interested in the land shall, unless the agreement otherwise provides, be binding on persons deriving title under or from
that person and be enforceable by the relevant authority against
those persons accordingly.

(4) Schedule 2 to the Forestry Act 1967 (power for tenant for 1967 c. 10.
life and others to enter into forestry dedication covenants) shall
apply to management agreements as it applies to forestry
dedication covenants.

PART II

(5) In this section " the relevant authority " means—

(a) as respects land in a National Park, the county planning authority ;

(b) as respects land in Greater London, the Greater London Council or the London borough council ; and

(c) as respects any other land, the local planning authority.

(6) The powers conferred by this section on a relevant authority shall be in addition to and not in derogation of any powers conferred on such an authority by or under any enactment.

Experimental schemes.

40. For subsections (1) and (2) of section 4 of the 1968 Act (under which the Countryside Commission may submit for the Secretary of State's approval proposals for experimental schemes in relation to particular areas and are required to carry out proposals approved by him) there shall be substituted the following subsection—

" (1) The Commission, after consultation with such local authorities and other bodies as appear to the Commission to have an interest, may from time to time make and carry out or promote the carrying out of any experimental scheme designed to facilitate the enjoyment of the countryside, or to conserve or enhance its natural beauty or amenity, which—

(a) in relation to the countryside generally or to any particular area involves the development or application of new methods, concepts or techniques, or the application or further development of existing methods, concepts or techniques ; and

(b) is designed to illustrate the appropriateness of the scheme in question for the countryside generally or for any particular area."

Duties of agriculture Ministers with respect to the countryside.

1944 c. 28.

41.—(1) The advice for the giving of which free of charge the Minister of Agriculture, Fisheries and Food and the Secretary of State are required by section 1(1) of the Agriculture (Miscellaneous Provisions) Act 1944 to make provision through such organisation as they consider appropriate shall include—

(a) advice to persons carrying on agricultural businesses on the conservation and enhancement of the natural beauty and amenity of the countryside ;

(b) advice to such persons on diversification into other enterprises of benefit to the rural economy ; and

(c) advice to government departments and other bodies exercising statutory functions on the promotion and furtherance of such diversification as is mentioned in paragraph (b).

(2) In the exercise of his general duty under section 4(2) of the Small Landholders (Scotland) Act 1911 of promoting the in- 1911 c. 49. terests of agriculture and other rural industries, and without prejudice to the generality of that duty, the Secretary of State shall make provision, through such organisation as he considers appropriate, for the giving of such advice as is mentioned in paragraphs (*a*), (*b*) and (*c*) of subsection (1).

(3) Where an application for a grant under a scheme made under section 29 of the Agriculture Act 1970 (farm capital grants) 1970 c. 40 is made as respects expenditure incurred or to be incurred for the purposes of activities on land which is in a National Park or an area specified for the purposes of this subsection by the Ministers, the appropriate Minister—

(*a*) shall, so far as may be consistent with the purposes of the scheme and the said section 29, so exercise his functions thereunder as to further the conservation and enhancement of the natural beauty and amenity of the countryside and to promote its enjoyment by the public ; and

(*b*) where the relevant authority have objected to the making of the grant on the ground that the activities in question have had or will have an adverse effect on the natural beauty or amenity of the countryside or its enjoyment by the public, shall not make the grant except after considering the objection and, in the case of land in England, after consulting with the Secretary of State ;

and this subsection shall have effect, in its application to Scotland, as if references to the amenity of the countryside were omitted.

(4) Where, in consequence of an objection by the relevant authority, an application for a grant as respects expenditure to be incurred is refused on the ground that the activities in question will have such an effect as is mentioned in subsection (3)(*b*), the relevant authority shall, within three months of their receiving notice of the appropriate Minister's decision, offer to enter into, in the terms of a draft submitted to the applicant, a management agreement—

(*a*) imposing restrictions as respects those activities ; and

(*b*) providing for the making by them of payments to the applicant.

(5) In this section—

" agricultural business " and " the appropriate Minister " have the same meanings as in the said section 29 ;

" management agreement "—

> (*a*) in relation to England and Wales, means an agreement under section 39 ;

1967 c. 86.
> (*b*) in relation to Scotland, means an agreement under section 49A of the Countryside (Scotland) Act 1967 ;

" the relevant authority "—

> (*a*) in relation to England and Wales, has the same meaning as in section 39 ;

> (*b*) in relation to Scotland, means the authority exercising district planning functions.

(6) Subsection (1) extends only to England and Wales and subsection (2) extends only to Scotland.

National Parks

Notification of agricultural operations on moor and heath in National Parks.

42.—(1) The Ministers may, if satisfied that it is expedient to do so, by order apply subsection (2) to any land which is comprised in a National Park and which appears to them to consist of or include moor or heath.

(2) Subject to subsection (3), no person shall—

(*a*) by ploughing or otherwise convert into agricultural land any land to which this subsection applies and which is moor or heath which has not been agricultural land at any time within the preceding 20 years ; or

(*b*) carry out on any such land any other agricultural operation or any forestry operation which (in either case) appears to the Ministers to be likely to affect its character or appearance and is specified in the order applying this subsection to that land.

(3) Subsection (2) shall not apply in relation to any operation carried out, or caused or permitted to be carried out, by the owner or occupier of the land if—

(*a*) one of them has, after the coming into force of the order, given the county planning authority written notice of a proposal to carry out the operation, specifying its nature and the land on which it is proposed to carry it out ; and

(*b*) one of the conditions specified in subsection (4) is satisfied.

(4) The said conditions are—

(*a*) that the county planning authority have given their consent to the carrying out of the operation ;

(*b*) where that authority have neither given nor refused their consent, that three months have expired from the giving of the notice ; and

(c) where that authority have refused their consent, that twelve months have expired from the giving of the notice.

(5) A person who, without reasonable excuse, contravenes subsection (2) shall be liable—

    (a) on summary conviction, to a fine not exceeding the statutory maximum ;

    (b) on conviction on indictment, to a fine.

(6) Where the county planning authority are given notice under this section in respect of any land, the authority shall forthwith send copies of the notice to the Ministers, the Nature Conservancy Council and the Countryside Commission.

(7) In considering for the purposes of this section whether land has been agricultural land within the preceding 20 years, no account shall be taken of any conversion of the land into agricultural land which was unlawful under the provisions of this section or section 14 of the 1968 Act.

(8) An order under this section shall be made by statutory instrument which shall be subject to annulment in pursuance of a resolution of either House of Parliament.

(9) The said section 14 (which is superseded by this section) shall cease to have effect ; but this section shall have effect as if any order under that section in force immediately before the coming into force of this section had been made under this section.

43.—(1) Every county planning authority whose area comprises the whole or any part of a National Park shall—

Maps of National Parks showing certain areas of moor or heath.

    (a) before the expiration of the period of two years beginning with the commencement date, prepare a map of the Park or the part thereof showing any areas of moor or heath the natural beauty of which it is, in the opinion of the authority, particularly important to conserve ; and

    (b) at such intervals thereafter as they think fit (but not less than once ·in any year), review the particulars contained in the map and make such revisions thereof (if any) as may be requisite.

(2) The authority shall cause a map prepared or revised in pursuance of subsection (1) to be printed, and shall cause copies thereof to be put on sale to the public at such price as the authority may determine.

PART II
Grants and
loans for
purposes of
National
Parks.

44.—(1) Without prejudice to section 11 of the 1949 Act (general powers of local planning authorities in relation to National Parks), a county planning authority may give financial assistance by way of grant or loan, or partly in one way and partly in the other, to any person in respect of expenditure incurred by him in doing anything which in the opinion of the authority is conducive to the attainment, in any National Park the whole or part of which is comprised in that authority's area, of any of the following purposes, that is to say, the conservation and enhancement of the natural beauty of that Park and the promotion of its enjoyment by the public.

(2) On making a grant or loan under this section a county planning authority may impose such conditions as they think fit, including (in the case of a grant) conditions for repayment in specified circumstances.

(3) A county planning authority shall so exercise their powers under subsection (2) as to ensure that any person receiving a grant or loan under this section in respect of premises to which the public are to be admitted, whether on payment or otherwise, shall, in the means of access both to and within the premises, and in the parking facilities and sanitary conveniences to be available (if any), make provision, insofar as it is in the circumstances both practicable and reasonable, for the needs of members of the public visiting the premises who are disabled.

Power to
vary order
designating
National
Park.

45. The Countryside Commission (as well as the Secretary of State) shall have power to make an order amending an order made under section 5 of the 1949 Act designating a National Park, and—

(a) section 7(5) and (6) of that Act (consultation and publicity in connection with orders under section 5 or 7) shall apply to an order under this section as they apply to an order under section 7(4) of that Act with the substitution for the reference in section 7(5) to the Secretary of State of a reference to the Countryside Commission ; and

(b) Schedule 1 to that Act (procedure in connection with the making and confirmation of orders under section 5 or 7) shall apply to an order under this section as it applies to an order designating a National Park.

Membership
of National
Park
authorities
1972 c. 70.

46.—(1) In Part I of Schedule 17 to the Local Government Act 1972 (discharge of planning and countryside functions in National Parks) in paragraph 11 after the words " one third " there shall be inserted the words " (to the nearest whole number) ".

(2) After paragraph 12 of that Schedule there shall be inserted the following paragraph—

" 12A.—(1) The members of a joint planning board, special planning board or National Park Committee established for an area being or comprising the whole or any part of a National Park shall include members (in this paragraph referred to as ' district council members ') who are appointed by district councils whose districts comprise any part of that Park (in this paragraph referred to as ' relevant district councils ').

(2) The number of district council members of such a board or Committee shall be equal to—

(a) the number of relevant district councils ; or

(b) one seventh (to the nearest whole number) of the members of the board or Committee,

whichever is the less ; and for the purposes of this subparagraph any casual vacancy in the membership of the board or Committee shall be disregarded.

(3) The district council members shall be appointed by such of the relevant district councils as may be agreed between those councils or as in default of agreement may be determined by the Secretary of State.

(4) The district council members shall hold office for a period of one year and shall be eligible for reappointment ; and section 102 (5) above shall apply in relation to a district council member appointed under this paragraph as it applies in relation to a member of a committee appointed under that section."

(3) In paragraph 14 of that Schedule for the words " subject to paragraph 11 above " there shall be substituted the words " subject to paragraphs 11 and 12A above ".

(4) In the case of a joint planning board, special planning board or National Park Committee established for an area being or comprising the whole or any part of a National Park, members who are members of relevant district councils (within the meaning of the said paragraph 12A) and are neither members of a county council nor persons appointed in pursuance of the said paragraph 11 shall cease to be members of the board or Committee as from the coming into force of this section.

Miscellaneous and supplemental

47.—(1) Schedule 13 shall have effect as respects the Coun- Provisions tryside Commission. with respect

(2) The Secretary of State may, with the approval of the to the Countryside Treasury, make to the Countryside Commission out of moneys Commission.

Provisions with respect to the Countryside Commission.

PART II

provided by Parliament grants of such amount and subject to such conditions (if any) as he may, with the approval of the Treasury, think fit.

(3) Sections 2, 4 and 95 of the 1949 Act and section 3 of the 1968 Act (which are superseded by this section) shall cease to have effect.

Duties of water authorities etc. with regard to nature conservation and the countryside.

1973 c. 37.

48.—(1) For subsection (1) of section 22 of the Water Act 1973 (duties with respect to nature conservation and amenity) there shall be substituted the following subsection—

" (1) In formulating or considering any proposals relating to the discharge of any of the functions of water authorities, those authorities and the appropriate Minister or Ministers—

(a) shall, so far as may be consistent with the purposes of this Act and of the Land Drainage Act 1976, so exercise their functions with respect to the proposals as to further the conservation and enhancement of natural beauty and the conservation of flora, fauna and geological or physiographical features of special interest;

(b) shall have regard to the desirability of protecting buildings or other objects or archaeological, architectural or historic interest; and

(c) shall take into account any effect which the proposals would have on the beauty of, or amenity in, any rural or urban area or on any such flora, fauna, features, buildings or objects."

(2) In subsection (3) of that section the words " not being land for the time being managed as a nature reserve " shall be omitted.

(3) After that subsection there shall be inserted the following subsections—

" (4) Where any land has been notified to a water authority under subsection (3) above, the authority shall consult with the Council before executing or carrying out any works or operations appearing to them to be likely to destroy or damage any of the flora, fauna, or geological or physiographical features by reason of which the land is of special interest.

(5) Subsection (4) above shall not apply in relation to any emergency operation particulars of which (including details of the emergency) are notified to the Council as soon as practicable after the commencement of the operation.

(6) References in this section to water authorities shall include references to internal drainage boards and the reference in subsection (3) above to the water authority in whose area the land is situated shall include a reference to the internal drainage board in whose district the land is situated."

49.—(1) This section applies to any land in a National Park or in the countryside if—

    (*a*) the public are allowed access to the land ; and

    (*b*) there is no power under any of the provisions of the 1949 Act and the 1968 Act for a local authority, a local planning authority or the Countryside Commission to appoint wardens as respects that land.

(2) Subject to subsections (3) and (4) the power· conferred on a local authority by section 92(1) of the 1949 Act (appointment of wardens) shall include a power, exercisable only with the agreement of the owner and of the occupier of any land to which this section applies, to appoint persons to act as wardens as respects that land.

(3) The only purpose for which wardens may be appointed by virtue of subsection (2) is to advise and assist the public.

(4) Notwithstanding the provisions of section 41(8) of the 1968 Act (Countryside Commission to be local authority for purposes of section 92 of the 1949 Act), nothing in this section shall be construed as conferring on the Countryside Commission any additional power to appoint wardens.

50.—(1) This section applies where—

    (*a*) the Nature Conservancy Council offer to enter into an agreement under section 16 of the 1949 Act or section 15 of the 1968 Act providing for the making by them of payments to—

        (i) a person who has given notice under section 28(5) or 29(4) ; or

        (ii) a person whose application for farm capital grant has been refused in consequence of an objection by the Council ; or

    (*b*) the relevant authority offer to enter into a management agreement providing for the making by them of payments to a person whose application for a farm capital grant has been refused in consequence of an objection by the authority.

(2) Subject to subsection (3), the said payments shall be of such amounts as may be determined by the offeror in accordance with guidance given by the Ministers.

(3) If the offeree so requires within one month of receiving the offer, the determination of those amounts shall be referred to an arbitrator (or, in Scotland, an arbiter) to be appointed, in default of agreement, by the Secretary of State ; and where the amounts determined by the arbitrator exceed those determined by the offeror, the offeror shall—

> (a) amend the offer so as to give effect to the arbitrator's (or, in Scotland, the arbiter's) determination ; or

> (b) except in the case of an offer made to a person whose application for a farm capital grant has been refused in consequence of an objection by the offeror, withdraw the offer.

(4) In this section—

> " farm capital grant " means a grant under a scheme made under section 29 of the Agriculture Act 1970 ;

1970 c. 40.

> " management agreement " and " the relevant authority " have the same meanings as in section 41.

Powers of entry.

51.—(1) Any person authorised in writing by the relevant authority may, at any reasonable time and (if required to do so) upon producing evidence that he is authorised, enter any land for any of the following purposes—

> (a) to ascertain whether an order should be made in relation to that land under section 29 or if an offence under that section is being, or has been, committed on that land ;

> (b) to ascertain the amount of any compensation payable under section 30 in respect of an interest in that land ;

> (c) to ascertain whether an order should be made in relation to that land under section 34 or if an offence under that section is being, or has been, committed on that land ;

> (d) to ascertain whether an order should be made in relation to that land under section 42 or if an offence under that section is being, or has been, committed on that land ;

but nothing in this subsection shall authorise any person to enter a dwelling.

(2) In subsection (1) " the relevant authority " means—

> (a) for the purposes of paragraphs (a) and (b) of that subsection, the Nature Conservancy Council ;

(*b*) for the purposes of paragraph (*c*) of that subsection, the Secretary of State or the relevant authority within the meaning of section 34 ;

(*c*) for the purposes of paragraph (*d*) of that subsection, the Ministers or the county planning authority.

(3) A person shall not demand admission as of right to any land which is occupied unless either—

(*a*) 24 hours notice of the intended entry has been given to the occupier ; or

(*b*) the purpose of the entry is to ascertain if an offence under section 29, 34 or 42 is being, or has been, committed on that land.

(4) Any person who intentionally obstructs a person acting in the exercise of any power conferred by subsection (1) shall be liable on summary conviction to a fine not exceeding £200.

52.—(1) In this Part, unless the context otherwise requires,— Interpretation of Part II.
" agricultural land " does not include land which affords rough grazing for livestock but is not otherwise used as agricultural land ;

" the Ministers ", in the application of this Part to England, means the Secretary of State and the Minister of Agriculture, Fisheries and Food, and, in the application of this Part to Scotland or Wales, means the Secretary of State.

(2) In the application of this Part to England and Wales—

(*a*) references to a local planning authority shall be construed, except as respects Greater London, as references to a county planning authority and a district planning authority and, as respects Greater London, as references to a London borough council ; and

(*b*) references to a county planning authority shall be construed, as respects Greater London, as references to a London borough council ;

and in the application of this Part to Scotland references to a local planning authority shall be construed as references to a regional planning authority, a general planning authority and a district planning authority.

(3) References in this Part to the conservation of the natural beauty of any land shall be construed as including references to the conservation of its flora, fauna and geological and physiographical features.

(4) Section 114 of the 1949 Act shall apply for the construction of this Part.

PART II   **(5)** Any power or duty which under this Part (except sections 41 and 42(1)) falls to be exercised or performed by or in relation to the Ministers may, in England, be exercised or performed by or in relation to either of them.

PART III

PUBLIC RIGHTS OF WAY

Ascertainment of public rights of way

Duty to keep definitive map and statement under continuous review.

53.—(1) In this Part " definitive map and statement ", in relation to any area, means, subject to section 57(3),—

    (a) the latest revised map and statement prepared in definitive form for that area under section 33 of the 1949 Act ; or

    (b) where no such map and statement have been so prepared, the original definitive map and statement prepared for that area under section 32 of that Act ; or

    (c) where no such map and statement have been so prepared, the map and statement prepared for that area under section 55(3).

(2) As regards every definitive map and statement, the surveying authority shall—

    (a) as soon as reasonably practicable after the commencement date, by order make such modifications to the map and statement as appear to them to be requisite in consequence of the occurrence, before that date, of any of the events specified in subsection (3) ; and

    (b) as from that date, keep the map and statement under continuous review and as soon as reasonably practicable after the occurrence, on or after that date, of any of those events, by order make such modifications to the map and statement as appear to them to be requisite in consequence of the occurrence of that event.

(3) The events referred to in subsection (2) are as follows—

    (a) the coming into operation of any enactment or instrument, or any other event, whereby—

        (i) a highway shown or required to be shown in the map and statement has been authorised to be stopped up, diverted, widened or extended ;

        (ii) a highway shown or required to be shown in the map and statement as a highway of a particular description has ceased to be a highway of that description ; or

        (iii) a new right of way has been created over land in the area to which the map relates, being a right of way such that the land over which the right subsists is a public path ;

(b) the expiration, in relation to any way in the area to which the map relates, of any period such that the enjoyment by the public of the way during that period raises a presumption that the way has been dedicated as a public path ;

(c) the discovery by the authority of evidence which (when considered with all other relevant evidence available to them) shows—

(i) that a right of way which is not shown in the map and statement subsists or is reasonably alleged to subsist over land in the area to which the map relates, being a right of way to which this Part applies ;

(ii) that a highway shown in the map and statement as a highway of a particular description ought to be there shown as a highway of a different description ; or

(iii) that there is no public right of way over land shown in the map and statement as a highway of any description, or any other particulars contained in the map and statement require modification.

(4) The modifications which may be made by an order under subsection (2) shall include the addition to the statement of particulars as to—

(a) the position and width of any public path or byway open to all traffic which is or is to be shown on the map ; and

(b) any limitations or conditions affecting the public right of way thereover.

(5) Any person may apply to the authority for an order under subsection (2) which makes such modifications as appear to the authority to be requisite in consequence of the occurrence of one or more events falling within paragraph (b) or (c) of subsection (3) ; and the provisions of Schedule 14 shall have effect as to the making and determination of applications under this subsection.

(6) Orders under subsection (2) which make only such modifications as appear to the authority to be requisite in consequence of the occurrence of one or more events falling within paragraph (a) of subsection (3) shall take effect on their being made ; and the provisions of Schedule 15 shall have effect as to the making, validity and date of coming into operation of other orders under subsection (2).

PART III
Duty to
reclassify
roads used as
public paths.

54.—(1) As regards every definitive map and statement, the surveying authority shall, as soon as reasonably practicable after the commencement date,—

(a) carry out a review of such of the particulars contained in the map and statement as relate to roads used as public paths ; and

(b) by order make such modifications to the map and statement as appear to the authority to be requisite to give effect to subsections (2) and (3) ;

and the provisions of Schedule 15 shall have effect as to the making, validity and date of coming into operation of orders under this subsection.

(2) A definitive map and statement shall show every road used as a public path by one of the three following descriptions namely—

(a) a byway open to all traffic ;

(b) a bridleway ;

(c) a footpath,

and shall not employ the expression " road used as a public path " to describe any way.

(3) A road used as a public path shall be shown in the definitive map and statement as follows—

(a) if a public right of way for vehicular traffic has been shown to exist, as a byway open to all traffic ;

(b) if paragraph (a) does not apply and public bridleway rights have not been shown not to exist, as a bridleway ; and

(c) if neither paragraph (a) nor paragraph (b) applies, as a footpath.

(4) Each way which, in pursuance of an order under subsection (1), is shown in the map and statement by any of the three descriptions shall, as from the coming into operation of the order, be a highway maintainable at the public expense ; and each way which, in pursuance of paragraph 9 of Part III of Schedule 3 to the 1968 Act, is so shown shall continue to be so maintainable.

(5) In this section " road used as a public path " means a way which is shown in the definitive map and statement as a road used as a public path.

(6) In subsections (2)(a) and (5) of section 51 of the 1949 Act (long distance routes) references to roads used as public paths shall include references to any way shown in a definitive map and statement as a byway open to all traffic.

(7) Nothing in this section or section 53 shall limit the opera PART III tion of traffic orders under the Road Traffic Regulation Act 1967 c. 76. 1967 or oblige a highway authority to provide, on a way shown in a definitive map and statement as a byway open to all traffic, a metalled carriage-way or a carriage-way which is by any other means provided with a surface suitable for the passage of vehicles.

55.—(1) No survey under sections 27 to 32 of the 1949 Act, or No further review under section 33 of that Act, shall be begun after the surveys or commencement date; and where on that date a surveying reviews under authority have not completed such a survey or review begun the 1949 Act. earlier, the Secretary of State may, after consultation with the authority, direct the authority—

  (a) to complete the survey or review; or

  (b) to abandon the survey or review to such extent as may be specified in the direction.

(2) Where such a survey or review so begun is abandoned, the Secretary of State shall give such notice of the abandonment as appears to him requisite.

(3) Where, in relation to any area, no such survey has been so begun or such a survey so begun is abandoned, the surveying authority shall prepare for that area a map and statement such that, when they have been modified in accordance with the provisions of this Part, they will serve as the definitive map and statement for that area.

(4) Where such a survey so begun is abandoned after a draft map and statement have been prepared and the period for making representations or objections has expired, the authority shall by order modify the map and statement prepared under subsection (3) so as—

  (a) to give effect to any determination or decision of the authority under section 29(3) or (4) of the 1949 Act in respect of which either there is no right of appeal or no notice of appeal has been duly served ;

  (b) to give effect to any decision of the Secretary of State under section 29(6) of that Act ; and

  (c) to show any particulars shown in the draft map and statement with respect to which no representation or objection has been duly made, or in relation to which all such representations or objections had been withdrawn.

(5) Where such a review so begun is abandoned after a draft map and statement have been prepared and the period for making representations or objections has expired, the authority

PART III   shall by order modify the map and statement under review so as—

> (a) to give effect to any decision of the Secretary of State under paragraph 4(4) of Part II of Schedule 3 to the 1968 Act ; and
>
> (b) to show any particulars shown in the draft map and statement but not in the map and statement under review, and to omit any particulars shown in the map and statement under review but not in the draft map and statement, being (in either case) particulars with respect to which no representation or objection has been duly made, or in relation to which all such representations or objections have been withdrawn.

(6) Orders under subsection (4) or (5) shall take effect on their being made.

Effect of definitive map and statement.

56.—(1) A definitive map and statement shall be conclusive evidence as to the particulars contained therein to the following extent, namely—

> (a) where the map shows a footpath, the map shall be conclusive evidence that there was at the relevant date a highway as shown on the map, and that the public had thereover a right of way on foot, so however that this paragraph shall be without prejudice to any question whether the public had at that date any right of way other than that right ;
>
> (b) where the map shows a bridleway, the map shall be conclusive evidence that there was at the relevant date a highway as shown on the map, and that the public had thereover at that date a right of way on foot and a right of way on horseback or leading a horse, so however that this paragraph shall be without prejudice to any question whether the public had at that date any right of way other than those rights ;
>
> (c) where the map shows a byway open to all traffic, the map shall be conclusive evidence that there was at the relevant date a highway as shown on the map, and that the public had thereover at that date a right of way for vehicular and all other kinds of traffic ;
>
> (d) where the map shows a road used as a public path, the map shall be conclusive evidence that there was at the relevant date a highway as shown on the map, and that the public had thereover at that date a right of way on foot and a right of way on horseback or leading a horse, so however that this paragraph shall be without prejudice to any question whether the

public had at that date any right of way other than
those rights ; and PART III

(e) where by virtue of the foregoing paragraphs the map
is conclusive evidence, as at any date, as to a highway
shown thereon, any particulars contained in the statement as to the position or width thereof shall be
conclusive evidence as to the position or width thereof
at that date, and any particulars so contained as to
limitations or conditions affecting the public right of
way shall be conclusive evidence that at the said date
the said right was subject to those limitations or conditions, but without prejudice to any question whether
the right was subject to any other limitations or conditions at that date.

(2) For the purposes of this section " the relevant date "—

(a) in relation to any way which is shown on the map otherwise than in pursuance of an order under the foregoing
provisions of this Part, means the date specified in
the statement as the relevant date for the purposes of
the map ;

(b) in relation to any way which is shown on the map in
pursuance of such an order, means the date which, in
accordance with subsection (3), is specified in the order
as the relevant date for the purposes of the order.

(3) Every order under the foregoing provisions of this Part
shall specify, as the relevant date for the purposes of the order,
such date, not being earlier than six months before the making
of the order, as the authority may determine.

(4) A document purporting to be certified on behalf of the
surveying authority to be a copy of or of any part of a definitive
map or statement as modified in accordance with the provisions
of this Part shall be receivable in evidence and shall be deemed,
unless the contrary is shown, to be such a copy.

(5) Where it appears to the Secretary of State that paragraph
(d) of subsection (1) can have no further application, he may
by order made by statutory instrument repeal that paragraph.

57.—(1) An order under the foregoing provisions of this Part Supple-
shall be in such form as may be prescribed by regulations made mentary
by the Secretary of State, and shall contain a map, on such scale provisions as
as may be so prescribed, showing the modifications to which the to definitive
order relates. maps and
statements.

(2) Regulations made by the Secretary of State may prescribe
the scale on which maps are to be prepared under section 55(3),

PART III and the method of showing in definitive maps and statements anything which is required to be so shown.

(3) Where, in the case of a definitive map and statement for any area which have been modified in accordance with the foregoing provisions of this Part, it appears to the surveying authority expedient to do so, they may prepare a copy of that map and statement as so modified ; and where they do so, the map and statement so prepared, and not the map and statement so modified, shall be regarded for the purposes of the foregoing provisions of this Part as the definitive map and statement for that area.

(4) The statement prepared under subsection (3) shall specify, as the relevant date for the purposes of the map, such date, not being earlier than six months before the preparation of the map and statement, as the authority may determine.

(5) As regards every definitive map and statement, the surveying authority shall keep—

(a) a copy of the map and statement ; and

(b) copies of all orders under this Part modifying the map and statement,

available for inspection free of charge at all reasonable hours at one or more places in each district comprised in the area to which the map and statement relate and, so far as appears practicable to the surveying authority, a place in each parish so comprised ; and the authority shall be deemed to comply with the requirement to keep such copies available for inspection in a district or parish if they keep available for inspection there a copy of so much of the map and statement and copies of so many of the orders as relate to the district or parish.

(6) Notwithstanding anything in subsection (5), an authority shall not be required to keep available for inspection more than one copy of—

(a) any definitive map and statement ; or

(b) each order under this Part modifying the map and statement,

if, as respects the area to which that map and statement relate, a subsequent map and statement have been prepared under subsection (3) ; and the said single copies may be kept in such place in the area of the authority as they may determine.

(7) Every surveying authority shall take such steps as they consider expedient for bringing to the attention of the public the provisions of this Part including, in particular, section 53(5) and subsection (5).

(8) Regulations under this section shall be made by statutory instrument which shall be subject to annulment in pursuance of a resolution of either House of Parliament.

PART III

58.—(1) Subject to subsection (2), the foregoing provisions of this Part shall not apply to any area to which this subsection applies; and this subsection applies to any area which, immediately before 1st April 1965, formed part of the administrative county of London.

Application of ss. 53 to 57 to inner London.

(2) A London borough council may by resolution adopt the said foregoing provisions as respects any part of their area specified in the resolution, being a part to which subsection (1) applies, and those provisions shall thereupon apply accordingly.

(3) Where by virtue of a resolution under subsection (2), the said foregoing provisions apply to any area, those provisions shall have effect in relation thereto as if for references to the commencement date there were substituted references to the date on which the resolution comes into operation.

Miscellaneous and supplemental

59.—(1) If, in a case not falling within subsection (2), the occupier of a field or enclosure crossed by a right of way to which this Part applies permits a bull to be at large in the field or enclosure, he shall be liable on summary conviction to a fine not exceeding £200.

Prohibition on keeping bulls on land crossed by public rights of way.

(2) Subsection (1) shall not apply to any bull which—

(a) does not exceed the age of ten months; or

(b) is not of a recognised dairy breed and is at large in any field or enclosure in which cows or heifers are also at large.

(3) Nothing in any byelaws, whenever made, shall make unlawful any act which is, or but for subsection (2) would be, made unlawful by subsection (1).

(4) In this section " recognised dairy breed " means one of the following breeds, namely, Ayrshire, British Friesian, British Holstein, Dairy Shorthorn, Guernsey, Jersey and Kerry.

(5) The Secretary of State may by order add any breed to, or remove any breed from, subsection (4); and an order under this subsection shall be made by statutory instrument which shall be subject to annulment in pursuance of a resolution of either House of Parliament.

PART III
Regulation
of traffic on
public rights
of way.
1967 c. 76.

60. The Road Traffic Regulation Act 1967 shall have effect in relation to any footpath, bridleway or byway open to all traffic as if—

(a) any reference to traffic included a reference to foot passengers and persons driving, riding or leading horses or other animals of draught or burden ; and

(b) any reference in section 1(3A) or 12 to foot passengers included a reference to such persons as aforesaid.

61.—(1) Section 134 of the Highways Act 1980 (ploughing of footpath or bridleway) shall have effect subject to the amendments provided for by subsections (2) to (9).

(2) Subsection (3) (7 days' notice of intention to plough) shall be omitted.

(3) In subsection (4) (duty to restore surface of footpath or bridleway), for paragraphs (a) and (b) there shall be substituted the following paragraphs—

" (a) not later than 2 weeks from the time when the occupier began to plough the footpath or bridleway, or

(b) if prevented from doing so by exceptional weather conditions, as soon as practicable thereafter,".

(4) In subsection (5) (failure to comply with subsection (3) or (4)) the words " (3) or " shall be omitted, for paragraphs (a) and (b) there shall be substituted the words " to a fine not exceeding £200 " and for the words " subsection (4) ", in the second place where they occur, there shall be substituted the words " that subsection ".

(5) After that subsection there shall be inserted the following subsection—

" (5A) A person who ploughs any footpath, bridleway or other highway otherwise than in the exercise of a right to plough it shall be guilty of an offence and liable to a fine not exceeding £200."

(6) In subsection (6) (enforcement of subsections (3) to (5)) for the words " subsections (3) to (5) above as respects any footpath or bridleway " there shall be substituted the words " subsections (4) to (5A) above as respects any footpath, bridleway or other highway ".

(7) In subsection (7) (proceedings by parish or community councils) after the words " subsection (4) " there shall be inserted the words " or (5A) ".

(8) In subsection (8) (power of competent authority to restore surface of footpath or bridleway) for the words " footpath or bridleway " there shall be substituted the words " footpath, bridleway or other highway ".

(9) In subsection (10) (competent authorities for the purposes of subsections (8) and (9)) for the words " footpath or bridleway ", in both places where they occur, there shall be substituted the words " footpath, bridleway or other highway ".

(10) In section 135(1) of the said Act of 1980 (temporary diversion of footpath or bridleway ploughed up under section 134) the words " 6 or " and " 6 weeks or " shall be omitted.

62. A local authority may appoint such number of persons as appears to the authority to be necessary or expedient to act as wardens as respects a footpath, bridleway or byway open to all traffic which is both in the countryside and in the area of the authority, and the purpose for which the wardens may be so appointed is to advise and assist the public in connection with the use of the path or way.

Appointment of wardens for public rights of way.

63. The enactments mentioned in Schedule 16 (which relate to the making and confirmation of certain orders creating, extinguishing or diverting footpaths and bridleways) shall have effect subject to the amendments provided for in that Schedule.

Orders creating, extinguishing or diverting footpaths and bridleways.

64. At the end of section 25 of the Highways Act 1980 (creation of footpath or bridleway by agreement) there shall be inserted the following subsection—

Publication of dedication of footpaths and bridleways.

1980 c. 66.

" (6) As soon as may be after the dedication of a footpath or bridleway in accordance with a public path creation agreement, the local authority who are party to the agreement shall give notice of the dedication by publication in at least one local newspaper circulating in the area in which the land to which the agreement relates is situated.".

65.—(1) In section 27 of the 1968 Act (signposting of footpaths and bridleways) for the words " or bridleway ", wherever they occur, there shall be substituted the words " bridleway or byway " ; and for the words " and bridleways " in subsection (6) of that section there shall be substituted the words " bridleways and byways ".

Signposting of byways open to all traffic.

(2) After subsection (7) of that section there shall be inserted the following subsection—

" (8) In this section " byway " means a byway open to all traffic, that is to say, a highway over which the public have a right of way for vehicular and all other kinds of traffic, but which is used by the public mainly for the purposes for which footpaths and bridleways are so used."

PART III
Interpretation
of Part III.

66.—(1) In this Part—

" bridleway " means a highway over which the public have the following, but no other, rights of way, that is to say, a right of way on foot and a right of way on horseback or leading a horse, with or without a right to drive animals of any description along the highway ;

" byway open to all traffic " means a highway over which the public have a right of way for vehicular and all other kinds of traffic, but which is used by the public mainly for the purpose for which footpaths and bridleways are so used ;

" definitive map and statement " has the meaning given by section 53(1) ;

" footpath " means a highway over which the public have a right of way on foot only, other than such a highway at the side of a public road ;

" horse " includes a pony, ass and mule, and " horseback " shall be construed accordingly ;

" public path " means a highway being either a footpath or a bridleway ;

" right of way to which this Part applies " means a right of way such that the land over which the right subsists is a public path or a byway open to all traffic ;

" surveying authority ", in relation to any area, means the county or London borough council whose area includes that area.

(2) A highway at the side of a river, canal or other inland navigation shall not be excluded from any definition contained in subsection (1) by reason only that the public have a right to use the highway for purposes of navigation, if the highway would fall within that definition if the public had no such right thereover.

(3) The provisions of section 30(1) of the 1968 Act (riding of pedal cycles on bridleways) shall not affect the definition of bridleway in subsection (1) and any rights exercisable by virtue of those provisions shall be disregarded for the purposes of this Part.

PART IV

MISCELLANEOUS AND GENERAL

Application
to Crown.

67.—(1) Subject to the following provisions of this section, Part II, except section 51, and Part III shall apply to Crown land, that is to say, land an interest in which belongs to Her Majesty in the right of the Crown or the Duchy of Lancaster

or to the Duchy of Cornwall, and land an interest in which   PART IV
belongs to a Government department or is held in trust for
Her Majesty for the purposes of a Government department.

(2) No order shall be made under section 29, 34, 36 or 42 in
relation to Crown land unless the appropriate authority has
consented to the making of that order.

(3) An agreement under section 39 as respects any interest in
Crown land, other than an interest held by or on behalf of
the Crown, shall not have effect unless approved by the appropriate authority.

(4) Section 101(11) of the 1949 Act (Crown land) shall apply
for the construction of references in this section to the appropriate authority.

68. The Secretary of State may, after consultation with the Appli-
Council of the Isles of Scilly, by order made by statutory instru- cation to
ment provide for the application of the provisions of Part II or the Isles of
III to the Isles of Scilly as if those Isles were a separate county ; Scilly.
and any such order may provide for the application of those
provisions to those Isles subject to such modifications as may
be specified in the order.

69.—(1) Where a body corporate is guilty of an offence Offences by
under this Act and that offence is proved to have been com- bodies
mitted with the consent or connivance of, or to be attributable corporate
to any neglect on the part of, any director, manager, secretary etc.
or other similar officer of the body corporate or any person
who was purporting to act in any such capacity he, as well as
the body corporate, shall be guilty of that offence and shall be
liable to be proceeded against and punished accordingly.

(2) Where the affairs of a body corporate are managed by its
members subsection (1) shall apply in relation to the acts and
defaults of a member in connection with his functions of management as if he were a director of the body corporate.

70.—(1) There shall be defrayed out of money provided by Financial
Parliament— provisions.

    (a) any administrative expenses incurred by any Minister
        of the Crown under this Act ; and

    (b) any increase attributable to the provisions of this Act
        in the sums payable out of money so provided under
        any other enactment.

(2) Any sums received by a Minister of the Crown under this
Act shall be paid into the Consolidated Fund.

PART IV
General
interpretation.
1949 c. 97.
1968 c. 41.

71. In this Act—

" the 1949 Act " means the National Parks and Access to the Countryside Act 1949 ;

" the 1968 Act " means the Countryside Act 1968 ;

" the commencement date ", in relation to any provision of this Act and any area, means the date of the coming into force of that provision in that area ;

" London borough council " includes the Common Council of the City of London ;

" modifications " includes additions, alterations and omissions, and cognate expressions shall be construed accordingly ;

" statutory maximum ", in relation to a fine on summary conviction, means—

1980 c. 43.

(a) in England and Wales, the prescribed sum within the meaning of section 32 of the Magistrates' Courts Act 1980 (at the passing of this Act £1,000) ; and

1975 c. 21.

(b) in Scotland, the prescribed sum within the meaning of section 289B of the Criminal Procedure (Scotland) Act 1975 (at the passing of this Act £1,000).

Minor
amendments.
1935 c. 47.

72.—(1) Section 4 of the Restriction of Ribbon Development Act 1935 (power to fence roads subject to restrictions) shall have effect, in relation to any area in the countryside of which walls of a particular construction are a feature, as if references to fences included references to walls of that construction ; and in exercising their powers under that section in relation to any such area, a highway authority shall have regard to the desirability of exercising the powers conferred by the foregoing provisions of this subsection.

1946 c. 73.

(2) In section 20(2) of the Hill Farming Act 1946 (penalty for contravening regulations with respect to the burning of heather and grass) as originally enacted for the words from " five pounds " onwards there shall be substituted the words " £200 ".

(3) In section 27 of that Act (penalty for contravening the provisions of that Act relating to muirburn) for the words from " five pounds " onwards there shall be substituted the words " £200 ".

1948 c. 45.

(4) In section 39 of the Agriculture (Scotland) Act 1948 for the words " the First Schedule to the Protection of Birds Act 1954 " there shall be substituted the words " Schedule 1 to the Wildlife and Countryside Act 1981 ".

(5) In section 11(1) of the 1949 Act (general powers of local planning authorities in relation to National Parks) after the word " accomplishment " there shall be inserted the words " of any ".

(6) In section 74(4) of the Public Health Act 1961 (power to 1961 c. 64. reduce numbers of pigeons and other birds in built-up areas), for the words " the Protection of Birds Act 1954 " there shall be substituted the words " Part I of the Wildlife and Countryside Act 1981 ".

(7) In section 2(8) of the 1968 Act (publicity and information services) for the words from " encouraging " onwards there shall be substituted the words " informing persons resorting to the countryside of their rights and obligations ".

(8) In section 15(1) of that Act (areas of special scientific interest) the words " which is not for the time being managed as a nature reserve but " shall be omitted.

(9) In section 37 of that Act (protection for interests in the countryside) for the words " and the Act of 1949 " there shall be substituted the words " the Act of 1949 and the·Wildlife and Countryside Act 1981 ".

(10) The functions of a county council under this Act as a local planning authority shall be included among the functions of such a council to which Part I of Schedule 17 to the Local 1972 c. 70. Government Act 1972 (planning and countryside functions in National Parks) applies.

(11) In section 31(10) of the Highways Act 1980 (dedication 1980 c. 66. of way as highway presumed after public use for 20 years), for the words from " subsection (4) " to " that section " there shall be substituted the words " section 56(1) of the Wildlife and Countryside Act 1981 (which provides that a definitive map and statement " and the words " or of that subsection " onwards shall be omitted.

(12) Section 80 of that Act (power of highway authority to fence highways) shall have effect in relation to any area in the countryside of which walls of a particular construction are a feature, as if references to fences included references to walls of that construction ; and in exercising their powers under that section in relation to any such area, a highway authority shall have regard to the desirability of exercising the powers conferred by the foregoing provisions of this subsection.

(13) In section 136(4) of that Act (time when hedges may not be required to be cut or pruned) immediately before the words " between the last day of September and the first day of April " there shall be inserted the word " except ".

PART IV
1981 c. 37.

(14) In section 4(5) of the Zoo Licensing Act 1981 (grant or refusal of licence) the entries relating to the Protection of Birds Acts 1954 to 1967 and the Conservation of Wild Creatures and Wild Plants Act 1975 shall be omitted and there shall be added at the end the following entry—

" Part I of the Wildlife and Countryside Act 1981 ".

Repeals and savings.

73.—(1) The enactments mentioned in Schedule 17 are hereby repealed to the extent specified in the third column of that Schedule.

(2) Nothing in the repeals made by this section shall affect the operation of sections 27 to 32 of the 1949 Act in relation to any survey begun before the commencement date.

(3) Nothing in the repeals made by this section shall affect the operation of sections 33 and 34 of the 1949 Act and Parts II, III and IV of Schedule 3 to the 1968 Act in relation to any review begun before the commencement date.

1975 c. 48.

1973 c. 57.

(4) Notwithstanding the repeal by this section of the Conservation of Wild Creatures and Wild Plants Act 1975, section 9 of the Badgers Act 1973 shall continue to have effect with the amendment made by section 16 of the said Act of 1975.

Short title commencement and extent.

74.—(1) This Act may be cited as the Wildlife and Countryside Act 1981.

(2) The following provisions of this Act, namely—

Part II, except sections 29 to 32, 41 and 46 to 48 and Schedule 13 ;

sections 59 to 62 and 65 and 66 ; and

Part IV, except section 72(4), (6) and (14) and section 73(1) so far as relating to Part II of Schedule 17,

shall come into force on the expiration of the period of one month beginning with the passing of this Act.

(3) The remaining provisions of this Act shall come into force on such day as the Secretary of State may by order made by statutory instrument appoint and different days may be appointed under this subsection for different provisions, different purposes or different areas.

(4) An order under subsection (3) may make such transitional provision as appears to the Secretary of State to be necessary or expedient in connection with the provisions thereby brought into force.

(5) The following provisions of this Act, namely—
    sections 39, 40 and 42 to 49 and Schedule 13 ; and
    Part III,
do not extend to Scotland.

(6) This Act, except section 15(1) and Schedule 10 and, so far as regards any enactment mentioned in Schedule 17 that so extends, section 73 and that Schedule, does not extend to Northern Ireland.

Sections 1, 2, 4,
6, 19 and 22.

SCHEDULES

SCHEDULE 1

BIRDS WHICH ARE PROTECTED BY SPECIAL PENALTIES

PART I

AT ALL TIMES

Common name	Scientific name
Avocet	Recurvirostra avosetta
Bee-eater	Merops apiaster
Bittern	Botaurus stellaris
Bittern, Little	Ixobrychus minutus
Bluethroat	Luscinia svecica
Brambling	Fringilla montifringilla
Bunting, Cirl	Emberiza cirlus
Bunting, Lapland	Calcarius lapponicus
Bunting, Snow	Plectrophenax nivalis
Buzzard, Honey	Pernis apivorus
Chough	Pyrrhocorax pyrrhocorax
Corncrake	Crex crex
Crake, Spotted	Porzana porzana
Crossbills (all species)	Loxia
Curlew, Stone	Burhinus oedicnemus
Divers (all species)	Gavia
Dotterel	Charadrius morinellus
Duck, Long-tailed	Clangula hyemalis
Eagle, Golden	Aquila chrysaetos
Eagle, White-tailed	Haliaetus albicilla
Falcon, Gyr	Falco rusticolus
Fieldfare	Turdus pilaris
Firecrest	Regulus ignicapillus
Garganey	Anas querquedula
Godwit, Black-tailed	Limosa limosa
Goshawk	Accipiter gentilis
Grebe, Black-necked	Podiceps nigricollis
Grebe, Slavonian	Podiceps auritus
Greenshank	Tringa nebularia
Gull, Little	Larus minutus
Gull, Mediterranean	Larus melanocephalus
Harriers (all species)	Circus
Heron, Purple	Ardea purpurea
Hobby	Falco subbuteo
Hoopoe	Upupa epops
Kingfisher	Alcedo atthis
Kite, Red	Milvus milvus
Merlin	Falco columbarius
Oriole, Golden	Oriolus oriolus
Osprey	Pandion haliaetus
Owl, Barn	Tyto alba
Owl, Snowy	Nyctea scandiaca

Common name	Scientific name	SCH. 1
Peregrine	Falco peregrinus	
Petrel, Leach's	Oceanodroma leucorhoa	
Phalarope, Red-necked	Phalaropus lobatus	
Plover, Kentish	Charadrius alexandrinus	
Plover, Little Ringed	Charadrius dubius	
Quail, Common	Coturnix coturnix	
Redstart, Black	Phoenicurus ochruros	
Redwing	Turdus iliacus	
Rosefinch, Scarlet	Carpodacus erythrinus	
Ruff	Philomachus pugnax	
Sandpiper, Green	Tringa ochropus	
Sandpiper, Purple	Calidris maritima	
Sandpiper, Wood	Tringa glareola	
Scaup	Aythya marila	
Scoter, Common	Melanitta nigra	
Scoter, Velvet	Melanitta fusca	
Serin	Serinus serinus	
Shorelark	Eremophila alpestris	
Shrike, Red-backed	Lanius collurio	
Spoonbill	Platalea leucorodia	
Stilt, Black-winged	Himantopus himantopus	
Stint, Temminck's	Calidris temminckii	
Swan, Bewick's	Cygnus bewickii	
Swan, Whooper	Cygnus cygnus	
Tern, Black	Chlidonias niger	
Tern, Little	Sterna albifrons	
Tern, Roseate	Sterna dougallii	
Tit, Bearded	Panurus biarmicus	
Tit, Crested	Parus cristatus	
Treecreeper, Short-toed	Certhia brachydactyla	
Warbler, Cetti's	Cettia cetti	
Warbler, Dartford	Sylvia undata	
Warbler, Marsh	Acrocephalus palustris	
Warbler, Savi's	Locustella luscinioides	
Whimbrel	Numenius phaeopus	
Woodlark	Lullula arborea	
Wryneck	Jynx torquilla	

PART II

DURING THE CLOSE SEASON

Common name	Scientific name
Goldeneye	Bucephala clangula
Goose, Greylag (in Outer Hebrides, Caithness, Sutherland and Wester Ross only)	Anser anser
Pintail	Anas acuta

NOTE. The common name or names given in the first column of this Schedule are included by way of guidance only ; in the event of any dispute or proceedings, the common name or names shall not be taken into account.

SCHEDULE 2

BIRDS WHICH MAY BE KILLED OR TAKEN

PART I

OUTSIDE THE CLOSE SEASON

Common name	Scientific name
Capercaillie	Tetrao urogallus
Coot	Fulica atra
Duck, Tufted	Aythya fuligula
Gadwall	Anas strepera
Goldeneye	Bucephala clangula
Goose, Canada	Branta canadensis
Goose, Greylag	Anser anser
Goose, Pink-footed	Anser brachyrhynchus
Goose, White-fronted (in England and Wales only)	Anser albifrons
Mallard	Anas platyrhynchos
Moorhen	Gallinula chloropus
Pintail	Anas acuta
Plover, Golden	Pluvialis apricaria
Pochard	Aythya ferina
Shoveler	Anas clypeata
Snipe, Common	Gallinago gallinago
Teal	Anas crecca
Wigeon	Anas penelope
Woodcock	Scolopax rusticola

PART II

BY AUTHORISED PERSONS AT ALL TIMES

Common name	Scientific name
Crow	Corvus corone
Dove, Collared	Streptopelia decaocto
Gull, Great Black-backed	Larus marinus
Gull, Lesser Black-backed	Larus fuscus
Gull, Herring	Larus argentatus
Jackdaw	Corvus monedula
Jay	Garrulus glandarius
Magpie	Pica pica
Pigeon, Feral	Columba livia
Rook	Corvus frugilegus
Sparrow, House	Passer domesticus
Starling	Sturnus vulgaris
Woodpigeon	Columba palumbus

NOTE. The common name or names given in the first column of this Schedule are included by way of guidance only; in the event of any dispute or proceedings, the common name or names shall not be taken into account.

SCHEDULE 3

BIRDS WHICH MAY BE SOLD

PART I

ALIVE AT ALL TIMES IF RINGED AND BRED IN CAPTIVITY

Common name	Scientific name
Blackbird	Turdus merula
Brambling	Fringilla montifringilla
Bullfinch	Pyrrhula pyrrhula
Bunting, Reed	Emberiza schoeniclus
Chaffinch	Fringilla coelebs
Dunnock	Prunella modularis
Goldfinch	Carduelis carduelis
Greenfinch	Carduelis chloris
Jackdaw	Corvus monedula
Jay	Garrulus glandarius
Linnet	Carduelis cannabina
Magpie	Pica pica
Owl, Barn	Tyto alba
Redpoll	Carduelis flammea
Siskin	Carduelis spinus
Starling	Sturnus vulgaris
Thrush, Song	Turdus philomelos
Twite	Carduelis flavirostris
Yellowhammer	Emberiza citrinella

PART II

DEAD AT ALL TIMES

Common name	Scientific name
Pigeon, Feral	Columba livia
Woodpigeon	Columba palumbus

PART III

DEAD FROM 1ST SEPTEMBER TO 28TH FEBRUARY

Common name	Scientific name
Capercaillie	Tetrao urogallus
Coot	Fulica atra
Duck, Tufted	Aythya fuligula
Mallard	Anas platyrhynchos
Pintail	Anas acuta
Plover, Golden	Pluvialis apricaria
Pochard	Aythya ferina
Shoveler	Anas clypeata
Snipe, Common	Gallinago gallinago
Teal	Anas crecca
Wigeon	Anas penelope
Woodcock	Scolopax rusticola

NOTE. The common name or names given in the first column of this Schedule are included by way of guidance only; in the event of any dispute or proceedings, the common name or names shall not be taken into account.

SCHEDULE 4

BIRDS WHICH MUST BE REGISTERED AND RINGED IF KEPT IN CAPTIVITY

Common name	Scientific name
Avocet	Recurvirostra avosetta
Bee-eater	Merops apiaster
Bittern	Botaurus stellaris
Bittern, Little	Ixobrychus minutus
Bluethroat	Luscinia svecica
Bunting, Cirl	Emberiza cirlus
Bunting, Lapland	Calcarius lapponicus
Bunting, Snow	Plectrophenax nivalis
Chough	Pyrrhocorax pyrrhocorax
Corncrake	Crex crex
Crake, Spotted	Porzana porzana
Crossbills (all species)	Loxia
Curlew, Stone	Burhinus oedicnemus
Divers (all species)	Gavia
Dotterel	Charadrius morinellus
Duck, Long-tailed	Clangula hyemalis
Falcons (all species)	Falconidae
Fieldfare	Turdus pilaris
Firecrest	Regulus ignicapillus
Godwit, Black-tailed	Limosa limosa
Grebe, Black-necked	Podiceps nigricollis
Grebe, Slavonian	Podiceps auritus
Greenshank	Tringa nebularia
Hawks, True (except Old world vultures) that is to say, Buzzards, Eagles, Harriers, Hawks and Kites (all species in each case)	Accipitridae (except the genera Aegypius, Gypaetus, Gypohierax, Gyps, Neophron, Sarcogyps and Trigonoceps)
Hoopoe	Upupa epops
Kingfisher	Alcedo atthis
Oriole, Golden	Oriolus oriolus
Osprey	Pandion haliaetus
Petrel, Leach's	Oceanodroma leucorhoa
Phalarope, Red-necked	Phalaropus lobatus
Plover, Kentish	Charadrius alexandrinus
Plover, Little ringed	Charadrius dubius
Quail, Common	Coturnix coturnix
Redstart, Black	Phoenicurus ochruros
Redwing	Turdus iliacus
Rosefinch, Scarlet	Carpodacus erythrinus
Ruff	Philomachus pugnax
Sandpiper, Green	Tringa ochropus
Sandpiper, Purple	Calidris maritima
Sandpiper, Wood	Tringa glareola
Scoter, Common	Melanitta nigra
Scoter, Velvet	Melanitta fusca
Serin	Serinus serinus
Shorelark	Eremophila alpestris
Shrike, Red-backed	Lanius collurio
Spoonbill	Platalea leucorodia
Stilt, Black-winged	Himantopus himantopus

Common name	Scientific name	Sch. 4
Stint, Temminck's	Calidris temminckii	
Tern, Black	Chlidonias niger	
Tern, Little	Sterna albifrons	
Tern, Roseate	Sterna dougallii	
Tit, Bearded	Panurus biarmicus	
Tit, Crested	Parus cristatus	
Treecreeper, Short-toed	Certhia brachydactyla	
Warbler, Cetti's	Cettia cetti	
Warbler, Dartford	Sylvia undata	
Warbler, Marsh	Acrocephalus palustris	
Warbler, Savi's	Locustella luscinioides	
Whimbrel	Numenius phaeopus	
Woodlark	Lullula arborea	
Wryneck	Jynx torquilla	

NOTE. The common name or names given in the first column of this Schedule are included by way of guidance only ; in the event of any dispute or proceedings, the common name or names shall not be taken into account.

SCHEDULE 5
ANIMALS WHICH ARE PROTECTED

Sections 9, 10, 22 and 24.

Common name	Scientific name
Adder (in respect of section 9(5) only)	Vipera berus
Bats, Horseshoe (all species)	Rhinolophidae
Bats, Typical (all species)	Vespertilionidae
Beetle, Rainbow Leaf	Chrysolina cerealis
Burbot	Lota lota
Butterfly, Chequered Skipper	Carterocephalus palaemon
Butterfly, Heath Fritillary	Mellicta athalia (otherwise known as Melitaea athalia)
Butterfly, Large Blue	Maculinea arion
Butterfly, Swallowtail	Papilio machaon
Cricket, Field	Gryllus campestris
Cricket, Mole	Gryllotalpa gryllotalpa
Dolphin, Bottle-nosed	Tursiops truncatus (otherwise known as Tursiops tursio)
Dolphin, Common	Delphinus delphis
Dragonfly, Norfolk Aeshna	Aeshna isosceles
Frog, Common (in respect of section 9(5) only)	Rana temporaria
Grasshopper, Wart-biter	Decticus verrucivorus
Lizard, Sand	Lacerta agilis
Lizard, Viviparous (in respect of section 9(5) only)	Lacerta vivipara
Moth, Barberry Carpet	Pareulype berberata
Moth, Black-veined	Siona lineata (otherwise known as Idaea lineata)
Moth, Essex Emerald	Thetidia smaragdaria
Moth, New Forest Burnet	Zygaena viciae
Moth, Reddish Buff	Acosmetia caliginosa

SCH. 5

Common name	Scientific name
Newt, Great Crested (otherwise known as Warty newt)	Triturus cristatus
Newt, Palmate (in respect of section 9(5) only)	Triturus helveticus
Newt, Smooth (in respect of section 9(5) only)	Triturus vulgaris
Otter, Common	Lutra lutra
Porpoise, Harbour (otherwise known as Common porpoise)	Phocaena phocaena
Slow-worm (in respect of section 9(5) only)	Anguis fragilis
Snail, Carthusian	Monacha cartusiana
Snail, Glutinous	Myxas glutinosa
Snail, Sandbowl	Catinella arenaria
Snake, Grass (in respect of section 9(5) only)	Natrix helvetica
Snake, Smooth	Coronella austriaca
Spider, Fen Raft	Dolomedes plantarius
Spider, Ladybird	Eresus niger
Squirrel, Red	Sciurus vulgaris
Toad, Common (in respect of section 9(5) only)	Bufo bufo
Toad, Natterjack	Bufo calamita

NOTE. The common name or names given in the first column of this Schedule are included by way of guidance only ; in the event of any dispute or proceedings, the common name or names shall not be taken into account.

Sections 11 and 22.

SCHEDULE 6

ANIMALS WHICH MAY NOT BE

KILLED OR TAKEN BY CERTAIN METHODS

Common name	Scientific name
Badger	Meles meles
Bats, Horseshoe (all species)	Rhinolophidae
Bats, Typical (all species)	Vespertilionidae
Cat, Wild	Felis silvestris
Dolphin, Bottle-nosed	Tursiops truncatus (otherwise known as Tursiops tursio)
Dolphin, Common	Delphinus delphis
Dormice (all species)	Gliridae
Hedgehog	Erinaceus europaeus
Marten, Pine	Martes martes
Otter, Common	Lutra lutra
Polecat	Mustela putorius

Common name	Scientific name	
Porpoise, Harbour (otherwise known as Common porpoise)	Phocaena phocaena	SCH. 6
Shrews (all species)	Soricidae	
Squirrel, Red	Sciurus vulgaris	

NOTE. The common name or names given in the first column of this Schedule are included by way of guidance only ; in the event of any dispute or proceedings, the common name or names shall not be taken into account.

SCHEDULE 7

Section 12.

PROTECTION OF CERTAIN MAMMALS

The Ground Game Act 1880

1.—(1) Notwithstanding the provisions of section 6 of the Ground Game Act 1880, it shall not be unlawful for the occupier of any land himself, or one other person authorised by him under section 1 of that Act, to use firearms for the purpose of killing ground game thereon between the expiration of the first hour after sunset and the commencement of the last hour before sunrise if (except where he has the exclusive right) the occupier has the written authority of the other person or one of the other persons entitled to kill and take the ground game on the land. 1880 c. 47.

(2) In this paragraph " ground game " means hares and rabbits.

The Agriculture (Scotland) Act 1948

2.—(1) Notwithstanding the provisions of section 50(1)(a) of the Agriculture (Scotland) Act 1948, it shall not be unlawful for the owner of the shooting rights on any land or any person holding those rights from him, or subject to sub-paragraph (2) below the occupier of any land, to use a firearm for the purpose of killing ground game thereon between the expiration of the first hour after sunset and the commencement of the last hour before sunrise. 1948 c. 45.

(2) The occupier of any land shall not use a firearm as mentioned in sub-paragraph (1) above unless (except where he has the exclusive right) he has first obtained the written authority of the other person or one of the other persons entitled to kill and take the ground game on the land.

(3) An occupier who is entitled, in terms of this paragraph, to use a firearm for the purpose of killing ground game may, subject to the provisions of section 1 of the Ground Game Act 1880, authorise one other person so to use a firearm.

(4) In this paragraph " ground game " means hares and rabbits.

The Dogs (Protection of Livestock) Act 1953

3.—(1) At the end of subsection (2) of section 1 of the Dogs (Protection of Livestock) Act 1953 (penalty where dog worries livestock on agricultural land) there shall be inserted the words " or

> (c) being at large (that is to say not on a lead or otherwise under close control) in a field or enclosure in which there are sheep ".

(2) After that subsection there shall be inserted the following subsection—

> " (2A) Subsection (2)(c) of this section shall not apply in relation to—

> > (a) a dog owned by, or in the charge of, the occupier of the field or enclosure or the owner of the sheep or a person authorised by either of those persons ; or

> > (b) a police dog, a guide dog, a trained sheep dog, a working gun dog or a pack of hounds."

The Deer Act 1963

4. For subsection (3) of section 10 of the Deer Act 1963 (general exceptions) there shall be substituted the following subsections—

> " (3) A person shall not be guilty of an offence under section 3(1)(c)(i) of this Act by reason of the use of any smooth-bore gun for the purpose of killing any deer if he shows that the deer had been so seriously injured otherwise than by his unlawful act or was in such a condition that to kill it was an act of mercy.

> (4) A person shall not be guilty of an offence under section 3(1)(c)(i) of this Act by reason of the use as a slaughtering instrument, for the purpose of killing any deer, of a smooth-bore gun which—

> > (a) is of not less gauge than 12 bore ;

> > (b) has a barrel less than 24 inches (609·6 millimetres) in length ; and

> > (c) is loaded with a cartridge purporting to contain shot none of which is less than ·203 inches (5·16 millimetres) in diameter (that is to say, size AAA or any larger size)."

5.—(1) After section 10 of that Act there shall be inserted the following section—

" Exceptions for authorised persons.

10A.—(1) Subject to subsection (3) of this section an authorised person shall not be guilty of an offence under section 1 of this Act by reason of—

> (a) the taking or killing of any deer by means of shooting ; or

(*b*) the injuring of any deer by means of shooting
in an attempt to take or kill it,

on any cultivated land, pasture or enclosed woodland.

(2) Subject to subsection (3) of this section an authorised person shall not be guilty of an offence under section 3(1)(*c*)(i) of this Act by reason of the use, for the purpose of taking or killing any deer on any land, of any smooth-bore gun of not less gauge than 12 bore which is loaded with—

> (*a*) a cartridge containing a single non-spherical projectile weighing not less than 350 grains (22·68 grammes) ; or
>
> (*b*) a cartridge purporting to contain shot each of which is 203 inches (5·16 millimetres) in diameter (that is to say, size AAA).

(3) An authorised person shall not be entitled to rely on the defence provided by subsection (1) or (2) of this section as respects anything done in relation to any deer on any land unless he shows that—

> (*a*) he had reasonable grounds for believing that deer of the same species were causing, or had caused, damage to crops, vegetables, fruit, growing timber or any other form of property on the land ;
>
> (*b*) it was likely that further damage would be so caused and any such damage was likely to be serious ; and
>
> (*c*) his action was necessary for the purpose of preventing any such damage.

(4) The Secretary of State and the agriculture Minister acting jointly may by order, either generally or in relation to any area or any species and description of deer specified in the order, repeal subsection (2) of this section or amend it by adding any firearm or ammunition or by altering the description of, or deleting, any firearm or ammunition mentioned in it, or by adding any further conditions which must be satisfied.

(5) Before making an order under subsection (4) of this section, the Secretary of State and the agriculture Minister shall consult organisations that appear to them to represent persons likely to be interested in or affected by the order.

(6) In this section—

> ' agriculture Minister ' means the Minister of Agriculture, Fisheries and Food in relation to England and the Secretary of State for Wales in relation to Wales ;
>
> ' authorised person ' means—
>
>> (*a*) the occupier of the land on which the action is taken ;

SCH. 7

(b) any member of the occupier's household normally resident on the occupier's land, acting with the written authority of the occupier ;

(c) any person in the ordinary service of the occupier on the occupier's land, acting with the written authority of the occupier ; or

(d) any person having the right to take or kill deer on the land on which the action is taken or any person acting with the written authority of a person having that right."

(2) In sections 1(1) and 3(1) of that Act for the words " sections 10 and 11 " there shall be substituted the words " sections 10, 10A and 11 ".

(3) For subsection (1) of section 12 of that Act (orders) there shall be substituted the following subsections—

" (1) Any power to make orders under this Act shall be exercisable by statutory instrument.

(1A) A statutory instrument containing an order under section 1(2) or 3(4) of this Act shall be subject to annulment in pursuance of a resolution of either House of Parliament.

(1B) No order under section 10A(4) of this Act shall be made unless a draft of the order has been laid before and approved by a resolution of each House of Parliament."

6.—(1) In paragraph 1 of Schedule 2 to that Act (prohibited firearms and ammunition) the words " of less gauge than 12 bore " shall be omitted.

(2) In paragraph 4 of that Schedule the words from " other than " onwards shall be omitted.

The Conservation of Seals Act 1970

1970 c. 30.

7.—(1) In subsection (1)(c) of section 10 of the Conservation of Seals Act 1970 (power to grant licences), the word " or " immediately following sub-paragraph (ii) shall be omitted and after sub-paragraph (iii) there shall be inserted the words " or

(iv) the protection of flora or fauna in an area to which subsection (4) of this section applies,".

(2) In subsection (3)(b) of that section for the words from " a nature reserve " onwards there shall be substituted the words " an area to which subsection (4) of this section applies ".

(3) After subsection (3) of that section there shall be inserted the following subsection—

" (4) This subsection applies to any area which—

(a) is a nature reserve within the meaning of section 15 of the National Parks and Access to the Countryside Act 1949 ;

(b) has been notified under section 28(1) of the Wildlife and Countryside Act 1981 (areas of special scientific interest) ;

(c) is an area to which section 29(3) of that Act (special protection for certain areas of special scientific interest) applies ; or

(d) has been designated as a marine nature reserve under section 36 of that Act."

The Badgers Act 1973

8. For subsections (2) and (3) of section 1 of the Badgers Act 1973 (possession of recently killed badgers etc.) there shall be substituted the following subsections—

1973 c. 57.

" (2) If, save as permitted by or under this Act, any person has in his possession or under his control any dead badger or any part of, or anything derived from, a dead badger, he shall be guilty of an offence.

(3) A person shall not be guilty of an offence under subsection (2) above if he shows that—

(a) the badger had not been killed, or had been killed otherwise than in contravention of the provisions of this Act ; or

(b) the badger or other thing in his possession or control had been sold (whether to him or any other person) and, at the time of the purchase, the purchaser had had no reason to believe that the badger had been killed in contravention of those provisions."

9.—(1) Section 7 of that Act (exceptions for authorised persons) shall be omitted.

(2) In section 2(c) of that Act for the words " subject to section 7(3) of this Act " there shall be substituted the words " save as permitted by or under this Act ".

(3) Section 6 of that Act (areas within which section 7(1) does not apply) shall be omitted.

(4) In subsection (2) of section 8 of that Act (general exceptions) paragraph (c) (live badger taken in circumstances in which, by virtue of section 7(1) or (2), the taking did not constitute an offence) shall be omitted.

(5) In section 11 of that Act (interpretation) the definitions of " area of special protection " and " authorised person " shall be omitted.

10.—(1) In section 8 of that Act (general exceptions), after subsection (1) there shall be inserted the following subsections—

" (1A) A person shall not be guilty of an offence under section 1(1) of this Act by reason of—

(a) the killing or taking or the attempted killing or taking of any badger, or

(b) the injuring of any badger in the course of taking it or attempting to kill or take it,

if he shows that his action was necessary for the purpose of preventing serious damage to land, crops, poultry or any other form of property.

SCH 7

(1B) The defence provided by subsection (1A) above shall not apply in relation to any action taken at any time if it had become apparent, before that time, that that action would prove necessary for the purpose mentioned in that subsection and either—

(a) a licence under section 9 of this Act authorising that action had not been applied for as soon as reasonably practicable after that fact had become apparent ; or

(b) an application for such a licence had been determined ".

(2) In section 9 of that Act (licences) at the end of subsection (1) there shall be inserted the following paragraph—

" (e) for the purpose of preventing serious damage to land, crops, poultry or any other form of property, to kill or take badgers within an area specified in the licence by any means so specified."

(3) In subsection (2)(b) of that section after the words " paragraph (d) " there shall be inserted the words " or (e) ".

(4) After subsection (3) of that section there shall be inserted the following subsection—

" (4) The Minister of Agriculture, Fisheries and Food and the Secretary of State shall from time to time consult with the Nature Conservancy Council as to the exercise of their functions under subsection (1)(e) above ; and neither of them shall grant a licence of any description unless he has been advised by the Council as to the circumstances in which, in the Council's opinion, licences of that description should be granted."

11.—(1) In subsection (1)(c) of section 10 of that Act (enforcement, penalties etc.) for the words from " any badger " onwards there shall be substituted the words " anything which may be evidence of the commission of the offence or may be liable to be forfeited under subsection (3) below ".

(2) In subsection (2) of that section for " £20 " there shall be substituted " £200 " and for " £100 " there shall be substituted " £1,000 ".

12. In section 11 of that Act (interpretation) for the definition of " local authority " there shall be substituted the following definition—

" ' sale ' includes hire, barter and exchange and cognate expressions shall be construed accordingly."

Sections 13, 22 and 24.

SCHEDULE 8

PLANTS WHICH ARE PROTECTED

Common name	Scientific name
Alison, Small	Alyssum alyssoides
Broomrape, Bedstraw	Orobanche caryophyllacea
Broomrape, Oxtongue	Orobanche loricata

Common name	Scientific name	SCH. 8
Broomrape, Thistle	Orobanche reticulata	
Calamint, Wood	Calamintha sylvatica	
Catchfly, Alpine	Lychnis alpina	
Cinquefoil, Rock	Potentilla rupestris	
Club-rush, Triangular	Scirpus triquetrus	
Cotoneaster, Wild	Cotoneaster integerrimus	
Cow-wheat, Field	Melampyrum arvense	
Cudweed, Jersey	Gnaphalium luteoalbum	
Diapensia	Diapensia lapponica	
Eryngo, Field	Eryngium campestre	
Fern, Dickie's Bladder	Cystopteris dickieana	
Fern, Killarney	Trichomanes speciosum	
Galingale, Brown	Cyperus fuscus	
Gentian, Alpine	Gentiana nivalis	
Gentian, Spring	Gentiana verna	
Germander, Water	Teucrium scordium	
Gladiolus, Wild	Gladiolus illyricus	
Hare's-ear, Sickle-leaved	Bupleurum falcatum	
Hare's-ear, Small	Bupleurum baldense	
Heath, Blue	Phyllodoce çaerulea	
Helleborine, Red	Cephalanthera rubra	
Knawel, Perennial	Scleranthus perennis	
Knotgrass, Sea	Polygonum maritimum	
Lady's-slipper	Cypripedium calceolus	
Lavender, Sea	{ Limonium paradoxum { Limonium recurvum	
Leek, Round-headed	Allium sphaerocephalon	
Lettuce, Least	Lactuca saligna	
Lily, Snowdon	Lloydia serotina	
Marsh-mallow, Rough	Althaea hirsuta	
Orchid, Early Spider	Ophrys sphegodes	
Orchid, Fen	Liparis loeselii	
Orchid, Ghost	Epipogium aphyllum	
Orchid, Late Spider	Ophrys fuciflora	
Orchid, Lizard	Himantoglossum hircinum	
Orchid, Military	Orchis militaris	
Orchid, Monkey	Orchis simia	
Pear, Plymouth	Pyrus cordata	
Pink, Cheddar	Dianthus gratianopolitanus	
Pink, Childling	Petroraghia nanteuilii	
Sandwort, Norwegian	Arenaria norvegica	
Sandwort, Teesdale	Minuartia stricta	
Saxifrage, Drooping	Saxifraga cernua	
Saxifrage, Tufted	Saxifraga cespitosa	
Solomon's-seal, Whorled	Polygonatum verticillatum	
Sow-thistle, Alpine	Cicerbita alpina	
Spearwort, Adder's-tongue	Ranunculus ophioglossifolius	
Speedwell, Spiked	Veronica spicata	
Spurge, Purple	Euphorbia peplis	
Starfruit	Damasonium alisma	
Violet, Fen	Viola persicifolia	
Water-plantain, Ribbon leaved	Alisma gramineum	
Wood-sedge, Starved	Carex depauperata	

154 Wildlife and Countryside Act 1981

Sch. 8	Common name	Scientific name
	Woodsia, Alpine	Woodsia alpina
	Woodsia, Oblong	Woodsia ilvensis
	Wormwood, Field	Artemisia campestris
	Woundwort, Downy	Stachys germanica
	Woundwort, Limestone	Stachys alpina
	Yellow-rattle, Greater	Rhinanthus serotinus

NOTE. The common name or names given in the first column of this Schedule are included by way of guidance only ; in the event of any dispute or proceedings, the common name or names shall not be taken into account.

Sections 14 and 22.

SCHEDULE 9
ANIMALS AND PLANTS TO WHICH SECTION 14 APPLIES

PART I
ANIMALS WHICH ARE ESTABLISHED IN THE WILD

Common name	Scientific name
Bass, Large-mouthed Black	Micropterus salmoides
Bass, Rock	Ambloplites rupestris
Bitterling	Rhodeus sericeus
Budgerigar	Melopsittacus undulatus
Capercaillie	Tetrao urogallus
Coypu	Myocastor coypus
Dormouse, Fat	Glis glis
Duck, Carolina Wood	Aix sponsa
Duck, Mandarin	Aix galericulata
Duck, Ruddy	Oxyura jamaicensis
Eagle, White-tailed	Haliaetus albicilla
Frog, Edible	Rana esculenta
Frog, European Tree (otherwise known as Common tree frog)	Hyla arborea
Frog, Marsh	Rana ridibunda
Gerbil, Mongolian	Meriones unguiculatus
Goose, Canada	Branta canadensis
Goose, Egyptian	Alopochen aegyptiacus
Heron, Night	Nycticorax nycticorax
Lizard, Common Wall	Podarcis muralis
Marmot, Prairie (otherwise known as Prairie dog)	Cynomys
Mink, American	Mustela vison
Newt, Alpine	Triturus alpestris
Parakeet, Ring-necked	Psittacula krameri
Partridge, Chukar	Alectoris chukar
Partridge, Rock	Alectoris graeca
Pheasant, Golden	Chrysolophus pictus
Pheasant, Lady Amherst's	Chrysolophus amherstiae
Pheasant, Reeves'	Syrmaticus reevesii
Pheasant, Silver	Lophura nycthemera
Porcupine, Crested	Hystrix cristata
Porcupine, Himalayan	Hystrix hodgsonii

Common name	Scientific name
Pumpkinseed (otherwise known as Sun-fish or Pond-perch)	Lepomis gibbosus
Quail, Bobwhite	Colinus virginianus
Rat, Black	Rattus rattus
Squirrel, Grey	Sciurus carolinensis
Terrapin, European Pond	Emys orbicularis
Toad, African Clawed	Xenopus laevis
Toad, Midwife	Alytes obstetricans
Toad, Yellow-bellied	Bombina variegata
Wallaby, Red-necked	Macropus rufogriseus
Wels (otherwise known as European catfish)	Silurus glanis
Zander	Stizostedion lucioperca

PART II

PLANTS

Common name	Scientific name
Hogweed, Giant	Heracleum mantegazzianum
Kelp, Giant	Macrocystis pyrifera
Knotweed, Japanese	Polygonum cuspidatum
Seaweed, Japanese	Sargassum muticum

NOTE. The common name or names given in the first column of this Schedule are included by way of guidance only ; in the event of any dispute or proceedings, the common name or names shall not be taken into account.

SCHEDULE 10

Section 15.

AMENDMENTS OF THE ENDANGERED SPECIES (IMPORT AND EXPORT) ACT 1976

PART I

THE AMENDMENTS

Licences

1.—(1) After subsection (3) of section 1 of the 1976 Act (restriction on importation and exportation of certain animals and plants) there shall be inserted the following subsections—

" (3A) Subsection (3) above shall not apply in relation to an application of any description if the scientific authority concerned has advised the Secretary of State as to whether licences should be issued in pursuance of applications of that description and, if so, their terms.

(3B) Where the Secretary of State is satisfied that the issue of a licence authorising the importation or exportation of any item which—

(a) is part of or derives from or is made wholly or partly from an animal of any of the kinds to which Schedule 1 or a plant of any of the kinds to which Schedule 2 to this Act for the time being applies ; but

Sᴄʜ. 10

(*b*) is not an item to which Schedule 3 to this Act for the time being applies,

would facilitate the importation or exportation of that item, he may, if he considers it expedient to do so, issue such a licence."

(2) In subsections (4), (5), (6) and (7) of that section after the words "subsection (2)" there shall be inserted the words "or (3B)".

(3) In subsection (4) of that section after paragraph (*a*) there shall be inserted the following paragraphs—

"(*aa*) may be issued either to all persons, to persons of a class or to a particular person ;

(*ab*) may be subject to compliance with any specified conditions," ;

and in paragraph (*c*) of that subsection for the words from "a period" to "shorter" there shall be substituted the word "such".

Expenses of returning animals and plants to the wild

2. After subsection (8) of section 1 of the 1976 Act there shall be inserted the following subsection—

"(9) Where, in the case of a live animal or plant of any kind which is condemned or deemed to be condemned as forfeited, the Commissioners of Customs and Excise incur any expenses in connection with, or with a view to—

(*a*) its return to the wild ; or

(*b*) its being kept at premises (whether within or outside the United Kingdom) which are suitable for the keeping of animals or plants of that kind,

those expenses may be recovered, as a debt due to the Crown, from the importer or intending exporter of the animal or plant or any person possessing or having control of it at the time of its seizure.

In this subsection expressions which are also used in the Customs and Excise Management Act 1979 have the same meanings as in that Act."

Powers of entry

3. After the subsection inserted by paragraph 2 as subsection (9) of section 1 of the 1976 Act there shall be inserted the following subsections—

"(10) Any person duly authorised in writing by the Secretary of State may, at any reasonable time and (if required to do so) upon producing evidence that he is so authorised, enter any premises where animals of any of the kinds to which Schedule 1 or plants of any of the kinds to which Schedule 2 to this Act for the time being applies are kept (whether temporarily or permanently) in order to ascertain whether any of the animals or plants kept there have been imported contrary to this section.

(11) Any person who wilfully obstructs a person acting under subsection (10) above shall be liable on summary conviction to a fine not exceeding £200."

Power to modify Schedules

4.—(1) In paragraph (*c*) of section 3 of the 1976 Act (power to modify Schedules) after the word " conservation " there shall be inserted the words " in any area " and after the word " endangered " there shall be inserted the word " there ".

(2) After paragraph (*d*) of that section there shall be inserted the following paragraph—

" (*dd*) to restrict the importation of animals or plants of any kind which appear to the Secretary of State to be unlikely to survive for any appreciable time if they are kept in the United Kingdom ;".

Sale of certain animals or plants or their derivatives

5.—(1) In subsection (1) of section 4 of the 1976 Act (offences to sell etc. things imported contrary to section 1 or their derivatives) for the words " Subject to subsection (2) " there shall be substituted the words " Subject to subsections (1B) and (2) ", after the words " has in his possession " there shall be inserted the words " or transports " and the words " and in the following provisions " onwards shall be omitted.

(2) After that subsection there shall be inserted the following subsections—

" (1A) Subject to subsections (1B) and (2) below, a person who sells, offers or exposes for sale, or has in his possession or transports for the purpose of sale—

(*a*) a live or dead animal of any of the kinds to which Schedule 4 to this Act for the time being applies or an egg or other immature stage of such an animal ;

(*b*) a live or dead plant of any of the kinds to which Schedule 5 to this Act for the time being applies ; or

(*c*) any part of or anything which derives from or is made wholly or partly from anything referred to in paragraph (*a*) or (*b*) above,

shall be guilty of an offence ; but nothing in this subsection shall apply in relation to anything falling within subsection (1) above or anything which has been imported, or is a part of or derives from or is made wholly or partly from anything which has been imported, before the passing of the Wildlife and Countryside Act 1981.

(1B) Subsections (1) and (1A) above do not apply to anything done under and in accordance with the terms of a licence issued by the Secretary of State ; and subsections (4) to (7) of section 1 above shall apply in relation to a licence issued under this subsection as they apply in relation to a licence issued under subsection (2) of that section.

(1C) In the following provisions of this section " restricted article " means anything falling within subsection (1) or (1A) above."

(3) In subsection (2) of that section after the words " subsection (1) " there shall be inserted the words " or (1A) ".

SCH. 10   (4) In subsection (5) of that section after the words "subsection (1)" there shall be inserted the words ", (1A)".

(5) In subsection (6) of that section after the words "references to" there shall be inserted the word "hire".

(6) After Schedule 3 to the 1976 Act there shall be inserted as Schedule 4 the Schedule set out in Part II of this Schedule.

(7) After the Schedule inserted in the 1976 Act by sub-paragraph (6) there shall be inserted as Schedule 5 the Schedule set out in Part III of this Schedule.

Supplemental

6. In section 13(2) of the 1976 Act (substitution in Northern Ireland of references to the Department of Agriculture for Northern Ireland for references to the Secretary of State in specified provisions) for the words " 1(2), (3) and (4), 2(4) " there shall be substituted the words " 1(2) to (4) and (10), 2(4), 4(1B) ".

PART II
SCHEDULE INSERTED AS SCHEDULE 4
SCHEDULE 4
ANIMALS THE SALE ETC. OF WHICH IS RESTRICTED

This Schedule applies to the following kinds of animal, namely—

MAMMALS

1. The kinds of mammal specified in the first column below—

Marsupials

Kind	Common name
Bettongia	Rat kangaroo
Caloprymnus campestris	Desert rat-kangaroo
Lagorchestes hirsutus	Western hare-wallaby
Lagostrophus fasciatus	Banded hare-wallaby
Onychogalea fraenata	Bridle nail-tailed wallaby
Onychogalea lunata	Crescent nail-tailed wallaby
Lasiorhinus krefftii	Queensland hairy-nosed wombat
Chaeropus ecaudatus	Pig-footed bandicoot
Macrotis lagotis	Rabbit-bandicoot
Macrotis leucura	Lesser rabbit-bandicoot
Perameles bougainville	Western barred bandicoot
Sminthopsis longicaudata	Long-tailed dunnart
Sminthopsis psammophila	Sandhill dunnart
Thylacinus cynocephalus	Tasmanian wolf

Primates

Kind	Common name
Allocebus	Hairy-eared dwarf lemur
Cheirogaleus	Dwarf lemurs
Hapalemur	Gentle lemurs
Lemur	Lemurs
Lepilemur	Sportive and weasel lemurs
Microcebus	Mouse lemurs
Phaner	Fork-marked mouse lemurs
Avahi	Avahis (otherwise known as Woolly indris)
Indri	Indris
Propithecus	Sifakas

Kind	Common name	Sch. 10
Daubentonia madagascarien-sis	Aye-aye	
Callimico goeldii	Goeldi's marmoset (otherwise known as Goeldi's tamarin)	
Callithrix aurita	White eared marmoset	
Callithrix flaviceps	Buff-headed marmoset	
Leontopithecus	Maned tamarin (otherwise known as Golden tamarin)	
Saguinus bicolor	Pied tamarin	
Saguinus geoffroyi	Geoffroy's tamarin	
Saguinus leucopus	White-footed tamarin	
Saguinus oedipus	Cotton-headed tamarin	
Alouatta palliata (otherwise known as Alouatta villosa)	Mantled howler	
Ateles geoffroyi frontatus	Black-browed spider monkey	
Ateles geoffroyi panamensis	Red spider monkey	
Brachyteles arachnoides	Woolly spider monkey	
Cacajao	Uakaris	
Chiropotes albinasus	White-nosed saki	
Saimiri oerstedii	Red-backed squirrel monkey	
Cercocebus galeritus galeritus	Tana River mangabey	
Cercopithecus diana	Diana monkey	
Colobus badius kirkii	Kirk's red colobus (otherwise known as Zanzibar red colobus)	
Colobus badius rufomitratus	Tana River red colobus	
Macaca silenus	Lion-tailed macaque	
Nasalis larvatus	Proboscis monkey	
Papio leucophaeus (otherwise known as Mandrillus leucophaeus)	Drill	
Papio sphinx (otherwise known as Mandrillus sphinx)	Mandrill	
Presbytis entellus	Langur (otherwise known as Entellus langur or True langur)	
Presbytis geei	Golden langur	
Presbytis pileatus	Caped langur	
Presbytis potenziani	Mentawi leaf monkey	
Pygathrix nemaeus	Douc langur	
Rhinopithecus roxellanae	Snub-nosed langur	
Simias concolor	Mentawi snub-nosed langur	
Hylobates	Gibbons	
Symphalangus syndactylus	Siamang	
Pongidae	Great apes	

Edentates

Priodontes giganteus (otherwise known as Priodontes maximus)	Giant armadillo	

Sch. 10

Pangolins

Kind	Common name
Manis temmincki	South African pangolin

Rabbits and hares

Kind	Common name
Caprolagus hispidus	Assam rabbit (otherwise known as Hispid hare)
Romerolagus diazi	Volcano rabbit

Rodents

Kind	Common name
Cynomys mexicanus	Mexican prairie marmot
Leporillus conditor	Australian sticknest rat
Pseudomys fumeus	Smoky mouse
Pseudomys praeconis	Shark Bay mouse
Xeromys myoides	False water rat
Zyzomys pendunculatus	Central thick-tailed rat
Chinchilla (except any domestic form of Chinchilla laniger)	Chinchilla

Cetaceans

Kind	Common name
Lipotes vexillifer	Chinese river dolphin
Physeter catodon (otherwise known as Physeter macrocephalus)	Sperm whale
Platanista gangetica	Ganges dolphin
Platanista minor	Indus river dolphin
Sotalia	Humpbacked dolphins
Sousa	Humpbacked dolphins
Neophocaena phocaenoides	Finless porpoise
Phocoena sinus	Cochito
Balaena mysticetus	Greenland right whale (otherwise known as Bowhead whale)
Balaenoptera borealis	Sei whale
Balaenoptera musculus	Blue whale
Balaenoptera physalus	Common rorqual
Eschrichtius	Grey whales
Eubalaena	Right whales
Megaptera novaeangliae	Humpback whale

Carnivores

Kind	Common name
Speothos venaticus	Bush dog
Vulpes velox hebes	Northern kit fox
Helarctos malayanus	Sun bear
Selenarctos thibetanus	Asiatic black bear
Tremarctos ornatus	Spectacled bear
Ursus arctos isabellinus	Brown bear
Ursus arctos nelsoni	Mexican brown bear
Ursus arctos pruinosus	Tibetan brown bear
Aonyx microdon	Cameroon clawless otter
Enhydra lutris nereis	Southern sea otter
Lutra felina	Marine otter
Lutra longicaudis	South American otter
Lutra lutra	Eurasian otter
Lutra provocax	Southern river otter

Kind	Common name	SCH. 10
Mustela nigripes	Black-footed ferret	
Pteronura brasiliensis	Giant otter	
Prionodon pardicolor	Spotted linsang	
Hyaena brunnea	Brown hyaena	
Acinonyx jubatus	Cheetah	
Felis bengalensis bengalensis	Leopard cat	
Felis concolor coryi	Florida puma	
Felis concolor costaricensis	Costa Rica puma	
Felis concolor cougar	Eastern puma	
Felis jacobita	Andean cat	
Felis rufa escuinapae	Mexican bobcat	
Felis marmorata	Marbled cat	
Felis nigripes	Black-footed cat	
Felis pardalis mearnsi	Costa Rica ocelot	
Felis pardalis mitis	Brazilian ocelot	
Felis planiceps	Flat-headed cat	
Felis rubiginosa	Rusty spotted cat	
Felis temmincki	Asiatic golden cat	
Felis tigrina oncilla	Little spotted cat	
Felis wiedii nicaraguae	Nicaraguan margay	
Felis wiedii salvinia	Guatemalan margay	
Felis yagouaroundi cacomitli	Jaguarundi	
Felis yagouaroundi fossata	Jaguarundi	
Felis yagouaroundi panamensis	Jaguarundi	
Felis yagouaroundi tolteca	Jaguarundi	
Neofelis nebulosa	Clouded leopard	
Panthera leo persica	Asiatic lion	
Panthera onca	Jaguar	
Panthera pardus	Leopard	
Panthera tigris	Tiger	
Panthera uncia	Snow leopard	

Seals

Kind	Common name
Arctocephalus townsendi	Guadelupe fur seal
Monachus	Monk seals

Elephants

Kind	Common name
Elephas maximus	Asian elephant

Sea-cows

Kind	Common name
Dugong dugon	Dugong (otherwise known as Sea-cow)
Trichechus inunguis	Amazonian manatee
Trichechus manatus	West Indian manatee

Odd-toed ungulates

Kind	Common name
Equus grevyi	Grevy's zebra
Equus hemionus hemionus	Mongolian wild ass
Equus hemionus khur	Indian wild ass
Equus przewalskii	Przewalski's horse
Equus zebra zebra	Cape mountain zebra
Tapirus bairdii	Central American tapir
Tapirus indicus	Malayan tapir (otherwise known as Indian tapir)

Sch. 10

Kind	Common name
Tapirus pinchaque	Mountain tapir (otherwise known as Woolly tapir)
Rhinocerotidae	Rhinoceroses

Even-toed ungulates

Kind	Common name
Babyrousa babyrussa	Babirusa
Sus salvanius	Pygmy hog
Vicugna vicugna	Vicugna
Axis calamianensis	Calamian deer
Axis kuhli	Bawean deer
Axis porcinus annamiticus	Thai hog deer
Blastocerus dichotomus	Marsh deer
Cervus duvauceli	Swamp deer
Cervus elaphus hanglu	Kashmir stag (otherwise known as Hanglu)
Cervus eldi	Brow-antlered deer
Dama mesopotamica	Persian fallow deer
Hippocamelus antisiensis	Peruvian huemal
Hippocamelus bisulcus	Chilean huemal
Moschus moschiferus moschiferus	Himalayan musk deer
Ozotoceros bezoarticus	Pampas deer
Pudu pudu	Chilean pudu
Antilocapra americana peninsularis	Lower California pronghorn
Antilocapra americana sonoriensis	Sonoran pronghorn
Bison bison athabascae	Wood bison
Bos gaurus	Gaur
Bos mutus	Wild yak
Bubalus depressicornis	Lowland anoa
Bubalus mindorensis	Tamaraw
Bubalus quarlesi	Mountain anoa
Capra falconeri chiltanensis	Markhor
Capra falconeri jerdoni	Markhor
Capra falconeri megaceros	Markhor
Capricornis sumatraensis	Serow
Hippotragus niger variani	Giant sable antelope
Nemorhaedus goral	Goral
Novibos sauveli	Koupray
Oryx leucoryx	Arabian oryx
Ovis ammon hodgsoni	Great Tibetan sheep
Ovis orientalis ophion	Cyprian mouflon
Ovis vignei	Urial
Pantholops hodgsoni	Tibetan antelope
Rupicapra rupicapra ornata	Abrussi chamois

BIRDS

2. The kinds of bird specified in the first column below—

Rheas

Pterocnemia pennata	Lesser rhea

Tinamous

Tinamus solitarius	Solitary tinamou

Kind	*Common name*	SCH. 10
	Penguins	
Spheniscus humboldti	Humboldt penguin	
	Grebes	
Podilymbus gigas	Atitlan grebe	
	Albatrosses	
Diomedea albatrus	Short-tailed albatross	
	Pelican-like birds	
Sula abbotti	Abbot's booby	
Fregata andrewsi	Christmas Island frigatebird	
	Storks	
Ciconia ciconia boyciana	Japanese white stork	
Geronticus eremita	Bald ibis	
Nipponia nippon	Japanese crested ibis	
	Waterfowl	
Anas aucklandica nesiotis	Campbell Island Flightless teal	
Anas laysanensis	Laysan duck	
Anas oustaleti	Marianas Island duck (otherwise known as Marianas Mallard)	
Branta canadensis leucopareia	Aleutian Canada goose	
Branta sandvicensis	Hawaiian goose (otherwise known as Nene)	
Cairina scutulata	White-winged wood duck	
Rhodonessa caryophyllacea	Pink-headed duck	
	Diurnal Birds of Prey	
Cathartidae	New world vultures	
Pandion haliaetus	Osprey	
Accipitridae	True hawks	
Sagittarius serpentarius	Secretary bird	
Falconidae	Falcons	
	Gamebirds	
Aburria jacutinga	Black-fronted curassow (otherwise known as Black-fronted guan)	
Aburria pipile	White-headed curassow (otherwise known as Piping guan)	
Catreus wallichii	Cheer pheasant	
Colinus virginianus ridgwayi	Masked bobwhite	
Crax blumenbachii	Red-billed curassow	
Crax mitu	Razor-billed curassow	
Crossoptilon crossoptilon	White Eared-pheasant	
Crossoptilon mantchuricum	Brown Eared-pheasant	
Lophophorus impejanus	Himalayan monal	
Lophophorus lhuysii	Chinese monal	
Lophophorus sclateri	Sclater's monal	
Lophura edwardsi	Edward's pheasant	
Lophura imperialis	Imperial pheasant	

Kind	Common name
Lophura swinhoei	Swinhoe's pheasant
Macrocephalon maleo	Maleo Fowl
Oreophasis derbianus	Horned guan
Penelope albipennis	White-winged guan
Polyplectron emphanum	Palawan peacock pheasant
Syrmaticus ellioti	Elliot's pheasant
Syrmaticus humiae	Hume's pheasant (otherwise known as Bar-tailed pheasant)
Syrmaticus mikado	Mikado pheasant
Tetraogallus caspius	Caspian snowcock
Tetraogallus tibetanus	Tibetan snowcock
Tragopan blythii	Blyth's tragopan
Tragopan caboti	Cabot's tragopan
Tragopan melanocephalus	Western tragopan
Tympanuchus cupido attwateri	Attwater's prairie chicken

Cranes and rails

Grus americana	Whooping crane
Grus canadensis nesiotes	Cuban sandhill crane
Grus canadensis pulla	Mississippi sandhill crane
Grus japonensis	Manchurian crane (otherwise known as Japanese crane)
Grus leucogeranus	Siberian White crane
Grus monacha	Hooded crane
Grus nigricollis	Black-necked crane
Grus vipio	White-necked crane (otherwise known as White-naped crane)
Tricholimnas sylvestris	Lord Howe wood-rail
Rhynochetos jubatus	Kagu
Chlamydotis undulata	Houbara bustard
Choriotis nigriceps (otherwise known as Ardeotis nigriceps)	Great Indian bustard
Eupodotis bengalensis	Bengal florican

Waders and Gulls

Numenius borealis	Eskimo curlew
Tringa guttifer	Spotted greenshank (otherwise known as Nordmann's greenshank)
Larus relictus	Relict gull

Pigeons and doves

Caloenas nicobarica	Nicobar pigeon
Ducula mindorensis	Mindoro imperial pigeon

Parrots

Kind	*Common name*
Amazona arausiaca	Red-necked parrot (otherwise known as Red-necked amazon)
Amazona barbadensis	Yellow-shouldered parrot (otherwise known as Yellow-shouldered amazon)
Amazona brasiliensis	Red-tailed parrot (otherwise known as Red-tailed amazon
Amazona guildingii	St. Vincent parrot (otherwise known as St. Vincent amazon)
Amazona imperialis	Imperial parrot (otherwise known as Imperial amazon)
Amazona leucocephala	Cuban parrot (otherwise known as Cuban amazon)
Amazona pretrei	Red-spectacled parrot (otherwise known as Red-spectacled amazon)
Amazona rhodocorytha (otherwise known as Amazona dufresniana rhodocorytha)	Red-crowned parrot (otherwise known as Red-crowned amazon)
Amazona versicolor	St Lucia parrot (otherwise known as St Lucia amazon)
Amazona vinacea	Vinaceous parrot (otherwise known as Vinaceous amazon)
Amazona vittata	Puerto Rico parrot (otherwise known as Puerto Rican amazon)
Anodorhynchus glaucus	Glaucous macaw
Anodorhynchus leari	Lear's macaw
Aratinga guaruba	Golden parakeet (otherwise known as Golden conure)
Cyanopsitta spixii	Spix's macaw
Cyanoramphus auriceps forbesi	Forbes' parakeet
Cyanoramphus novaezelandiae	Red-fronted parakeet
Cyclopsitta diophthalma coxeni (otherwise known as Opopsitta diophthalma coxeni)	Coxen's fig parrot
Geopsittacus occidentalis	Australian night parrot
Neophema chrysogaster	Orange-bellied parakeet (otherwise known as Orange-bellied parrot)
Pezoporus wallicus	Ground parrot

Kind	*Common name*
Pionopsitta pileata	Red-capped parrot (otherwise known as Pileated parrot)
Psephotus chrysopterygius	Golden-shouldered parakeet (otherwise known as Golden-shouldered parrot or Hooded parakeet)
Psephotus pulcherrimus	Paradise parrot
Psittacula echo (otherwise known as Psittacula krameri echo)	Mauritius parakeet (otherwise known as Mauritius ring-necked parakeet)
Psittacus erithacus princeps	Fernando Po grey parrot
Pyrrhura cruentata	Blue-throated conure
Rhynchopsitta pachyrhyncha	Thick-billed parrot
Rhynchopsitta terrisi	Maroon-fronted parrot
Strigops habroptilus	Kakapo (otherwise known as Owl parrot)

Hummingbirds

Ramphodon dohrnii	Hook-billed hermit

Trogons

Pharomachrus mocinno costaricensis	Costa Rican quetzal (otherwise known as Resplendent quetzal)
Pharomachrus mocinno mocinno	Magnificent quetzal (otherwise known as Resplendent quetzal)

Owls

Tytonidae	Barn owls
Strigidae	Typical owls

Hornbills

Buceros bicornis (otherwise known as Buceros homrai)	Great pied hornbill
Rhinoplax vigil	Helmeted hornbill

Woodpeckers

Campephilus imperialis	Imperial woodpecker
Dryocopus javensis richardsi	Tristram's woodpecker (otherwise known as White-bellied black woodpecker)

Songbirds

Cotinga maculata	Banded cotinga
Xipholena atropurpurea	White-winged cotinga
Pitta kochi	Koch's pitta

Kind	Common name	
Atrichornis clamosa	Noisy scrub-bird	Sch. 10
Leucopsar rothschildi	Rothschild's mynah	
Dasyornis brachypterus longirostris	Western bristlebird	
Dasyornis broadbenti littoralis	Western rufous bristlebird	
Picathartes gymnocephalus	White-necked rockfowl (otherwise known as Yellow-headed rockfowl or Guinea bear-headed rockfowl)	
Picathartes oreas	Grey-necked rockfowl (otherwise known as Cameroon bare-headed rockfowl or Red-headed rockfowl)	
Zosterops albogularis	White-breasted silver-eye	
Meliphaga cassidix	Helmeted honeyeater	
Spinus cucullatus (otherwise known as Carduelis cucullatus)	Red siskin	

REPTILES

3. The kinds of reptile specified in the first column below—

Crocodilians

Alligator sinensis	Chinese alligator
Caiman crocodilus apaporiensis	Rio Apaporis caiman (otherwise known as Spectacled caiman)
Caiman latirostris	Broad-nosed caiman
Melanosuchus niger	Black caiman
Crocodylus acutus	American crocodile
Crocodylus cataphractus	African slender-snouted crocodile (otherwise known as African sharp-nosed crocodile)
Crocodylus intermedius	Orinoco crocodile
Crocodylus moreletii	Morelet's crocodile
Crocodylus niloticus	Nile crocodile
Crocodylus novaeguineae mindorensis	Philippine crocodile
Crocodylus palustris	Mugger (otherwise known as Marsh crocodile or Broad-snouted crocodile)
Crocodylus porosus	Estuarine crocodile (otherwise known as Salt-water crocodile)
Crocodylus rhombifer	Cuban crocodile
Crocodylus siamensis	Siamese crocodile

Sch. 10	
Kind	*Common name*
Osteolaemus tetraspis	West African dwarf crocodile
Tomistoma schlegelii	False gharial (otherwise known as False gavial)
Gavialis gangeticus	Indian gharial (otherwise known as Indian gavial)

Iguanas

Brachylophus	Fijian iguanas
Cyclura	Caribbean rock iguanas
Sauromalus varius	San Esteban Island chuckwalla

Lizards

Varanus bengalensis	Bengal monitor (otherwise known as Indian monitor or Common monitor)
Varanus flavescens	Yellow monitor
Varanus griseus	Desert monitor (otherwise known as Agra monitor or Grey monitor)
Varanus komodoensis	Komodo dragon

Snakes

Acrantophis	Madagascar boas
Bolyeria	Round island boas
Casarea	Round island boas
Epicrates inornatus	Yellow tree boa
Epicrates subflavus	Jamaican boa
Python molurus molurus	Indian python (otherwise known as Indian rock python)
Sanzinia madagascariensis	Madagascar boa

Tuatara

Sphenodon punctatus	Tuatara

Chelonians

Batagur baska	River terrapin (otherwise known as Tuntong)
Geoclemys hamiltonii (otherwise known as Damonia hamiltonii)	Black pond turtle (otherwise known as Spotted pond turtle)
Melanochelys tricarinata (otherwise known as Geoemyda tricarinata or Nicoria tricarinata)	Three-keeled turtle (otherwise known as Three-keeled land tortoise)
Kachuga tecta tecta	Indian tent turtle (otherwise known as Indian sawback turtle or Roofed turtle or Dura turtle)

Kind	Common name	SCH. 10
Morenia ocellata	Burmese swamp turtle	
Terrapene coahuila	Aquatic box turtle (otherwise known as Water box turtle)	
Geochelone elephantopus (otherwise known as Testudo elephantopus)	Galapagos giant tortoise	
Geochelone radiata (otherwise known as Testudo radiata)	Radiated tortoise (otherwise known as Rayed tortoise)	
Geochelone yniphora (otherwise known as Testudo yniphora)	Madagascar tortoise (otherwise known as Rayed tortoise or Angonoka)	
Gopherus flavomarginatus (otherwise known as Crophemus polyphemus flavomarginatus)	Mexican gopher tortoise	
Psammobates geometricus (otherwise known as Testudo geometricus)	Geometric tortoise	
Cheloniidae	Sea turtles	
Dermochelys coriacea	Leatherback turtle (otherwise known as Leathery turtle or Luth)	
Lissemys punctata punctata	Indian flap-shelled turtle	
Trionyx ater	Cuatro Cienegas soft-shell turtle (otherwise known as Black soft-shelled turtle)	
Trionyx gangeticus	Ganges soft-shelled turtle (otherwise known as Indian soft-shelled turtle)	
Trionyx hurum	Peacock-marked soft-shelled turtle	
Trionyx nigricans	Dark-coloured soft-shelled turtle	
Pseudemydura umbrina	Short-necked turtle (otherwise known as Western swamp turtle)	

AMPHIBIANS

4. The kinds of amphibian specified in the first column below—

Andrias davidianus (otherwise known as Megalobatrachus davidianus)	Chinese giant salamander
Andrias japonicus (otherwise known as Megalobatrachus japonicus)	Japanese giant salamander
Atelopus varius zeteki	Golden frog (otherwise known as Zetek's frog)
Bufo periglenes	Golden toad (otherwise known as Orange toad)
Bufo superciliaris	Cameroon toad
Nectophrynoides	Viviparous toads

FISH

5. The kinds of fish specified in the first column below—

Kind	Common name
Acipenser brevirostrum	Shortnose sturgeon
Scleropages formosus	Asiatic bonytongue
Coregonus alpenae	Longjaw cisco
Chasmistes cujus	Cui-ui
Probarbus jullieni	Ikan temolek
Pangasianodon gigas	Giant catfish
Stizostedion vitreum glaucum	Blue walleye
Cynoscion macdonaldi	Drum fish

MOLLUSCS

6. The kinds of mollusc specified below—

Conradilla caelata

Dromus dromas

Epioblasma florentina curtisi (otherwise known as Dysnomia florentina curtisi)

Epioblasma florentina florentina (otherwise known as Dysnomia florentina florentina)

Epioblasma sampsoni (otherwise known as Dysnomia sampsoni)

Epioblasma sulcata perobliqua (otherwise known as Dysnomia sulcata perobliqua)

Epioblasma torulosa gubernaculum (otherwise known as Dysnomia torulosa gubernaculum)

Epioblasma torulosa torulosa (otherwise known as Dysnomia torulosa torulosa)

Epioblasma turgidula (otherwise known as Dysnomia turgidula)

Epioblasma walkeri (otherwise known as Dysnomia walkeri)

Fusconaia cuneolus

Fusconaia edgariana

Lampsilis higginsi

Lampsilis orbiculata orbiculata

Lampsilis satura

Lampsilis verescens

Plethobasus cicatricosus

Plethobasus cooperianus

Pleurobema plenum

Potamilus capax (otherwise known as Proptera capax)

Quadrula intermedia

Quadrula sparsa

Toxolasma cylindrella (otherwise known as Carunculina cylindrella)

Unio nickliniana (otherwise known as Megalonaias nickliniana)

Unio tampicoensis tecomatensis (otherwise known as Lampsilis tampicoensis tecomatensis)

Villosa trabalis (otherwise known as Micromya trabalis)

NOTE. The second column of this Schedule gives a common name or names, where available, and is included by way of guidance only; in the event of any dispute or proceedings, only the first column is to be taken into account.

SCHEDULE INSERTED AS SCHEDULE 5

SCHEDULE 5

PLANTS THE SALE ETC. OF WHICH IS RESTRICTED

This Schedule applies to the kinds of plant specified in the second column below—

Family	*Kind*
Apocynaceae	Pachypodium namaquanum
Araceae	Alocasia sanderana
Cactaceae	Ariocarpus agavoides
	Ariocarpus scapharostrus
	Aztekium ritteri
	Echinocereus lindsayi
	Obregonia denegrii
	Pelecyphora aselliformis
	Pelecyphora strobiliformis
Caryocaraceae	Caryocar costaricense
Caryophyllaceae	Gymnocarpus przewalskii
	Melandrium mongolicus
	Silene mongolica
	Stellaria pulvinata
Cupressaceae	Fitzroya cupressoides
	Pilgerodendron uviferum
Cycadaceae	Mirocycas calocoma
Gentianaceae	Prepusa hookeriana
Humiriaceae	Vantanea barbourii
Juglandaceae	Engelhardtia pterocarpa
Leguminosae	Ammopiptanthus mongolicum
	Cynometra hemitomophylla
	Platymiscium pleiostachyum
	Tachigalia versicolor
Liliaceae	Aloe albida
	Aloe pillansii
	Aloe polyphylla
	Aloe thorncropftii
	Aloe vossii
Melastomataceae	Lavoisiera itambana
Meliaceae	Guarea longipetiola
Moraceae	Batocarpus costaricensis
Nepenthaceae	Nepenthes rajah
Orchidaceae	Cattleya skinneri
	Cattleya trianae
	Didiciea cunninghamii
	Laelia jongheana
	Laelia lobata
	Lycaste virginalis var alba
	Peristeria elata
	Renanthera imschootiana
	Vanda coerulea

Family—cont.	Kind—cont.
Pinaceae	Abies guatemalensis
	Abies nebrodensis
Podocarpaceae	Podocarpus costalis
	Podocarpus parlatorei
Proteaceae	Orothamnus zeyheri
	Protea odorata
Rubiaceae	**Balmea stormae**
Sarraceniaceae	Sarracenia alabamensis alabamensis
	Sarracenia jonesii
	Sarracenia oreophila
Saxifragaceae (otherwise known as Grossulariaceae)	Ribes sardoum
Stangeriaceae	Stangeria eriopus
Ulmaceae	Celtis aetnensis
Welwitschiaceae	Welwitschia bainesii
Zamiaceae	Encephalartos
Zingiberaceae	Hedychium philippinense

Sections 29 and 34.

SCHEDULE 11

PROCEDURE IN CONNECTION WITH CERTAIN ORDERS UNDER PART II

Coming into operation

1.—(1) An original order or a restrictive amending order shall take effect on its being made.

(2) It shall be the duty of the Secretary of State to consider every original order or restrictive amending order made by him or a relevant authority, and any such order shall cease to have effect nine months after it is made unless the Secretary of State has previously given notice under paragraph 6 that he has considered it and does not propose to amend or revoke it or he has amended or revoked it or, in the case of an order made by such an authority, the authority has revoked it.

(3) An amending or revoking order, other than a restrictive amending order, made by a relevant authority shall be submitted by the authority to the Secretary of State for confirmation and shall not take effect until confirmed by him.

(4) Subject to paragraphs 3(1) and 4(4), an amending or revoking order, other than a restrictive amending order, made by the Secretary of State shall not take effect until confirmed by him.

(5) An amending or revoking order requiring confirmation shall, by virtue of this sub-paragraph, stand revoked if the Secretary of State gives notice under paragraph 6 that the order is not to be confirmed.

Publicity for orders

2.—(1) Where an order takes effect immediately, the authority making the order (whether the relevant authority or the Secretary of State) shall give notice—

(a) setting out the order or describing its general effect and in either case stating that it has taken effect ;

(b) naming a place in the area in which the land to which the order relates is situated where a copy of the order may be inspected free of charge at all reasonable hours ; and

(c) specifying the time (not being less than 28 days from the date of the first publication of the notice) within which, and the manner in which, representations or objections with respect to the order may be made.

(2) Where an order requires confirmation, the authority making the order shall give notice—

(a) setting out the order or describing its general effect and in either case stating that it has been made and requires confirmation ; and

(b) stating in relation to it the matters specified in sub-paragraph (1)(b) and (c).

(3) Subject to sub-paragraph (4), the notice to be given under sub-paragraph (1) or (2) shall be given—

(a) by publication in the Gazette and also at least one local newspaper circulating in the area in which the land to which the order relates is situated ;

(b) by serving a like notice on every owner and occupier of any of that land ; and

(c) in the case of a notice given by the Secretary of State, by serving a like notice on the relevant authority in whose area the land to which the order relates is situated.

(4) The Secretary of State may, in any particular case, direct that it shall not be necessary to comply with sub-paragraph (3)(b) ; but if he so directs in the case of any land, then in addition to publication the notice shall be addressed to " The owners and any occupiers " of the land (describing it) and a copy or copies of the notice shall be affixed to some conspicuous object or objects on the land.

Unopposed orders

3.—(1) Where an order made by a relevant authority takes effect immediately and no representations or objections are duly made in respect of it or any so made are withdrawn,—

(a) the Secretary of State shall as soon as practicable after considering it decide either to take no action on the order or to make an order amending or revoking it (subject, however, to paragraph 5) ; and

(b) the amending or revoking order shall take effect immediately, but it shall not require confirmation and no representation or objection with respect to it shall be entertained.

(2) Where an order requiring confirmation is made and no representations or objections are duly made in respect of it or any so made are withdrawn, the Secretary of State may confirm the order (with or without modifications).

Opposed orders

4.—(1) If any representation or objection duly made with respect to an order is not withdrawn, then, as soon as practicable in the case of an order having immediate effect and before confirming an order requiring confirmation, the Secretary of State shall either—

(a) cause a local inquiry to be held ; or

SCH 11 (*b*) afford any person by whom a representation or objection has been duly made and not withdrawn an opportunity of being heard by a person appointed by the Secretary of State for the purpose.

(2) On considering any representations or objections duly made and the report of any person appointed to hold the inquiry or to hear representations or objections, the Secretary of State—

    (*a*) shall, if the order has already taken effect, decide either to take no action on the order or to make an order (subject, however, to paragraph 5) amending or revoking the order as the Secretary of State thinks appropriate in the light of the report, representations or objections, without consulting the relevant authority where that authority made the order ; or

    (*b*) if the order requires confirmation, may confirm it (with or without modifications).

1972 c. 70.
1973 c. 65. (3) The provisions of subsections (2) to (5) of section 250 of the Local Government Act 1972 or subsections (4) to (8) of section 210 of the Local Government (Scotland) Act 1973 (which relate to the giving of evidence at, and defraying the cost of, local inquiries) shall apply in relation to any inquiry held under this paragraph as they apply in relation to a local inquiry which a Minister causes to be held under subsection (1) of that section.

(4) An amending or revoking order made by virtue of this paragraph shall take effect immediately, but it shall not require confirmation and no representation or objection with respect to it shall be entertained.

Restriction on power to amend orders or confirm them with modifications

5. The Secretary of State shall not by virtue of paragraph 3(1) or 4(2) amend an order which has taken effect, or confirm any other order with modifications, so as to extend the area to which an original order applies.

Notice of final decision on orders

6.—(1) The Secretary of State shall as soon as practicable after making an order by virtue of paragraph 3(1) or 4(2) give notice—

    (*a*) setting out the order or describing its general effect and in either case stating that it has taken effect ; and

    (*b*) stating the name of the place in the area in which the land to which the order relates is situated where a copy of the order may be inspected free of charge at all reasonable hours.

(2) The Secretary of State shall give notice of any of the following decisions of his as soon as practicable after making the decision—

    (*a*) a decision under paragraph 3(1) or 4(2) to take no action on an order which has already taken effect ;

    (*b*) a decision to confirm or not to confirm an order requiring confirmation under this Schedule.

(3) A notice under this paragraph of a decision to confirm an order shall—

> (a) set out the order as confirmed or describe its general effect, and in either case state the day on which the order took effect;
>
> (b) state the name of the place in the area in which the land to which the order relates is situated where a copy of the order as confirmed may be inspected free of charge at all reasonable hours.

(4) A notice under this paragraph shall be given by publishing it in accordance with paragraph 2(3) and serving a copy of it on any person on whom a notice was required to be served under paragraph 2(3) or (4).

Proceedings for questioning validity of orders

7.—(1) This paragraph applies to any order which has taken effect and as to which the Secretary of State has given notice under paragraph 6 of a decision of his to take no action or to amend the order in accordance with paragraph 3 or 4; and in this paragraph "the relevant notice" means any such notice.

(2) If any person is aggrieved by an order to which this paragraph applies and desires to question its validity on the ground that it is not within the powers of section 29 or 34, as the case may be, or that any of the requirements of this Schedule have not been complied with in relation to it, he may within six weeks from the date of the relevant notice make an application to the Court under this paragraph.

(3) On any such application the Court may, if satisfied that the order is not within those powers or that the interests of the applicant have been substantially prejudiced by a failure to comply with any of those requirements—

> (a) in England and Wales, quash the order, or any provision of the order, either generally or in so far as it affects the interests of the applicant; or
>
> (b) in Scotland, make such declarator as seems to the Court to be appropriate.

(4) Except as provided by this paragraph, the validity of an order shall not be questioned in any legal proceedings whatsoever.

(5) In this paragraph "the Court" means the High Court in relation to England and Wales and the Court of Session in relation to Scotland.

Interpretation

8. In this Schedule—

> "amending order" and "revoking order" mean an order which amends or, as the case may be, revokes a previous order;
>
> "the Gazette" means—
>
>> (a) if the order relates in whole or in part to England and Wales, the London Gazette;

SCH. 11   (*b*) if the order relates in whole or in part to Scotland, the Edinburgh Gazette ;

" order " means an order under section 29 or 34 ;

" original order " means an order other than an amending or revoking order ;

" the relevant authority " has the same meaning as in section 34 ;

" restrictive amending order " means an amending order which extends the area to which a previous order applies.

Section 36.

SCHEDULE 12
PROCEDURE IN CONNECTION WITH ORDERS UNDER
SECTION 36
Consultation

1. Before making an order, the Secretary of State shall consult with such persons as he may consider appropriate.

Publicity for draft orders

2.—(1) Before making an order, the Secretary of State shall prepare a draft of the order and give notice—

(*a*) stating that he proposes to make the order and the general effect of it ;

(*b*) naming a place in the area in which the land to which the draft order relates is situated where a copy of the draft order, and of any byelaws made or proposed to be made by a relevant authority for the protection of the area specified in the draft order, may be inspected free of charge, and copies thereof may be obtained at a reasonable charge, at all reasonable hours ; and

(*c*) specifying the time (not being less than 28 days from the date of the first publication of the notice) within which, and the manner in which, representations or objections with respect to the draft order may be made.

(2) Subject to sub-paragraph (3), the notice to be given under sub-paragraph (1) shall be given—

(*a*) by publication in the Gazette and also at least one local newspaper circulating in the area in which the land to which the draft order relates is situated ;

(*b*) by serving a like notice on—

(i) every person in whom is vested an interest in or right over any of that land ;

(ii) every relevant authority whose area includes any of that land ; and

(iii) such other bodies as may be prescribed or as the Secretary of State may consider appropriate ; and

(*c*) by causing a copy of the notice to be displayed in a prominent position—

(i) at council offices in the locality of the land to which the draft order relates ; and

(ii) at such other places as the Secretary of State may consider appropriate.

(3) The Secretary of State may, in any particular case, direct that it shall not be necessary to comply with sub-paragraph (2)(*b*)(i).

(4) Subject to sub-paragraph (3), sub-paragraph (2)(*b*) and (*c*) shall be complied with not less than 28 days before the expiration of the time specified in the notice.

Unopposed orders

3. If no representations or objections are duly made, or if any so made are withdrawn, the Secretary of State may make the order with or without modifications.

Opposed orders

4.—(1) If any representation or objection duly made is not withdrawn the Secretary of State shall, before making the order, either—

(*a*) cause a local inquiry to be held ; or

(*b*) afford any person by whom a representation or objection has been duly made and not withdrawn an opportunity of being heard by a person appointed by the Secretary of State for the purpose.

(2) On considering any representations or objections duly made and the report of the person appointed to hold the inquiry or hear representations or objections, the Secretary of State may make the order with or without modifications.

Restriction on power to make orders with modifications

5.—(1) The Secretary of State shall not make an order with modifications so as—

(*a*) to affect land not affected by the draft order ; or

(*b*) to authorise the making of any byelaw not authorised by the draft order,

except after complying with the requirements of sub-paragraph (2).

(2) The said requirements are that the Secretary of State shall—

(*a*) give such notice as appears to him requisite of his proposal so to modify the order, specifying the time (which shall not be less than 28 days from the date of the first publication of the notice) within which, and the manner in which, representations or objections with respect to the proposal may be made ;

(*b*) hold a local inquiry or afford any person by whom any representation or objection has been duly made and not withdrawn an opportunity of being heard by a person appointed by the Secretary of State for the purpose ; and

(*c*) consider the report of the person appointed to hold the inquiry or to hear representations or objections.

Local inquiries

6.—(1) The provisions of subsections (2) to (5) of section 250 of the Local Government Act 1972 or subsections (4) to (8) of section 210 1972 c. 70.

of the Local Government (Scotland) Act 1973 (which relate to the giving of evidence at, and defraying the cost of, local inquiries) shall apply in relation to any inquiry held under paragraph 4 or 5 as they apply in relation to a local inquiry which a Minister causes to be held under subsection (1) of that section.

(2) A local inquiry caused to be held under paragraph 4 or 5 before the making of an order may be held concurrently with any local inquiry caused to be held before the confirmation of byelaws made by a relevant authority for the protection of the area specified in the order.

Notice of making of orders

7.—(1) As soon as practicable after an order is made, the Secretary of State shall give notice—

(a) describing the general effect of the order as made and stating the date on which it took effect ; and

(b) naming a place in the area in which the land to which the order relates is situated where a copy of the order as made may be inspected free of charge, and copies thereof may be obtained at a reasonable charge, at all reasonable hours.

(2) A notice under sub-paragraph (1) shall be given—

(a) by publication in the manner required by paragraph 2(2)(a) ;

(b) by serving a like notice on any persons on whom notices were required to be served under paragraph 2(2)(b) ; and

(c) by causing like notices to be displayed in the like manner as the notices required to be displayed under paragraph 2(2)(c).

Proceedings for questioning validity of orders

8.—(1) If any person is aggrieved by an order which has taken effect and desires to question its validity on the ground that it is not within the powers of section 36 or that any of the requirements of this Schedule have not been complied with in relation to it, he may within 42 days from the date of publication of the notice under paragraph 7 make an application to the Court under this paragraph.

(2) On any such application the Court may, if satisfied that the order is not within those powers or that the interests of the applicant have been substantially prejudiced by a failure to comply with those requirements—

(a) in England and Wales, quash the order, or any provision of the order, either generally or in so far as it affects the interests of the applicant ; or

(b) in Scotland, make such declarator as seems to the Court to be appropriate.

(3) Except as provided by this paragraph, the validity of an order shall not be questioned in any legal proceedings whatever.

(4) In this paragraph " the Court " means the High Court in relation to England and Wales and the Court of Session in relation to Scotland.

Supplemental

9.—(1) In this Schedule—

" area " includes district ;

" council offices " means offices or buildings acquired or provided by a local authority ;

" the Gazette " means—

(a) if the order relates in whole or in part to England and Wales, the London Gazette ;

(b) if the order relates in whole or in part to Scotland, the Edinburgh Gazette ;

" order " means an order under section 36 ;

" prescribed " means prescribed by regulations made by the Secretary of State ;

and expressions to which a meaning is assigned by section 36 have the same meanings in this Schedule as in that section.

(2) References in this Schedule to land include references to any waters covering it ; and for the purposes of this Schedule any area in Great Britain which is bounded by tidal waters or parts of the sea shall be taken to include—

(a) the waters adjacent to that area up to the seaward limits of territorial waters ; and

(b) the land covered by the said adjacent waters.

(3) Regulations under this Schedule shall be made by statutory instrument which shall be subject to annulment in pursuance of a resolution of either House of Parliament.

SCHEDULE 13

PROVISIONS WITH RESPECT TO THE COUNTRYSIDE COMMISSION

Status

1. The Commission shall be a body corporate.

2. The Commission shall not be regarded as the servant or agent of the Crown, or as enjoying any status, immunity or privilege of the Crown ; and the Commission's property shall not be regarded as property of, or property held on behalf of, the Crown.

Members

3.—(1) The Commission shall consist of a chairman and such number of other members as the Secretary of State may determine, of whom one may be appointed to be deputy chairman.

(2) The members of the Commission shall be appointed by the Secretary of State and shall hold and vacate office in accordance with such terms as may be prescribed by or under regulations made by the Secretary of State and, on vacating office, shall be eligible for re-appointment.

SCH. 13

(3) Regulations under sub-paragraph (2) shall be made by statutory instrument which shall be subject to annulment in pursuance of a resolution of either House of Parliament.

(4) A member may at any time by notice in writing to the Secretary of State resign his office.

4.—(1) The Commission—

(a) shall pay to their members such remuneration and allowances (if any) as the Secretary of State may, with the approval of the Minister, determine ; and

(b) as regards any member in whose case the Secretary of State may, with the approval of the Minister, so determine, shall pay such pension to or in respect of him, or make such payments towards the provision of such pension as the Secretary of State may, with the Minister's approval, determine.

(2) If a person ceases to be a member of the Commission, and it appears to the Secretary of State that there are special circumstances which make it right that he should receive compensation, the Secretary of State may, with the approval of the Minister, require the Commission to pay to that person a sum of such amount as the Secretary of State may, with the Minister's approval, determine.

Committee for Wales

5.—(1) The Commission shall, after consultation with the Secretary of State, appoint a Committee for Wales.

(2) The membership of the Committee for Wales shall consist partly of persons who are members of the Commission, one of whom shall be the chairman of the Committee, and partly of persons, not exceeding such number as the Secretary of State may for the time being approve, who are not members of the Commission.

(3) The Commission may, after consulting the Secretary of State and subject to such conditions as they think appropriate, delegate any of their functions in Wales to the Committee for Wales, including (for Wales) their advisory functions under section 2 of the 1968 Act, and their duty of making recommendations under that section in respect of local authorities' applications for Exchequer grants.

(4) The Commission may, in the case of such members of the Committee for Wales as are not members of the Commission, pay to them such reasonable allowances in respect of—

(a) expenses properly incurred in the performance of their duties ;

(b) loss of remunerative time ; or

(c) additional expenses (other than as aforesaid) necessarily incurred by them for the purpose of enabling them to perform their duties, being expenses to which they would not otherwise have been subject,

as the Secretary of State may, with the approval of the Minister, determine.

Procedure

6. The procedure (including the quorum) of the Commission shall be such as they may determine.

7. The validity of any proceeding of the Commission shall not be affected by any vacancy among the members thereof or by any defect in the appointment of a member thereof.

SCH. 13

Staff

8.—(1) The Commission shall appoint—

(a) with the approval of the Secretary of State, a chief officer and

(b) such number of other employees as they may with the approval of the Secretary of State and the Minister determine.

(2) The Commission shall pay to their employees such remuneration and allowances as they may with the approval of the Secretary of State and the Minister determine.

(3) In the case of any person to be employed by them on and after the appointed day who immediately before that day was a civil servant, the Commission shall ensure that, so long as he is engaged in duties reasonably comparable to those in which he was engaged immediately before the coming into force of this Schedule, the terms and conditions of his employment, taken as a whole, are not less favourable than those which he then enjoyed.

(4) In relation to any person who—

(a) is a civil servant before the appointed day ; and

(b) is as from that day employed by the Commission,

Schedule 13 to the Employment Protection (Consolidation) Act 1978 (ascertainment, for the purposes of that Act and section 119 of the Employment Protection Act 1975, of the length of an employee's period of employment and whether that employment has been continuous) shall have effect as if his service as a civil servant had been employment under the Commission.

1978 c. 44.

1975 c. 71.

9.—(1) The Commission shall in the case of such of their employees as they may with the approval of the Secretary of State and the Minister determine,—

(a) pay such pension to or in respect of them ;

(b) make such payments towards the provision of such pensions ; or

(c) provide and maintain such schemes (whether contributory or not) for the payment of such pensions,

as they may with the approval of the Secretary of State and the Minister determine.

(2) In this paragraph any reference to the payment of pensions to or in respect of the Commission's employees includes a reference to the payment of pensions by way of compensation to or in respect of any of the Commission's employees who suffer loss of office or employment or loss or diminution of emoluments.

10.—(1) Employment with the Commission shall be included among the kinds of employment to which a superannuation scheme under section 1 of the Superannuation Act 1972 can apply, and

1972 c. 11.

Sch. 13 accordingly in Schedule 1 to that Act (in which those kinds of employment are listed) the words " Countryside Commission " shall be inserted after the words " Monopolies Commission ".

(2) The Commission shall pay to the Minister at such times in each financial year as may be determined by the Minister, subject to any directions of the Treasury, sums of such amounts as he may so determine for the purposes of this paragraph as being equivalent to the increase during the year of such liabilities of his under the Principal Civil Service Pension Scheme as are attributable to the provision of pensions to or in respect of persons who are, or have been, in the service of the Commission in so far as that increase results from the service of those persons during that financial year and to the expense to be incurred in administering those pensions.

Accounts and report

11.—(1) The Commission shall keep proper accounts and other records, and shall prepare for each financial year a statement of account in such form as the Secretary of State with the approval of the Treasury may direct and submit those statements of account to the Secretary of State at such time as he may with the approval of the Treasury direct.

(2) The Secretary of State shall, as respects each financial year, send the Commission's statement of accounts to the Comptroller and Auditor General not later than the end of November following the year.

(3) The Comptroller and Auditor General shall examine, certify and report on the statement of accounts and lay copies of it, together with his report, before each House of Parliament.

12. The Commission shall furnish the Secretary of State with such returns, accounts and other information with respect to their property and activities or proposed activities as he may from time to time require, and shall afford to the Secretary of State facilities for the verification of information so furnished and for that purpose permit any person authorised in that behalf by the Secretary of State to inspect and make copies of the Commission's accounts, books, documents or papers and give that person such explanation of them as he may reasonably require.

13.—(1) The Commission shall, as soon as possible after the end of each financial year, make to the Secretary of State a report on the discharge by them of their functions under the 1949 Act, the 1968 Act and this Act during that year.

(2) Without prejudice to the generality of sub-paragraph (1), but subject to the provisions of sub-paragraph (3), the report of the Commission for any year shall include—

(a) a statement of the action taken by the Commission to promote the enjoyment of the countryside by members of the public who are disabled ; and (*b*) a record of all questions with which the Commission have been concerned during that year and which appear to the Commission to be of general public interest, indicating the purport of any representations or recommendations made by the Commission with respect thereto, and the conclusions (if any) reached thereon.

(3) The report of the Commission for any year shall set out any direction given by the Secretary of State during that year under section 3 of the 1949 Act unless the Secretary of State has notified to the Commission his opinion that it is against the interests of national security so to do.

(4) The Secretary of State shall lay a copy of every report of the Commission under this paragraph before each House of Parliament.

Land

14. The Commission, for the purpose of providing themselves with office or other accommodation in connection with the exercise of any of their functions, may, with the approval of the Secretary of State, acquire land, erect and maintain buildings or other structures thereon, and, when the land is no longer required for such purpose, dispose of it.

15. Any land occupied by the Commission shall, for the purpose of any rate on property, be treated as if it were property occupied by or on behalf of the Crown for public purposes.

Interpretation

16. In this Schedule—

" appointed day " means the day appointed for the coming into force of this Schedule ;

" the Commission " means the Countryside Commission ;

" financial year " means the period commencing with the appointed day and ending with 31st March following that day, and each successive period of twelve months ;

" the Minister " means the Minister for the Civil Service ;

" pension " includes allowance or gratuity.

SCHEDULE 14

Section 53.

APPLICATIONS FOR CERTAIN ORDERS UNDER PART III

Form of applications

1. An application shall be made in the prescribed form and shall be accompanied by—

(*a*) a map drawn to the prescribed scale and showing the way or ways to which the application relates ; and

(*b*) copies of any documentary evidence (including statements of witnesses) which the applicant wishes to adduce in support of the application.

SCH. 13

SCH. 14

Notice of applications

2.—(1) Subject to sub-paragraph (2), the applicant shall serve a notice stating that the application has been made on every owner and occupier of any land to which the application relates.

(2) If, after reasonable inquiry has been made, the authority are satisfied that it is not practicable to ascertain the name or address of an owner or occupier of any land to which the application relates, the authority may direct that the notice required to be served on him by sub-paragraph (1) may be served by addressing it to him by the description " owner " or " occupier " of the land (describing it) and by affixing it to some conspicuous object or objects on the land.

(3) When the requirements of this paragraph have been complied with, the applicant shall certify that fact to the authority.

(4) Every notice or certificate under this paragraph shall be in the prescribed form.

Determination by authority

3.—(1) As soon as reasonably practicable after receiving a certificate under paragraph 2(3), the authority shall—

(a) investigate the matters stated in the application ; and

(b) after consulting with every local authority whose area includes the land to which the application relates, decide whether to make or not to make the order to which the application relates.

(2) If the authority have not determined the application within twelve months of their receiving a certificate under paragraph 2(3), then, on the applicant making representations to the Secretary of State, the Secretary of State may, after consulting with the authority, direct the authority to determine the application before the expiration of such period as may be specified in the direction.

(3) As soon as practicable after determining the application, the authority shall give notice of their decision by serving a copy of it on the applicant and any person on whom notice of the application was required to be served under paragraph 2(1).

Appeal against a decision not to make an order

4.—(1) Where the authority decide not to make an order, the applicant may, at any time within 28 days after service on him of notice of the decision, serve notice of appeal against that decision on the Secretary of State and the authority.

(2) If on considering the appeal the Secretary of State considers that an order should be made, he shall give to the authority such directions as appear to him necessary for the purpose.

Interpretation

5.—(1) In this Schedule—

" application " means an application under section 53(5) ;

" local authority " means a district council, the Greater London Sch. 14
Council, a parish or community council or the parish
meeting of a parish not having a separate parish council ;
" prescribed " means prescribed by regulations made by the
Secretary of State.

(2) Regulations under this Schedule shall be made by statutory
instrument which shall be subject to annulment in pursuance of a
resolution of either House of Parliament.

SCHEDULE 15

Sections 53
and 54.

PROCEDURE IN CONNECTION WITH CERTAIN ORDERS UNDER PART III

Consultation

1. Before making an order, the authority shall consult with every
local authority whose area includes the land to which the order
relates.

Coming into operation

2. An order shall not take effect until confirmed· either by the
authority or the Secretary of State under paragraph 6 or by the
Secretary of State under paragraph 7.

Publicity for orders

3.—(1) On making an order, the authority shall give notice in the
prescribed form—

(a) describing the general effect of the order and stating that
it has been made and requires confirmation ;

(b) naming a place in the area in which the land to which the
order relates is situated where a copy of the order may be
inspected free of charge, and copies thereof may be obtained
at a reasonable charge, at all reasonable hours ; and

(c) specifying the time (not being less than 42 days from the date
of the first publication of the notice) within which, and the
manner in which, representations or objections with respect
to the order may be made.

(2) Subject to sub-paragraph (4), the notice to be given under sub-
paragraph (1) shall be given—

(a) by publication in at least one local newspaper circulating in
the area in which the land to which the order relates
is situated ;

(b) by serving a like notice on—

(i) every owner and occupier of any of that land ;

(ii) every local authority whose area includes any of
that land ;

(iii) every person on whom notice is required to be
served in pursuance of sub-paragraph (3) ; and

(iv) such other persons as may be prescribed in relation to the area in which that land is situated or as the
authority may consider appropriate ; and

SCH. 15

(c) by causing a copy of the notice to be displayed in a prominent position—

(i) at the ends of so much of any way as is affected by the order ;

(ii) at council offices in the locality of the land to which the order relates ; and

(iii) at such other places as the authority may consider appropriate.

(3) Any person may, on payment of such reasonable charge as the authority may consider appropriate, require an authority to give him notice of all such orders as are made by the authority during a specified period, are of a specified description and relate to land comprised in a specified area ; and in this sub-paragraph " specified " means specified in the requirement.

(4) The Secretary of State may, in any particular case, direct that it shall not be necessary to comply with sub-paragraph (2)(b)(i) ; but if he so directs in the case of any land, then in addition to publication the notice shall be addressed to " The owners and any occupiers " of the land (describing it) and a copy or copies of the notice shall be affixed to some conspicuous object or objects on the land.

(5) Sub-paragraph (2)(b) and (c) and, where applicable, sub-paragraph (4) shall be complied with not less than 42 days before the expiration of the time specified in the notice.

(6) A notice required to be served by sub-paragraph (2)(b) on the owner or occupier of any land, or on a local authority, shall be accompanied by a copy of so much of the order as relates to that land or, as the case may be, the area of that authority ; and a notice required to be served by that sub-paragraph on such other persons as may be prescribed or as the authority may consider appropriate shall be accompanied by a copy of the order.

(7) A notice required to be displayed by sub-paragraph (2)(c) at the ends of so much of any way as is affected by the order shall be accompanied by a plan showing the general effect of the order so far as it relates to that way.

(8) At any time after the publication of a notice under this paragraph and before the expiration of the period specified in the notice for the making of representations and objections, any person may require the authority to inform him what documents (if any) were taken into account in preparing the order and—

(a) as respects any such documents in the possession of the authority, to permit him to inspect them and take copies ; and

(b) as respects any such documents not in their possession, to give him any information the authority have as to where the documents can be inspected ;

and on any requirement being made under this sub-paragraph the authority shall comply therewith within 14 days of the making of the requirement.

(9) Nothing in sub-paragraph (8) shall be construed as limiting the documentary or other evidence which may be adduced at any local inquiry or hearing held under paragraph 7 or 8.

Representations or objections made with respect to abandoned surveys or reviews

4.—(1) This paragraph applies where a survey begun under sections 27 to 32 of the 1949 Act, or a review begun under section 33 of that Act, is abandoned after a draft map and statement have been prepared.

(2) If an order modifies the definitive map and statement so as—

(*a*) to show any particulars shown in the draft map and statement but not in the definitive map and statement ; or

(*b*) to omit any particulars shown in the definitive map and statement but not in the draft map and statement,

any representation or objection duly made with respect to the showing in or omission from the draft map and statement of those particulars shall be treated for the purposes of paragraphs 6 and 7 as a representation or objection duly made with respect to the corresponding modifications made by the order.

Severance of orders

5.—(1) Where at any time representations or objections duly made and not withdrawn relate to some but not all of the modifications made by an order, the authority may, by notice given to the Secretary of State, elect that, for the purposes of the following provisions of this Schedule, the order shall have effect as two separate orders—

(*a*) the one comprising the modifications to which the representations or objections relate ; and

(*b*) the other comprising the remaining modifications.

(2) Any reference in sub-paragraph (1) to an order includes a reference to any part of an order which, by virtue of one or more previous elections under that sub-paragraph, has effect as a separate order.

Unopposed orders

6.—(1) If no representations or objections are duly made, or if any so made are withdrawn, the authority may—

(*a*) confirm the order without modification ; or

(*b*) if they require any modification to be made, submit the order to the Secretary of State for confirmation by him.

(2) Where an order is submitted to the Secretary of State under sub-paragraph (1), the Secretary of State may confirm the order with or without modifications.

Opposed orders

7.—(1) If any representation or objection duly made is not withdrawn the authority shall submit the order to the Secretary of State for confirmation by him.

Sch. 15   (2) Where an order is submitted to the Secretary of State under sub-paragraph (1), the Secretary of State shall either—

(a) cause a local inquiry to be held ; or

(b) afford any person by whom a representation or objection has been duly made and not withdrawn an opportunity of being heard by a person appointed by the Secretary of State for the purpose.

(3) On considering any representations or objections duly made and the report of the person appointed to hold the inquiry or hear representations or objections, the Secretary of State may confirm the order with or without modifications.

Restriction on power to confirm orders with modifications

8.—(1) The Secretary of State shall not confirm an order with modifications so as—

(a) to affect land not affected by the order ;

(b) not to show any way shown in the order or to show any way not so shown ; or

(c) to show as a highway of one description a way which is shown in the order as a highway of another description,

except after complying with the requirements of sub-paragraph (2).

(2) The said requirements are that the Secretary of State shall—

(a) give such notice as appears to him requisite of his proposal so to modify the order, specifying the time (which shall not be less than 28 days from the date of the first publication of the notice) within which, and the manner in which, representations or objections with respect to the proposal may be made ;

(b) hold a local inquiry or afford any person by whom any representation or objection has been duly made and not withdrawn an opportunity of being heard by a person appointed by the Secretary of State for the purpose ; and

(c) consider the report of the person appointed to hold the inquiry or to hear representations or objections.

Local inquiries

9.—The provisions of subsections (2) to (5) of section 250 of the
1972 c. 70.   Local Government Act 1972 (which relate to the giving of evidence at, and defraying the cost of, local inquiries) shall apply in relation to any inquiry held under paragraph 7 or 8 as they apply in relation to a local inquiry which a Minister causes to be held under subsection (1) of that section.

Appointment of inspectors etc.

10.—(1) A decision of the Secretary of State under paragraph 6, 7 or 8 shall, except in such classes of case as may for the time being be prescribed or as may be specified in directions given by the Secretary of State, be made by a person appointed by the Secretary of State for the purpose instead of by the Secretary of State ; and a decision made by a person so appointed shall be treated as a decision of the Secretary of State.

(2) The Secretary of State may, if he thinks fit, direct that a decision which, by virtue of sub-paragraph (1) and apart from this sub-paragraph, falls to be made by a person appointed by the Secretary of State shall instead be made by the Secretary of State ; and a direction under this sub-paragraph shall state the reasons for which it is given and shall be served on the person, if any, so appointed, the authority and any person by whom a representation or objection has been duly made and not withdrawn.

(3) Where the Secretary of State has appointed a person to make a decision under paragraph 6, 7 or 8 the Secretary of State may, at any time before the making of the decision, appoint another person to make it instead of the person first appointed to make it.

(4) Where by virtue of sub-paragraph (2) or (3) a particular decision falls to be made by the Secretary of State or any other person instead of the person first appointed to make it, anything done by or in relation to the latter shall be treated as having been done by or in relation to the former.

(5) Regulations under this paragraph may provide for the giving of publicity to any directions given by the Secretary of State under this paragraph.

Notice of final decisions on orders

11.—(1) As soon as practicable after a decision to confirm an order is made or, in the case of a decision by the Secretary of State, as soon as practicable after receiving notice of his decision, the authority shall give notice—

(a) describing the general effect of the order as confirmed and stating that it has been confirmed (with or without modification) and the date on which it took effect ; and

(b) naming a place in the area in which the land to which the order relates is situated where a copy of the order as confirmed may be inspected free of charge, and copies thereof may be obtained at a reasonable charge, at all reasonable hours.

(2) A notice under sub-paragraph (1) shall be given—

(a) by publication in the manner required by paragraph 3(2)(a) ;

(b) by serving a like notice on any persons on whom notices were required to be served under paragraph 3(2)(b) or (4) ; and

(c) by causing like notices to be displayed in the like manner as the notices required to be displayed under paragraph 3(2)(c).

(3) A notice required to be served by sub-paragraph (2)(b) on the owner or occupier of any land, or on a local authority, shall be accompanied by a copy of so much of the order as confirmed as relates to that land or, as the case may be, the area of that authority ;

SCH. 15 and, in the case of an order which has been confirmed with modifications, a notice required to be served by that sub-paragraph on such other persons as may be prescribed or as the authority may consider appropriate shall be accompanied by a copy of the order as confirmed.

(4) As soon as practicable after a decision not to confirm an order or, in the case of a decision by the Secretary of State, as soon as practicable after receiving notice of his decision, the authority shall give notice of the decision by serving a copy of it on any persons on whom notices were required to be served under paragraph 3(2)(*b*) or (4).

Proceedings for questioning validity of orders

12.—(1) If any person is aggrieved by an order which has taken effect and desires to question its validity on the ground that it is not within the powers of section 53 or 54 or that any of the requirements of this Schedule have not been complied with in relation to it, he may within 42 days from the date of publication of the notice under paragraph 11 make an application to the High Court under this paragraph.

(2) On any such application the High Court may, if satisfied that the order is not within those powers or that the interests of the applicant have been substantially prejudiced by a failure to comply with those requirements, quash the order, or any provision of the order, either generally or in so far as it affects the interests of the applicant.

(3) Except as provided by this paragraph, the validity of an order shall not be questioned in any legal proceedings whatsoever.

Supplemental

13.—(1) The Secretary of State may, subject to the provisions of this Schedule, by regulations make such provision as to the procedure on the making, submission and confirmation of orders as appears to him to be expedient.

(2) In this Schedule—

" council offices " means offices or buildings acquired or provided by the authority or by a local authority ;

" local authority " means a district council, the Greater London Council, a parish or community council or the parish meeting of a parish not having a separate parish council ;

" order " means an order to which the provisions of this Schedule apply ;

" prescribed " means prescribed by regulations made by the Secretary of State.

(3) Regulations under this Schedule shall be made by statutory instrument which shall be subject to annulment in pursuance of a resolution of either House of Parliament.

SCHEDULE 16

Section 63.

ORDERS CREATING, EXTINGUISHING OR DIVERTING FOOTPATHS OR BRIDLEWAYS

The Town and Country Planning Act 1971

1.—(1) In sub-paragraph (1)(*b*) of paragraph 1 of Schedule 20 to the Town and Country Planning Act 1971 (procedure in connection with orders relating to footpaths and bridleways) after the word "charge" there shall be inserted the words "and copies thereof may be obtained at a reasonable charge".

1971 c. 78.

(2) In sub-paragraph (2) of that paragraph—

    (*a*) in head (*a*) the words "in the London Gazette and" shall be omitted ;

    (*b*) at the end of head (*b*) there shall be inserted the words—

        "(iv) every person on whom notice is required to be served in pursuance of sub-paragraph (2A) of this paragraph ; and

        (v) such other persons as may be prescribed in relation to the area in which that land is situated or as the authority may consider appropriate ; and " ; and

    (*c*) for head (*c*) there shall be substituted the following head—

        "(*c*) by causing a copy of the notice to be displayed in a prominent position—

        (i) at the ends of so much of any footpath or bridleway as is to be stopped up, diverted or extinguished by the order ;

        (ii) at council offices in the locality of the land to which the order relates ; and

        (iii) at such other places as the authority may consider appropriate ".

(3) After that sub-paragraph there shall be inserted the following sub-paragraph—

    "(2A) Any person may, on payment of such reasonable charge as the authority may consider appropriate, require an authority to give him notice of all such orders under section 210 or 214(1)(*b*) of this Act as are made by the authority during a specified period, are of a specified description and relate to land comprised in a specified area ; and in this sub-paragraph 'specified' means specified in the requirement."

(4) At the end of sub-paragraph (3) of that paragraph there shall be inserted the words "and 'council offices' means offices or buildings acquired or provided by a council or by the council of a parish or community or the parish meeting of a parish not having a separate parish council ".

(5) After sub-paragraph (4) of that paragraph there shall be inserted the following sub-paragraphs—

    "(5) Sub-paragraph (2)(*b*) and (*c*) and, where applicable, sub-paragraph (4) of this paragraph shall be complied with not less than 28 days before the expiration of the time specified in the notice.

SCH. 16

(6) A notice required to be served by sub-paragraph (2)(*b*)(i), (ii), (iii) or (v) of this paragraph shall be accompanied by a copy of the order.

(7) A notice required to be displayed by sub-paragraph (2)(*c*)(i) of this paragraph at the ends of so much of any way as is affected by the order shall be accompanied by a plan showing the general effect of the order so far as it relates to that way."

2. After paragraph 3 of that Schedule there shall be inserted the following paragraph—

" 3A.—(1) A decision of the Secretary of State under paragraph 3 of this Schedule shall, except in such classes of case as may for the time being be prescribed or as may be specified in directions given by the Secretary of State, be made by a person appointed by the Secretary of State for the purpose instead of by the Secretary of State ; and a decision made by a person so appointed shall be treated as a decision of the Secretary of State.

(2) The Secretary of State may, if he thinks fit, direct that a decision which, by virtue of sub-paragraph (1) of this paragraph and apart from this sub-paragraph, falls to be made by a person appointed by the Secretary of State shall instead be made by the Secretary of State ; and a direction under this sub-paragraph shall state the reasons for which it is given and shall be served on the person, if any, so appointed, the authority and any person by whom a representation or objection has been duly made and not withdrawn.

(3) Where the Secretary of State has appointed a person to make a decision under paragraph 3 of this Schedule the Secretary of State may, at any time before the making of the decision, appoint another person to make it instead of the person first appointed to make it.

(4) Where by virtue of sub-paragraph (2) or (3) of this paragraph a particular decision falls to be made by the Secretary of State or any other person instead of the person first appointed to make it, anything done by or in relation to the latter shall be treated as having been done by or in relation to the former.

(5) Regulations under this Act may provide for the giving of publicity to any directions given by the Secretary of State under this paragraph."

3.—(1) In paragraph 6 of that Schedule—

(*a*) for the words " a copy thereof " there shall be substituted the words " a copy of the order " ;

(*b*) after the words " free of charge " there shall be inserted the words " and copies thereof may be obtained at a reasonable charge " ; and

(*c*) for heads (*a*) and (*b*) there shall be substituted the following heads—

" (*a*) serve a like notice on any persons on whom notices were required to be served under paragraph 1(2)(*b*) or (4) of this Schedule ; and (*b*) cause like notices to be displayed in the like manner as the notices required to be displayed under paragraph 1(2)(*c*) of this Schedule: ".

(2) That paragraph as so amended shall be renumbered as paragraph 6(1) of that Schedule and after that provision as so renumbered there shall be inserted the following sub-paragraphs—

" (2) A notice required to be served by sub-paragraph (1)(*a*) of this paragraph on—

(*a*) a person on whom notice was required to be served by paragraph 1(2)(*b*)(i), (ii) or (iii) of this Schedule ; or

(*b*) in the case of an order which has been confirmed with modifications, a person on whom notice was required to be served by paragraph 1(2)(*b*)(v) of this Schedule, shall be accompanied by a copy of the order as confirmed.

(3) As soon as may be after a decision not to confirm an order under the said section 210 or 214(1)(*b*), the authority by whom the order was made shall give notice of the decision by serving a copy of it on any persons on whom notices were required to be served under paragraph 1(2)(*b*) or (4) of this Schedule. "

4. After that paragraph there shall be inserted the following paragraph—

" 7. As soon as may be after an order under section 210 or 214(1)(*b*) of this Act has come into operation otherwise than—

(*a*) on the date on which it was confirmed by the Secretary of State or confirmed as an unopposed order ; or

(*b*) at the expiration of a specified period beginning with that date,

the authority by whom the order was made shall give notice of its coming into operation by publication in at least one local newspaper circulating in the area in which the land to which the order relates is situated.".

The Highways Act 1980

5.—(1) In subsection (1) of section 119 of the Highways Act 1980 (diversion of footpaths and bridleways) for the words from the beginning to " or on to land " there shall be substituted the words " Where it appears to a council as respects a footpath or bridleway in their area (other than one that is a trunk road or a special road) that, in the interests of the owner, lessee or occupier of land crossed by the path or way or of the public, it is expedient that the line of the path or way, or part of that line, should be diverted (whether on to land of the same or ".

SCH. 16   (2) In subsection (5) of that section for the words "the council may require the owner, lessee or occupier on whose representations they are acting" there shall be substituted the words "on the representations of an owner, lessee or occupier of land crossed by the path or way, the council may require him".

6.—(1) In sub-paragraphs (1)(*b*) and 2(*b*) of paragraph 1 of Schedule 6 to that Act (procedure as to certain orders relating to footpaths and bridleways) after the words "free of charge" there shall be inserted the words "and copies thereof may be obtained at a reasonable charge".

(2) For sub-paragraph (3) of that paragraph there shall be substituted the following sub-paragraph—

"(3) The notices to be given under sub-paragraph (1) or (2) above shall be given—

(*a*) by publication in at least one local newspaper circulating in the area in which the land to which the order relates is situated ;

(*b*) by serving a like notice on—

(i) every owner, occupier and lessee (except tenants for a month or any period less than a month and statutory tenants within the meaning of the Rent (Agriculture) Act 1976 or the Rent Act 1977) of any of that land ;

(ii) every council, the council of every parish or community and the parish meeting of every parish not having a separate parish council, being a council, parish or community whose area includes any of that land ;

(iii) every person on whom notice is required to be served in pursuance of sub-paragraph (3A) or (3B) below ; and

(iv) such other persons as may be prescribed in relation to the area in which that land is situated or as the authority or, as the case may be, the Secretary of State may consider appropriate ; and

(*c*) by causing a copy of the notice to be displayed in a prominent position—

(i) at the ends of so much of any footpath or bridleway as is created, stopped up or diverted by the order ;

(ii) at council offices in the locality of the land to which the order relates ; and

(iii) at such other places as the authority or, as the case may be, the Secretary of State may consider appropriate."

(3) After that sub-paragraph there shall be inserted the following sub-paragraphs—

"(3A) Any person may, on payment of such reasonable charge as the authority may consider appropriate, require an authority to give him notice of all such public path creation orders, public path extinguishment orders and public path diversion orders as are made by the authority during a specified period, are of a specified description and relate to land comprised in a specified area ; and in this sub-paragraph " specified " means specified in the requirement.

(3B) Any person may, on payment of such reasonable charge as the Secretary of State may consider appropriate, require the Secretary of State to give him notice of all such draft public path creation orders, draft public path extinguishment orders and draft public path diversion orders as are prepared by the Secretary of State during a specified period, are of a specified description and relate to land comprised in a specified area ; and in this sub-paragraph " specified " means specified in the requirement.

(3C) The Secretary of State may, in any particular case, direct that it shall not be necessary to comply with sub-paragraph (3)(*b*)(i) above ; but if he so directs in the case of any land, then in addition to publication the notice shall be addressed to ' The owners and any occupiers ' of the land (describing it) and a copy or copies of the notice shall be affixed to some conspicuous object or objects on the land."

(4) After sub-paragraph (4) of that paragraph there shall be inserted the following sub-paragraphs—

"(4A) Sub-paragraph (3)(*b*) and (*c*) and, where applicable, sub-paragraphs (3C) and (4) above shall be complied with not less than 28 days before the expiration of the time specified in the notice.

(4B) A notice required to be served by sub-paragraph (3)(*b*)(i), (ii) or (iv) above shall be accompanied by a copy of the order.

(4C) A notice required to be displayed by sub-paragraph (3) (*c*)(i) above at the ends of so much of any way as is affected by the order shall be accompanied by a plan showing the general effect of the order so far as it relates to that way.

(4D) In sub-paragraph (3)(*c*)(ii) above ' council offices ' means offices or buildings acquired or provided by a council or by the council of a parish or community or the parish meeting of a parish not having a separate parish council."

7. After paragraph 2 of that Schedule there shall be inserted the following paragraph—

" 2A—(1) A decision of the Secretary of State under paragraph 2 above as respects an order made by an authority other than the Secretary of State shall, except in such classes of case as may for the time being be prescribed or as may be specified in directions given by the Secretary of State, be made by a person appointed by the Secretary of State for the purpose instead of by the Secretary of State; and a decision made by a person so appointed shall be treated as a decision of the Secretary of State.

(2) The Secretary of State may, if he thinks fit, direct that a decision which, by virtue of sub-paragraph (1) above and apart from this sub-paragraph, falls to be made by a person appointed by the Secretary of State shall instead be made by the Secretary of State; and a direction under this sub-paragraph shall state the reasons for which it is given and shall be served on the person, if any, so appointed, the authority and any person by whom a representation or objection has been duly made and not withdrawn.

(3) Where the Secretary of State has appointed a person to make a decision under paragraph 2 above the Secretary of State may, at any time before the making of the decision, appoint another person to make it instead of the person first appointed to make it.

(4) Where by virtue of sub-paragraph (2) or (3) above a particular decision falls to be made by the Secretary of State or any other person instead of the person first appointed to make it, anything done by or in relation to the latter shall be treated as having been done by or in relation to the former.

(5) Provision may be made by regulations of the Secretary of State for the giving of publicity to any directions given by the Secretary of State under this paragraph."

8.—(1) In paragraph 4 of that Schedule after the words " free of charge " there shall be inserted the words " and copies thereof may be obtained at a reasonable charge " and for heads (*a*) and (*b*) there shall be substituted the following heads—

" (*a*) serve a like notice on any persons on whom notices were required to be served under paragraph 1(3)(*b*), (3C) or (4) above ; and

(*b*) cause like notices to be displayed in the like manner as the notices caused to be displayed under paragraph 1(3)(*c*) above ; ".

(2) That paragraph as so amended shall be renumbered as paragraph 4(1) of that Schedule and after that provision as so renumbered there shall be inserted the following sub-paragraphs—

" (2) A notice required to be served by sub-paragraph (1)(*a*) above, on—

(*a*) a person on whom notice was required to be served by paragraph 1(3)(*b*)(i) or (ii) above ; or

(*b*) in the case of an order which has been confirmed or made with modifications, a person on whom notice was required to be served by paragraph 1(3)(*b*)(iv) above,

shall be accompanied by a copy of the order as confirmed or made.

(3) As soon as may be after a decision not to confirm an
order to which this Schedule applies, the authority by whom the
order was made shall give notice of the decision by serving a
copy of it on any persons on whom notices were required to
be served under paragraph 1(3)(*b*), (3C) or (4) above.".

Sch. 16

9. After that paragraph there shall be inserted the following paragraph—

" 4A. As soon as may be after an order to which this
Schedule applies has come into operation otherwise than—

(*a*) on the date on which it was confirmed or made by the
Secretary of State or confirmed as an unopposed order ;
or

(*b*) at the expiration of a specified period beginning with
that date,

the authority by whom the order was made or, in the case of
an order made by the Secretary of State, the Secretary of State
shall give notice of its coming into operation by publication in
at least one local newspaper circulating in the area in which
the land to which the order relates is situated."

Supplemental

10.—(1) The amendments made by the foregoing provisions of this
Schedule shall not apply in relation to any order if it was made or a
draft thereof was prepared, or a notice relating to it was given
under paragraph 1 of the relevant Schedule, before the commencement date.

(2) Any reference in this paragraph to Schedule 6 to the Highways
Act 1980 includes a reference to that Schedule as applied by paragraph 3 of the provisions of Part I of Schedule 3 to the 1968 Act
which relate to the Acquisition of Land (Authorisation Procedure)
Act 1946.

1980 c. 66.
1946 c. 49.

SCHEDULE 17

Section 73.

Enactments Repealed

Part I

Enactments repealed one month
after the passing of this Act

Chapter	Short title	Extent of repeal
12, 13 & 14 Geo. 6. c. 97.	The National Parks and Access to the Country-side Act 1949.	Section 23.
1968 c. 41.	The Countryside Act 1968.	Section 14. In section 15(1) the words " which is not for the time being managed as a nature reserve but ".

SCH. 17

Chapter	Short title	Extent of repeal
1973 c. 37.	The Water Act 1973.	In section 22(3) the words " not being land for the time being managed as a nature reserve".
1973 c. 54.	The Nature Conservancy Council Act 1973.	Section 3.
1973 c. 65.	The Local Government (Scotland) Act 1973.	In Schedule 27, in Part II, paragraph 101.
1980 c. 66.	The Highways Act 1980.	In section 134, subsection (3) and in subsection (5) the words " (3) or ". In section 135(1), the words " 6 or " and " 6 weeks or ".

PART II

ENACTMENTS REPEALED ON A DAY TO BE APPOINTED

Chapter	Short title	Extent of repeal
2 & 3 Geo. 5 c. 14.	The Protection of Animals (Scotland) Act 1912.	In section 9 the words " or any snare " and " or snare ".
12, 13 & 14 Geo. 6. c. 97.	The National Parks and Access to the Countryside Act 1949.	Sections 2 and 4. Sections 27 to 35. Section 38. Section 95.
2 & 3 Eliz. 2. c. 30.	The Protection of Birds Act 1954.	The whole Act.
1963 c. 33.	The London Government Act 1963.	In section 60, subsections (1) to (4).
1963 c. 36.	The Deer Act 1963.	In Schedule 2, in paragraph 1 the words " of less gauge than 12 bore " and in paragraph 4 the words from " other than " onwards.
1964 c. 59.	The Protection of Birds Act 1954 (Amendment) Act 1964.	The whole Act.
1967 c. 46.	The Protection of Birds Act 1967.	The whole Act.
1968 c. 41.	The Countryside Act 1968.	In section 1, subsection (4) and, in subsection (5), the words " and 2(1) " and the words " and in section 4(1) " onwards. Section 3. In Schedule 3, in Part I, the entry relating to the National Parks and Access to the Countryside Act 1949, and Parts II, III and IV.

Chapter	Short title	Extent of repeal
1970 c. 30.	The Conservation of Seals Act 1970.	In section 10(1)(*c*), the word " or " immediately following sub-paragraph (ii).
1971 c. 23.	The Courts Act 1971.	In Schedule 8, paragraph 31. In Schedule 9, in Part II, the entry relating to section 31 of the National Parks and Access to the Countryside Act 1949.
1971 c. 78.	The Town and Country Planning Act 1971.	In Schedule 20, in paragraph 1(2)(*a*), the words " in the London Gazette and ".
1972 c. 70.	The Local Government Act 1972.	In Schedule 17, paragraphs 22 to 33. In Schedule 29, paragraph 37.
1973 c. 37.	The Water Act 1973.	In Schedule 8, paragraph 67.
1973 c. 54.	The Nature Conservancy Council Act 1973.	In section 5(3) the words from the beginning to " save as aforesaid ". In Schedule 1, paragraphs 3, 5, 7 and 12(*a*) and (*c*).
1973 c. 57.	The Badgers Act 1973.	Sections 6 and 7. Section 8(2)(*c*). In section 11, the definitions of " area of special protection " and " authorised person ".
1973 c. 65.	The Local Government (Scotland) Act 1973.	In Schedule 27, in Part II, paragraphs 115 and 168.
1975 c. 21.	The Criminal Procedure (Scotland) Act 1975.	In Schedule 7C, the entries relating to the Protection of Birds Act 1954 and the Conservation of Wild Creatures and Wild Plants Act 1975.
1975 c. 48.	The Conservation of Wild Creatures and Wild Plants Act 1975.	The whole Act.
1976 c. 16.	The Statute Law (Repeals) Act 1976.	In Schedule 2, in Part II, the entry relating to the Protection of Birds Act 1967.
1976 c. 72.	The Endangered Species (Import and Export) Act 1976.	Section 13(6).
1977 c. 45.	The Criminal Law Act 1977.	In Schedule 6, the entries relating to the Protection of Birds Act 1954 and the Conservation of Wild Creatures and Wild Plants Act 1975.
1979 c. 2.	The Customs and Excise Management Act 1979.	In Schedule 4, in paragraph 12, in the Table the entry relating to the Protection of Birds Act 1954.
1980 c. 66.	The Highways Act 1980.	In section 31(10) the words " or of that subsection " onwards. Section 340(2)(*d*).
1981 c. 22.	The Animal Health Act 1981.	In Schedule 5, paragraph 1

SCH. 17

Chapter	Short title	Extent of repeal
1981 c. 37.	The Zoo Licensing Act 1981.	In section 4(5), the entries relating to the Protection of Birds Acts 1954 to 1967 and the Conservation of Wild Creatures and Wild Plants Act 1975.

Wildlife and Countryside Act 1981 197

(3) As soon as may be after a decision not to confirm an SCH. 16
order to which this Schedule applies, the authority by whom the
order was made shall give notice of the decision by serving a
copy of it on any persons on whom notices were required to
be served under paragraph 1(3)(b), (3C) or (4) above.".

9. After that paragraph there shall be inserted the following paragraph—

" 4A. As soon as may be after an order to which this
Schedule applies has come into operation otherwise than—

(a) on the date on which it was confirmed or made by the
Secretary of State or confirmed as an unopposed order ;
or

(b) at the expiration of a specified period beginning with
that date,

the authority by whom the order was made or, in the case of
an order made by the Secretary of State, the Secretary of State
shall give notice of its coming into operation by publication in
at least one local newspaper circulating in the area in which
the land to which the order relates is situated."

Supplemental

10.—(1) The amendments made by the foregoing provisions of this
Schedule shall not apply in relation to any order if it was made or a
draft thereof was prepared, or a notice relating to it was given
under paragraph 1 of the relevant Schedule, before the commencement date.

(2) Any reference in this paragraph to Schedule 6 to the Highways 1980 c. 66.
Act 1980 includes a reference to that Schedule as applied by paragraph 3 of the provisions of Part I of Schedule 3 to the 1968 Act
which relate to the Acquisition of Land (Authorisation Procedure) 1946 c. 49.
Act 1946.

SCHEDULE 17   Section 73.

ENACTMENTS REPEALED

PART I

ENACTMENTS REPEALED ONE MONTH
AFTER THE PASSING OF THIS ACT

Chapter	Short title	Extent of repeal
12, 13 & 14 Geo. 6. c. 97.	The National Parks and Access to the Country-side Act 1949.	Section 23.
1968 c. 41.	The Countryside Act 1968.	Section 14. In section 15(1) the words " which is not for the time being managed as a nature reserve but ".

SCH. 17

Chapter	Short title	Extent of repeal
1973 c. 37.	The Water Act 1973.	In section 22(3) the words " not being land for the time being managed as a nature reserve".
1973 c. 54.	The Nature Conservancy Council Act 1973.	Section 3.
1973 c. 65.	The Local Government (Scotland) Act 1973.	In Schedule 27, in Part II, paragraph 101.
1980 c. 66.	The Highways Act 1980.	In section 134, subsection (3) and in subsection (5) the words " (3) or ". In section 135(1), the words " 6 or " and " 6 weeks or ".

PART II

ENACTMENTS REPEALED ON
A DAY TO BE APPOINTED

Chapter	Short title	Extent of repeal
2 & 3 Geo. 5 c. 14.	The Protection of Animals (Scotland) Act 1912.	In section 9 the words " or any snare " and " or snare ".
12, 13 & 14 Geo. 6. c. 97.	The National Parks and Access to the Country-side Act 1949.	Sections 2 and 4. Sections 27 to 35. Section 38. Section 95.
2 & 3 Eliz. 2. c. 30.	The Protection of Birds Act 1954.	The whole Act.
1963 c. 33.	The London Government Act 1963.	In section 60, subsections (1) to (4).
1963 c. 36.	The Deer Act 1963.	In Schedule 2, in paragraph 1 the words " of less gauge than 12 bore " and in paragraph 4 the words from " other than " onwards.
1964 c. 59.	The Protection of Birds Act 1954 (Amendment) Act 1964.	The whole Act.
1967 c. 46.	The Protection of Birds Act 1967.	The whole Act.
1968 c. 41.	The Countryside Act 1968.	In section 1, subsection (4) and, in subsection (5), the words " and 2(1) " and the words " and in section 4(1) " onwards. Section 3. In Schedule 3, in Part I, the entry relating to the National Parks and Access to the Countryside Act 1949, and Parts II, III and IV.

Chapter	Short title	Extent of repeal
1970 c. 30.	The Conservation of Seals Act 1970.	In section 10(1)(c), the word " or " immediately following sub-paragraph (ii).
1971 c. 23.	The Courts Act 1971.	In Schedule 8, paragraph 31. In Schedule 9, in Part II, the entry relating to section 31 of the National Parks and Access to the Countryside Act 1949.
1971 c. 78.	The Town and Country Planning Act 1971.	In Schedule 20, in paragraph 1(2)(a), the words " in the London Gazette and ".
1972 c. 70.	The Local Government Act 1972.	In Schedule 17, paragraphs 22 to 33. In Schedule 29, paragraph 37.
1973 c. 37.	The Water Act 1973.	In Schedule 8, paragraph 67.
1973 c. 54.	The Nature Conservancy Council Act 1973.	In section 5(3) the words from the beginning to " save as aforesaid ". In Schedule 1, paragraphs 3, 5, 7 and 12(a) and (c).
1973 c. 57.	The Badgers Act 1973.	Sections 6 and 7. Section 8(2)(c). In section 11, the definitions of " area of special protection " and " authorised person ".
1973 c. 65.	The Local Government (Scotland) Act 1973.	In Schedule 27, in Part II, paragraphs 115 and 168.
1975 c. 21.	The Criminal Procedure (Scotland) Act 1975.	In Schedule 7C, the entries relating to the Protection of Birds Act 1954 and the Conservation of Wild Creatures and Wild Plants Act 1975.
1975 c. 48.	The Conservation of Wild Creatures and Wild Plants Act 1975.	The whole Act.
1976 c. 16.	The Statute Law (Repeals) Act 1976.	In Schedule 2, in Part II, the entry relating to the Protection of Birds Act 1967.
1976 c. 72.	The Endangered Species (Import and Export) Act 1976.	Section 13(6).
1977 c. 45.	The Criminal Law Act 1977.	In Schedule 6, the entries relating to the Protection of Birds Act 1954 and the Conservation of Wild Creatures and Wild Plants Act 1975.
1979 c. 2.	The Customs and Excise Management Act 1979.	In Schedule 4, in paragraph 12, in the Table the entry relating to the Protection of Birds Act 1954.
1980 c. 66.	The Highways Act 1980.	In section 31(10) the words " or of that subsection " onwards. Section 340(2)(d).
1981 c. 22.	The Animal Health Act 1981.	In Schedule 5, paragraph 1

SCH. 17

Chapter	Short title	Extent of repeal
1981 c. 37.	The Zoo Licensing Act 1981.	In section 4(5), the entries relating to the Protection of Birds Acts 1954 to 1967 and the Conservation of Wild Creatures and Wild Plants Act 1975.

APPENDIX A

NOTICE OF INTENTION TO CARRY OUT A LISTED OPERATION* WITHIN A SITE OF SPECIAL SCIENTIFIC INTEREST
(Please use capital letters for names and places)

Name, address and telephone number of applicant:

Location of operation (indicate on attached SSSI map or include sketch map or plan; give OS field numbers or grid references if possible):

Details of proposal (include proposed timing and likely duration of the work or activity):

Area of land affected:

Additional information (e.g. address of agent if relevant):

Signature ....

Name ....
(Block Capitals)
Date ....

Please return this form to:

(NCC Regional or Sub-Regional Office)

*An operation or activity falling into one of the categories listed by the NCC on the reverse of the SSSI notification.

202

SITES OF SPECIAL SCIENTIFIC INTEREST
Code of guidance

Over the past 30 years the Nature Conservancy Council has identified places in the countryside which are of special interest because of the animals, birds, insects or plants found in them, or because of the interesting rocks or features of the land itself.

These areas of special and exceptional value are known as Sites of Special Scientific Interest, or SSSIs for short, and deserve special protection. As some kinds of operations or developments can endanger them, new provisions were introduced in the Wildlife and Countryside Act 1981, which can, with goodwill, help to ensure that such protection is given.

This Code explains the provisions contained in the Wildlife and Countryside Act 1981 for the protection of SSSIs. It covers the new procedures for the Nature Conservancy Council to notify the existence of such sites, and the various arrangements that have now been established to try and put their protection on a sensible basis. It recognises the legitimate interests both of the owners and the tenants of such sites, and the wider interest in conservation. This Code has been prepared by the Ministers responsible, for the guidance of all those concerned, and has been approved by Parliament.

Contents

I *Introduction*

Statutory
References
(Wildlife and
Countryside
Act 1981 unless
otherwise
specified)

1 Over the past 30 years the Nature Conservancy Council has identified places in the countryside which are of special interest because of the animals, birds, insects or plants found in them, or because of the interesting rocks or features of the land itself. These areas of special and exceptional value are known as Sites of Special Scientific Interest, or SSSIs for short, and deserve special special protection(1).

As some kinds of operations or developments can endanger them, new provisions were introduced in the Wildlife and Countryside Act 1981, which can, with goodwill, help to ensure that such protection is given.

2 *The conservation and proper management of SSSIs is vital to the maintenance of Britain's wildlife in all its forms and owners, occupiers, Government Departments, statutory undertakers and others concerned are urged to co-operate by following the guidance contained in this code, in addition to complying with the legal obligations which it outlines.*

3 The following paragraphs set out how the new provisions work. They may appear complicated, but the NCC will be pleased to help with advice as to how they apply in any particular case. The NCC will also give advice on the management of SSSIs and may, in some circumstances, be able to assist with grants or payments under management agreements (see paragraphs 25–29). There may also be tax concessions available to SSSI owners. The NCC will provide details on request. A list of NCC Regional Offices is attached.

---

1 "The Selection of SSSIs", which sets out the relevant criteria, is available from the NCC on request.

II *Notification of SSSIs by the NCC*

Sites notified before 30 November 1981

Section 28(1)
(4) and (13)

4   Since 1949(2) the NCC has had a duty to notify SSSIs to local planning authorities. The Wildlife and Countryside Act 1981 provides that all such notifications made before 30 November 1981 shall remain valid but in addition the NCC is required to notify owners and occupiers that they have an SSSI on their land, specifying in the notification:

a the location of the site;
b the nature of the special interest; and
c any operations that appear likely to damage that interest (see paragraph 9).

This process will take some time and, in the interim, owners and occupiers who are aware of the existence of an SSSI on their land are asked to follow voluntarily the procedure set out in paragraph 14 in relation to any operations which might be damaging to the scientific interest of the site. If they are in doubt as to whether or not an operation might be damaging, the local office of the NCC will be pleased to advise.

5   Notification to owners and occupiers will be given in writing by the NCC and will include a map of the site. An NCC officer will be pleased to arrange a visit to provide further advice on request. Full notification details will be copied to the local planning authority, the Secretary of State and other relevant bodies.

Notification of SSSIs after 30 November 1981

Section 28(2)

6   In exercising its duty to notify any new SSSI, or an extension to an existing SSSI, the NCC is now required to give local planning

---

2 The National Parks and Access to the Countryside Act 1949 (Section 23).

authorities, owners and occupiers and the Secretary of State notice of its intentions. The notice will set out the terms of the proposed notification, which will specify:

a the location of the site (including a map)
b the nature of the special interest; and
c any operations that appear likely to damage that interest (see paragraph 9).

The proposed notification will also be sent to the appropriate Agriculture Department, the Forestry Commission, water authorities(3) and, where appropriate, internal drainage boards and other relevant bodies. The NCC will consider any representations or objections submitted in writing during the period specified in the notice, which must be at least 3 months, and will be pleased to discuss the proposals with owners and occupiers if requested.

7 Owners and occupiers who have received notice of a proposed notification should not, in advance of the NCC's final decision, carry out any operation specified in it without consulting the NCC.

8 Once the NCC has made a final decision to notify an SSSI it will send the notification (indicating the reasons for its conclusions where appropriate) to all owners and occupiers, the local planning authority, the Secretary of State and all other bodies to whom the original proposal was sent. The notification will set out in final form the particulars mentioned in paragraph 6(a) to (c) above.

Potentially damaging operations

9 To comply with the requirement to specify potentially damaging operations in an SSSI notification a list of such operations will be drawn up by the NCC for the whole of each SSSI. The NCC will discuss with individual owners and occupiers how it relates to particular landholdings within the site and will welcome comments from them. The inclusion of an operation in the list will ensure that the NCC is informed before any such operation is undertaken, but does not necessarily imply that it will object in any particular case.

Registration of SSSIs as a land charge

Section 28(11) and (12)

10 The NCC will register each SSSI in the appropriate local land

---

3 In Scotland the Regional or Islands Council, the River Purification Board, and the Central Scotland Water Development Board if appropriate.

charges registry(4) so that, when the land comprising an SSSI is sold, the new owner should become aware of the SSSI as a result of the searches carried out before purchase. In some instances a search may not be carried out (eg by those who inherit land). In order to prevent unwitting damage to an SSSI, owners and occupiers should try to ensure that new or prospective owners and occupiers are given the full details of the SSSI.

Statutory Undertakers

11 The NCC will inform statutory undertakers (eg electricity, gas and water authorities) of the full details of all SSSIs within the statutory undertakers' areas of operation and will ask to be consulted before any operations likely to damage SSSIs are carried out by an undertaker. Where statutory undertakers are owners or occupiers of SSSIs they are subject to the same obligations as any other owner or occupier, as set out in paragraph 14. Water authorities, including internal drainage boards, are also under an obligation(5) to consult the NCC before carrying out any works (other than emergency works notified to the Council as soon as possible after their commencement) which appear to them likely to damage or destroy the special features of an SSSI which the NCC has notified to them as being within their area.

Procedure for notification if owners or occupiers cannot be traced

Section 28(3)   **12** The NCC will make every effort to trace owners and occupiers but where it is unable to do so a notification will be served by attaching it to some conspicuous object on the land.

Removal of SSSI status

13 The NCC may decide that an SSSI, or part of an SSSI, no longer merits that status because of a reduction in the scientific value of the land due to natural or other causes. In such cases the NCC will inform all owners and occupiers, the local planning authority, the Secretary of State and other relevant bodies that the land in question is no longer an SSSI and arrange for cancellation of the entry in the local land charges registry.

---

4 In Scotland the General Register of Sasines or the Land Register of Scotland, as appropriate.
5 In Scotland, by administrative arrangement.

III *Notice of intended operations by owners and occupiers to the NCC*

Statutory obligation on owners and occupiers

14 The law now provides that owners and occupiers must not carry out (or cause or permit to be carried out) any operation listed in the SSSI notification unless the NCC has been given notice *in writing* of the intended operation, so that it may assess the likely effect on the scientific interest, and unless:

a it has been agreed in writing by the NCC; or
b it is carried out in accordance with a management agreement (see paragraphs 25–29); or
c 3 months have elapsed since written notice of the proposed operation was given to the NCC by the owner or occupier.

Section 28(8)   The above restrictions do not apply to any operation which is either authorised by a planning permission granted on application or carried out in response to an emergency. In the latter case the details of the emergency and the operation must be notified to the NCC as soon as practicable after the start of the operation (initially by telephone, if possible).

15 The NCC will make an initial response to the notice given by the owner or occupier within one calendar month of receipt, either giving its written consent or explaining its position (which may be that it wishes to discuss modifications or the possibility of entering into a management agreement).

16 Paragraphs 17–20 below contain additional advice on procedures for the following types of operations:

a Agricultural operations where an owner or occupier intends to seek farm capital grant.
b Forestry operations where Forestry Commission grant and/or a felling permission is sought.
c Operations with a general planning permission under a General Development Order.
d Operations requiring a planning application to be made.

Agricultural operations where an owner or occupier intends to seek farm capital grant(6)

17   Where an owner or occupier intends to seek farm capital grant and the NCC has given its written consent (see paragraphs 14–15) the owner or occupier may carry out the operation and claim grant. If, however, the NCC considers that the operation would be damaging to the scientific interest of the site the applicant and the Agricultural Development and Advisory Service (ADAS) (7) will be informed. If the proposed work is not an eligible item, or the applicant's business is not an eligible business, under the capital grant schemes, the applicant will be so informed. If the proposed work is eligible in principle for grant aid, ADAS will offer advice, having regard to the scientific interest of the site and the needs of the agricultural business, and assist the NCC and the applicant to resolve any differences between them. The Agriculture Minister, in considering grant applications, has a duty to exercise his functions so as to further the conservation of the special features of SSSIs, so far as is consistent with the purposes of the grant scheme. The course of events, in cases where the NCC does not consent to the proposed operation, will be as follows:

a If agreement is reached on modifications which are acceptable to the applicant and the NCC, then the NCC will give the applicant its written consent to the modified operation. A copy will also be sent to the appropriate Agriculture Department.

b If modifications cannot be agreed, the NCC will give the applicant and the appropriate Agriculture Department a detailed statement of its case for conservation and ADAS will provide the NCC and the applicant with an appraisal of the agricultural proposals including their feasibility.

c The NCC will, within 3 months of the applicant's original notice,

---

6 Farm capital grant means a grant under a scheme made by the Agriculture Ministers towards eligible capital expenditure incurred for the purpose of an agricultural business. Details of the schemes including the consultation procedures required in SSSIs and National Parks are set out in explanatory leaflets issued by the Agriculture Departments. In the case of capital grants to crofters and other eligible occupiers under the Crofting Counties Agricultural Grants (Scotland) Scheme 1972 the consent of the NCC does not obviate the need for prior approval by the Crofters Commission before operations are carried out.

7 In Scotland, the local office of the Department of Agriculture and Fisheries for Scotland.

advise the applicant and the appropriate Agriculture Department whether it wishes to object to the proposals on the grounds set out in its detailed statement of the case. (It is open to the NCC to offer a management agreement or to the owner or occupier to seek one at this stage).

Section 32

d In cases where the NCC objects the Secretary of State for Scotland or Wales, or in England the Minister of Agriculture in consultation with the Secretary of State for the Environment, will weigh both the agricultural and conservation cases and then determine whether or not he would refuse the grant on nature conservation grounds. The applicant and the NCC will be advised of the decision. Owners and occupiers are warned that grant may be refused if the work is carried out before the Minister makes his decision.

e If, as the result of an objection by the NCC, grant is refused on nature conservation grounds the NCC will, within 3 months of the decision, offer to enter into a management agreement with the applicant (see paragraphs 25–29).

f If the operation is eligible for grant, and grant is not refused on nature conservation grounds, then provided that three months have elapsed since his notice to the NCC, the owner or occupier may proceed and claim grant on completion of the work. It is however still open to the NCC to offer a management agreement.

Forestry operations where Forestry Commission grant and/or a felling permission is sought

18 Where grant and/or a felling permission is sought from the Forestry Commission and the proposed operation is specified in the notification as potentially damaging to the SSSI, owners or occupiers are required to give notice to the NCC as in paragraph 14. Discussions on the proposals will be conducted as part of the consultations with the applicant, the NCC and any other party concerned which the Forestry Commission is required to carry out in these circumstances. If agreement cannot be reached on these proposals or on alternative proposals and the NCC continues to object, the Forestry Commission, after reference to the appropriate Forestry Minister(8)

8 In England the Minister of Agriculture, Fisheries and Food, in Scotland and Wales the respective Secretaries of State.

(who in England will consult the Secretary of State for the Environment) will decide whether grant and/or felling permission will be refused on nature conservation grounds. Where grant or felling permission is so refused the NCC will, within three months of the decision, normally offer to enter into a management agreement (see paragraphs 25-29). If the operation is ineligible for grant or felling permission for reasons not connected with nature conservation, the applicant and the NCC will be informed accordingly.

Operations with a general planning permission under a General Development Order

19 Some operations specified in the NCC's notification as potentially damaging (eg, agricultural building or engineering work) may have general planning permission under a General Development Order(9). In such cases the guidance set out in paragraph 14 must be followed.

Operations requiring a planning application to be made

20 The NCC will not normally specify in an SSSI notification any operations which require a planning application to be made. The NCC would nevertheless welcome the opportunity to discuss any such operation with owners or occupiers before they submit a planning application so that it can advise them of any nature conservation implications.

(NB When a local planning authority receives an application for development on an SSSI it is required by law to consult the NCC and to take its advice into account in determining the application).

Offences and Penalties

Section 28(7) **21** Any owner or occupier who carries out a specified operation without complying with the relevant requirements outlined in paragraph 14 will be liable to a fine of up to £500.

---

9 For England and Wales — The Town and Country Planning General Development Order 1977. For Scotland — the Town and Country Planning General Development (Scotland) Order 1981.

The above orders permit certain development to be undertaken without a planning application having to be made.

IV *Information helpful to the NCC*

Changes to the scientific interest of an SSSI

22 The NCC would welcome information from owners or occupiers about changes in the scientific interest of any notified site.

Operations initiated by third parties

23 Owners and occupiers are reminded that it is an offence not only to carry out, but to cause or permit to be carried out, any damaging operation specified in the SSSI notification. If owners or occupiers are in any doubt about operations proposed by third parties they should consult the local office of the NCC.

Change of ownership, occupancy etc.

24 If an SSSI, or part of an SSSI, passes into the hands of a new owner or occupier, or if anything else occurs that affects the control or management of the site (eg, the transfer or creation of grazing rights) the local office of the NCC would be grateful to be informed.

V *Conservation options*

Management agreements

25 In promoting the conservation of SSSIs the NCC may in any circumstances, and particularly when it receives notice of an intention to carry out a specified operation, propose to enter into management agreements with owners or occupiers to safeguard or enhance the scientific interest. Owners or occupiers may also seek such an agreement at any time.

26 The effect of the agreement may simply be that the owner or occupier agrees to refrain from carrying out the operation that would cause damage; or it may in other cases extend to his taking positive action to safeguard the scientific interest of the site.

Section 50(2) **27** Where an agreement is made following notice of a specified operation, or following the refusal of grant as described in paragraph 17(d) or of grant or felling permission under paragraph 18, its financial provisions will be in accordance with guidelines to be given by Ministers (10).

28 An owner or occupier seeking any farm capital grant or Forestry Commission grant or felling permission may be unwilling to enter into a management agreement until his application is determined. If for this reason he does not accept the NCC's offer of an agreement, and it is eventually decided to refuse farm capital grant on nature conservation grounds the NCC will make a fresh offer to enter into a management agreement in accordance with paragraph 17(e). (The same will normally apply when forestry grant or felling permission is refused on nature conservation grounds).

29 Where owners or occupiers have indicated that they are willing to negotiate a management agreement, they should not carry out any potentially damaging operation during the process of negotiation without giving the NCC reasonable notice of their intention to do so.

10 The guidelines will be published under the title, "Wildlife and Countryside Act 1981 — Financial Guidelines for Management Agreements".

Arbitration arrangements

Section 50(3) **30** In the circumstances set out in paragraph 31 an owner or occupier who is dissatisfied with the financial terms of a management agreement offered by the NCC, or any revision of those terms resulting from subsequent negotiations, may, within one month of receiving the final offer, require the matter to be referred for determination to an arbitrator(11). The arbitrator may be appointed by agreement between the parties or, in default of such agreement, by the Secretary of State.

31 The circumstances in which an owner or occupier may seek arbitration are:

a Where an application for farm capital grant has been refused in consequence of an objection by the NCC on nature conservation grounds. In such circumstances the NCC will amend the offer in line with the amount determined by the arbitrator and, if the owner or occupier so wishes, is bound to conclude the agreement in those terms.

b Where an application for forestry grant or felling permission has been refused in consequence of an objection by the NCC on conservation grounds. In such circumstances the NCC will normally be prepared to conclude the agreement on the same basis as in (a) above if the owner or occupier so wishes.

c Cases not falling in (a) or (b) above, where an offer of an agreement is made by the NCC to a person who has given notice of intended operations (see paragraphs 14 and 35). In such cases, where the amounts determined by the arbitrator exceed those offered, the NCC will either amend the offer in line with the arbitrator's determination, or withdraw the offer, thus allowing the operation to proceed.

Sale or lease by agreement

32 If the NCC objects to a proposed operation it may offer to purchase or lease the site for management as a nature reserve or offer to introduce the owner to a non-government conservation body which may wish to do so. When the NCC purchases a site there are Capital Gains Tax advantages for the seller.

---

11 In Scotland the term is "arbiter".

Special Protection

33   If an area, in the view of the NCC, meets the criteria for a Nature Conservation Order, the NCC may apply to the Secretary of State for such an order (see paragraph 34).

VI *Special protection for certain areas*

Nature Conservation Orders

Section 29

34   Under the Wildlife and Countryside Act 1981 the Secretary of State (12) has the power to make orders (known as Nature Conservation Orders) in respect of land for the purpose of securing the survival of particular kinds of plant or animal, of complying with an international obligation or of conserving species or features of national importance. The effects of such an order are set out in paragraphs 35–37. The essential differences between these provisions and those applying to SSSIs generally are that:

a the restrictions on carrying out a specified operation apply to any person, whether or not he is, or is authorised by, the owner or occupier; and

b the period during which a specified operation may not be carried out is extended beyond 3 months if within certain time limits the NCC offers a management agreement, offers to acquire the land, or makes a compulsory purchase order.

35   An order will specify operations which are likely to cause damage which no person may carry out unless the owner or occupier has notified the NCC of a proposal to carry out such an operation and unless:

a the NCC has agreed to it in writing, or
b it is carried out in accordance with a management agreement (see paragraphs 25–29), or
c 3 months have elapsed since notice of the proposed operation was given to the NCC (subject to paragraphs 36–37).

The above restrictions do not apply to any operation which is either authorised by a planning permission granted on application or carried

---

12 In England Nature Conservation Orders will be made by the Secretary of State for the Environment, in Scotland by the Secretary of State for Scotland and in Wales by the Secretary of State for Wales.

out in response to an emergency. In the latter case the details must be notified to the NCC as soon as practicable after the start of the operation (initially by telephone, if possible).

36 Where the NCC considers that the operation would be damaging to the scientific interest it may, during this 3 month period, consult with the owner or occupier to find an acceptable way·of proceeding (this may include an offer to enter into a management agreement or an agreement to acquire the land). If, by the end of this period, such an agreement is offered but not concluded, the period during which the operation may not be carried out is extended as follows:

> **a** until the agreement is concluded, if this occurs within 12 months of giving notice;

> **b** in any other case the period ends 12 months after the notification of the proposed operation or 3 months after the rejection or withdrawal of the offer, whichever is the later (the purpose is to give the NCC time to decide whether to start compulsory purchase proceedings — see paragraph 37).

Compulsory Purchase

Section 29 (also Sections 16 and 17 of the National Parks and Access to the Country-side Act 1949)

37 The NCC may use its power to make a compulsory purchase order only where it is satisfied that it is unable to conclude a reasonable agreement under Section 16 of the National Parks and Access to the Countryside Act 1949. If the NCC makes such an order over land which is subject to a Nature Conservation Order within the period during which a proposed operation may not be carried out under paragraphs 35 or 36 above, that period is extended until the NCC has taken possession of the land, following confirmation of the order by the Secretary of State, or he decides not to confirm it, or the order is withdrawn by the NCC before confirmation.

Procedure for making Nature Conservation Orders

Section 29 and Schedule 11

38 Nature Conservation Orders will take effect immediately on being made by the Secretary of State. Notice of an order will be published in the London or Edinburgh Gazette and at least one local newspaper and will also be served on every owner and occupier of the land affected, except where the Secretary of State directs otherwise, eg when the owners cannot be traced. In such cases a notice will be attached to a conspicuous object on the land. Notices will set out the order, or describe its effect, state the date on which it took effect, name a place where copies of the order may be inspected and specify how representations or objections may be made. At least 28 days will be allowed for representations after the first publication of the notice.

39 If any representation or objection is not withdrawn, the Secretary of State will either arrange a local inquiry or allow an objector an opportunity to be heard. After considering any representations or objections and the report of any inquiry or hearing, the Secretary of State will announce his decision as to whether the order should stay in effect or be amended or revoked. If he does not do this within 9 months of the making of an order, it will cease to operate.

Compensation for Nature Conservation Orders

40 After a decision has been made that a Nature Conservation Order should stay in effect, owners and occupiers are entitled to claim compensation from the NCC for any depreciation in the value of an interest in land which is part of an agricultural unit, provided the depreciation is attributable to the making of the order. If the period during which a proposed operation may not be carried out is extended beyond 3 months, under paragraphs 36 or 37, compensation may be claimed for reasonable expenditure which has been rendered abortive or any other loss or damage directly attributable to the effects of the order.

Offences and Penalties

Section 29(8)
Section 31

41 A person is liable to a fine if he carries out an operation in contravention of a Nature Conservation Order. The courts are also empowered to make an order requiring that person to take certain actions to restore the land to its former condition. Failure to comply with such a court order may be punished by a fine of up to £1,000 and a further fine of up to £100 per day for as long as an offence continues. If operations to restore the land have not been carried out as ordered within a specified period the NCC has the power to enter the land, carry out the operations and recover reasonable expenses from the person against whom the order was made.

APPENDIX C

NATURE CONSERVANCY COUNCIL: REGIONAL OFFICES

ENGLAND

East Anglia
60 Bracondale, Norwich,
Norfolk NR1 2BE
Tel: Norwich (0603) 20558
(Essex; Norfolk; Suffolk)

East Midlands
PO Box 6
Godwin House
George Street
Huntingdon
Cambs PE18 6BU
Tel: Huntingdon (0480) 56191
(Bedfordshire;
Cambridgeshire;
Hertfordshire;
Leicestershire;
Lincolnshire;
Northamptonshire;
Nottinghamshire)

North East
Archbold House
Archbold Terrace
Newcastle-upon-Tyne
NE2 1EG
Tel: Newcastle-upon-Tyne
(0632) 816316
Cleveland; Durham;
Humberside; North
Yorkshire;
Northumberland; Tyne and
Wear)

North West
Blackwell
Bowness-on-Windermere
Windermere
Cumbria LA23 3JR
Tel: Windermere (09662) 5286
(Cumbria; Greater
Manchester; Lancashire;
Merseyside; South Yorkshire;
West Yorkshire)

South
Foxhold House,
Thornford Road
Crookham Common, Newbury
Berks RG15 8EL
Tel: Headley
(063523) 429/439/533
(Berkshire; Buckinghamshire;
Hampshire; Isle of Wight;
Oxfordshire; Wiltshire)

South-East
Zealds, Church Street, Wye
Ashford, Kent TN25 5BW
Tel: Wye (0233) 812525
(East Sussex; Greater London;
Kent; Surrey; West Sussex)

South-West
Roughmoor, Bishop's Hull,
Taunton, Somerset TA1 5AA
Tel: Taunton (0823) 83211
(Avon; Cornwall; Devon;
Dorset; Somerset)

ENGLAND (continued)

West Midlands
Attingham Park
Shrewsbury
Shropshire SY4 4TW
Tel: Upton Magna
(074377) 611
(Cheshire; Derbyshire;
Gloucestershire; Hereford &
Worcester; Peak District
National Park; Shropshire;
Staffordshire; Warwickshire;
West Midlands)

WALES

Dyfed-Powys
Plas Gogerddan
Aberystwyth
Dyfed SY23 3EB
Tel: Aberystwyth
(0970) 828351
(Dyfed, excluding Llanelli
Borough; Powys)

South
44 The Parade, Roath
Cardiff CF2 3AB
Tel: Cardiff (0222) 485111
(Gwent; Mid Glamorgan;
South Glamorgan; West
Glamorgan; Llanelli
Borough of Dyfed)

North
Plas Penrhos
Penrhos Road, Bangor
Gwynedd, LL57 2LQ
Tel: Bangor (0248) 55141
(Clywd; Gwynedd)

SCOTLAND

North-East
Wynne-Edwards House
17 Rubislaw Terrace
Aberdeen AB1 1XE
Tel: Aberdeen (0224) 572863
(Grampian Region; Nairn and
Badenoch and Strathspey
Districts of Highland Region;
Orkney Islands Area;
Shetland Islands Area)

South-East
12 Hope Terrace
Edinburgh
EH9 2AS
Tel: 031-447-4784
(Borders Region; Central
Region; Fife Region; Lothian
Region; Tayside Region)

North-West
Fraser Darling House
9 Culduthel Road
Inverness IV2 4AG
Tel: Inverness (0463) 39431
(Highland Region, excluding
Districts in North-East;
Western Isles Islands Area)

South-West
The Castle
Loch Lomond Park, Balloch
Dumbartonshire G83 8LY
Tel: Alexandria (0389) 58511
(Dumfries and Galloway
Region; Strathclyde Region)

COUNTRYSIDE COMMISSION REGIONAL OFFICE ADDRESSES

Office for Wales
8 Broad Street
Newtown
Powys SY16 2LU
Tel: (0686) 26799
(for Wales)

Northern
Warwick House
Grantham Road
Newcastle upon Tyne
NE2 1QF
Tel: (0632) 328252
(for Northumberland,
Cumbria, Durham, Tyne
& Wear, Cleveland)

North West
184 Deansgate
Manchester M3 3WB
Tel: 061-833 0316
(for Lancashire, Cheshire,
Merseyside, Greater
Manchester, the Peak
District of Derbyshire)

Midlands
Cumberland House
200 Broad Street
Birmingham B15 1TD
Tel: 021-632 6503/4
(for Shropshire, Staffordshire,
Hereford and Worcester,
West Midlands, Warwickshire,
Derbyshire except the Peak
District, Nottinghamshire,
Leicestershire,
Northamptonshire)

Head Office
John Dower House
Crescent Place
Cheltenham
Glos. GL50 3RA
Tel: 0242 21381

South West
Bridge House
Sion Place
Clifton Down
Bristol BS8 4AS
Tel: (0272) 732231
(for Gloucestershire, Avon,
Wiltshire, Somerset, Dorset,
Devon, Cornwall)

Greater London and South East
25 Savile Row
London W1X 2BT
Tel: 01-734 6010
(for Greater London, Kent,
Surrey, Berkshire,
Buckinghamshire, Oxfordshire,
East Sussex, West Sussex,
Hampshire, Isle of Wight).

Yorkshire and Humberside
8A Otley Road
Headingley
Leeds LS6 2AD
Tel: (0532) 742935/6
(for North, South and West
Yorkshire, Humberside)

Eastern
Terrington House
13/15 Hills Road
Cambridge CB2 1NL
Tel: (0223) 354462
(for Norfolk, Suffolk,
Cambridgeshire, Bedfordshire,
Essex, Hertfordshire,
Lincolnshire)

APPENDIX D

MODEL FORMS OF MANAGEMENT AGREEMENTS

The model format for a management agreement under section 39 of the Act is reproduced with the kind consent of the Countryside Commission. It has been prepared to assist planning authorities and owners and occupiers, and may need to be adapted to suit the circumstances of each case. The Countryside Commission welcome any comments on this model.

The model agreement used by the Nature Conservancy Council, and reproduced with their consent, is suitable for a management agreement to be made under section 15 of the Countryside Act 1968 in respect of Sites of Special Scientific Interest (SSSI). This is the form of agreement which the NCC may, and in certain cases, must offer to an owner or occupier who has notified that he intends to carry out activities that have been listed as potentially damaging to a SSSI. This agreement, and in particular the agreed management policy annexed to it, will need to be adapted to suit the circumstances of each case.

COUNTRYSIDE COMMISSION

MODEL FORMAT FOR MANAGEMENT AGREEMENT

MANAGEMENT AGREEMENT made the   day
of   198   BETWEEN

(hereinafter called 'the authority') of

the first part and AB of

of the second part CD of

of the third part EF of

of the fourth part and GH of

of the fifth part (the parties of the second third fourth and fifth parts together being hereinafter referred to as 'the other parties')

WHEREAS:

(1) Section 39 of the Wildlife and Countryside Act 1981 (hereinafter referred to as 'the 1981 Act') provides for the making of agreements between persons with an interest in land and a planning authority for the purpose of conserving or enhancing the natural beauty or amenity of land in the countryside or promoting its enjoyment by the public

(2) The authority is a planning authority for the area in which the land comprised in this agreement (hereinafter referred to as 'the managed land') is situated

(3) The other parties have the following interest(s) in the managed land—

    (a) the said AB is the estate owner in fee simple free from incumbrances of the managed land

    (b) the said CD is the agricultural/woodland *(specify)* tenant of [part of] the managed land

    (c) the said EF is entitled to [part of] the following sporting/fishing right(s) in the managed land that is to say EF has the right to [specify] on or over [that part of] the managed land

(d) the said GH is interested in the managed land as [specify]

NOW THEREFORE it is agreed between the authority and the other parties to this agreement as follows: —

1. ANY of the other parties whose interest in the managed land is changed terminated or disposed of shall within one month thereafter give notice in writing to the authority of such change termination or disposal

2. THE managed land is the area of land described in Part A and the extent of the interests of the other parties is described in Part B of the First Schedule hereto

3. THE authority and the other parties undertake to use their best endeavours to [conserve] [and] [enhance] [the appearance of the managed land] [and to] [promote the enjoyment of the countryside by the public over the managed land] In particular it is agreed that [here specify – see footnote 1] To these ends the authority undertakes to carry out at its own expense the works specified in Part A and the other parties undertake to carry out [at their own expense] [at the expense of the authority] the works specified in Part B and to adopt and maintain the land-use practices specified in Part C of the Second Schedule hereto In addition the other parties undertake to allow public access to the managed land on the conditions specified in Part D of that Schedule

4. (1) SUBJECT to sub-clauses (2) and (3) of this clause the authority shall pay to the other parties on the date of this agreement [and on the   day of   in each succeeding year] the sum of £   in consideration of the making of this agreement provided that if any of the parties shall terminate or dispose of his interest in the managed land or if his interest as aforesaid is terminated he shall if so required by the authority repay to the authority such proportion of any payment made to him under this clause as represents the proportion of the period after the termination or disposal of his interest as aforesaid

    (2) Any sum payable under sub-clause (1) hereof shall be apportioned by the authority between the other parties in

such manner as may from time to time be agreed in writing between the other parties and [and in default of such notification in such manner as may be determined by the authority] notified in writing to the authority by the other parties

(3) The amount payable by the authority under sub-clause (1) hereof may be reviewed and if the parties so agree varied with effect from the dates [e.g. five ten and fifteen years respectively] from [day of] [the date hereof] having regard to any change since the date hereof or the last review date as the case may be in the effect of this agreement on the value of the interests of the other parties in the managed land or the expenditure incurred by them for the purpose of complying with their obligations hereunder The party requiring such a review shall give notice in writing to that effect to the other parties (including the authority if not itself serving the notice) not more than twelve months nor less than six months before the dates from which any variation is to have effect as specified above [time to be of the essence of this clause]

5. (1) SUBJECT to the provisions of this clause this agreement shall subsist for a period of [e.g. twenty] years from [day of] [the date hereof]

(2) This agreement may be terminated—

(a) by the authority by giving to each of the other parties

or

(b) by any of the other parties by giving to the and to the remaining other parties

twelve months' notice in writing to expire at the end of a period of [e.g. six eleven or sixteen years] as the case may be from the said [day of] [date hereof]

(3) This agreement may be terminated as it affects the whole or any part of the managed land at any time by the authority giving notice in writing to all the other parties in the event of a breach by any of the other parties of any of the undertakings on their part contained in this agreement In the event of partial termination the amount payable under sub-clause 4(1) hereof may be reviewed with effect from the date of termination in accordance with sub-clause 4(3) excluding the provision relating to the service of a

prior notice requiring a review

(4) Termination under sub-clauses (2) or (3) hereof shall be without prejudice to any rights of the authority or of the other parties which may have accrued up to the date of termination

6. IN this agreement the expressions 'interest' and 'land' shall have the meanings assigned to them by Section 114(1) of the National Parks and Access to the Countryside Act 1949 and references to the conservation of the natural beauty of land shall be construed in accordance with Section 52(3) of the 1981 Act

7. THE authority shall pay to the other parties reasonable expenses [specify if appropriate] of and incidental to the preparation and granting of this agreement and any duplicate copy thereof and any stamp duty payable thereon

8. ANY dispute arising under this agreement between the authority and the other parties (or between the other parties) shall be referred to and determined by a single arbitrator to be agreed between the parties to the dispute or in default of agreement to be appointed on the request of [any of] the party(ies) by the President for the time being of the Royal Institution of Chartered Surveyors and in accordance with the provisions of the Arbitration Act 1950 or any statutory modification or re-enactment thereof for the time being in force

IN WITNESS whereof

FIRST SCHEDULE

Description of the Managed Land

Clause 2

Part A All that [here insert a description of the managed land and identify it by reference to a plan to be attached]

Part B .... [here specify the extent of the interests of the several other parties and identify them by reference to a plan to be attached]

SECOND SCHEDULE

Operation and Management of the Managed Land

Clause 3

Part A The authority undertakes to carry out the following specified works at its own expense – [see footnote 2]

Part B CD undertakes to carry out [at his own expense] the works shown against his interest – [see footnote 3]

Part C The other parties undertake for their respective interests to use the managed land in the following specified ways – [see footnote 4]

Part D The other parties undertake to allow the public to have access to the managed land as follows [specify means of access, routes, times and any other conditions agreed]

Footnote 1 e.g. the appearance of the managed land would be enhanced by reducing grazing and browsing of the semi-natural woodlands by deer or other wild animals and by farm stock in order to allow natural regeneration of these woodlands providing always that growth of the woodlands thus protected does not interfere with the enjoyment of scenery as viewed from specified vantage points

Footnote 2 e.g. the construction of a deer- and stock-proof fence to exclude deer rabbits hares and other grazing or browsing wild animals from the land lying between the public road A1234 and the upper limit of the natural tree-line on the hill and to maintain the same for the duration of this agreement

Footnote 3   e.g. the construction of internal stock-proof fences to sub-divide that part of the managed land within the deer fence so as to contain parcels of woodland where farm stock may be excluded and to maintain the same for the duration of this agreement

Footnote 4   e.g. farm stock shall be excluded from the fenced parcels of the managed land for the first ten years of this agreement in order to encourage natural regeneration of the woodlands and may be permitted to under-graze up to half of these areas thereafter by agreement with the authority Deer and other wild animals shall at all times be excluded from these areas

NATURE CONSERVANCY COUNCIL
AREAS OF SPECIAL SCIENTIFIC INTEREST
MODEL AGREEMENT
COUNTRYSIDE ACT 1968, SECTION 15

THIS AGREEMENT is made the   day of
19   BETWEEN
of
(hereinafter called "the Occupier/Owner" which expression
where the context so admits shall include 'his/its' successors
'in title/and assigns') of the one part and THE NATURE
CONSERVANCY COUNCIL (hereinafter called "the
Council") of the other part

The 'Occupier holds/Owner is the estate owner in fee simple
free from incumbrances of 'the pieces or parcels of land at
            in the Parish(s) of   in
the County of   (hereinafter
called "the land") containing in the whole '   acres/
hectares' or thereabouts and shown edged green on the
attached plan [eg on a yearly tenancy commencing on the
          day of   in each year *or* for a term of
years from the   day of   19   granted by a
lease dated the   day of   19   and made
between   of the one part and
of the other part] and the Council being of the opinion that
the land is of special interest by reason of its [flora fauna or
geological or physiographical features] have requested the
'Occupier/Owner' to enter into an agreement with respect to
the land under S.15 of the Countryside Act 1968 which the
'Occupier/Owner' has agreed to do on the following terms:

1. IN consideration of [*either* the sum of £   paid
    by the Council to the 'Occupier/Owner' (the receipt of
    which sum the Occupier/Owner hereby acknowledges)
    or the annual sum of £   hereinafter reserved]
    and the covenants and conditions hereinafter contained
    the 'Occupier/Owner' hereby agrees with the Council to
    the intent that (so far as practicable) such agreement
    shall bind the (Occupier's interest in the) land and every
    part therof in whosesoever hands the same may be that
    the Occuper/Owner and his/its successors 'in title/and
    assigns' during the subsistence of this Agreement:–

(a) will carry out the general estate management of the land in accordance with the Agreed Management Policy as defined in Clause 3 hereof and will not use the land or any part or parts thereof or permit or suffer the same to be used in any manner inconsistent with this Agreement including that Policy

(b) will permit the Council and members of their staff and all other persons authorised by the Council (1) to have access to the said land with or without vehicles over and along the routes coloured brown on the attached plan (2) to enter upon the land and every part or parts thereof from time to time and at all times for the purposes of inspecting the land and carrying out scientific observation research or experiment thereon without interruption (3) in connection with those purposes to erect on the land such hides fences or markers as the Council may consider necessary and maintain and remove the same and (4) to take from the land without charge all or any such specimens of flora and fauna (living or dead) or any other objects or substances of scientific interest as they may in their discretion require for their purposes

(c) will not 'assign/part with' 'his/its' interest in the land or any part thereof (and in this sub-clause the 'Occupier/Owner' expressly includes the personal representatives of the 'Occupier/Owner' unless 'his/its' 'successors in title/assignees' agreed with the Council to abide by the terms of this Agreement

2. THE Council hereby agrees with the 'Occupier/Owner' that subject to the due observance and performance of 'his/its' obligations hereunder the Council during the subsistence of this Agreement:–

(i) [will pay to the 'Occupier/Owner' the sum of £ in advance on the   day of   in each year the first payment being paid on the date hereof]

(ii) will comply with the terms of the Agreed Management Policy as defined in Clause 3 hereof so far as the Council is required to comply with the same

(iii) will furnish members of their staff and all other persons authorised by the Council to enter upon the land with written authority signed on behalf of the

Council to be produced to the 'Occupier/Owner' or 'his/its' duly authorised agent so often as either of them may reasonably request

3. THE expression "the Agreed Management Policy" used in this Agreement means the policy which has been drawn up and signed on behalf of each of the parties one copy being intended to be kept with each part of this Agreement and any variations of or amendments to such Policy which may from time to time be agreed between the parties. In the event of any incompatibility between the terms of this Agreement and those of the Agreed Management Policy the terms of this Agreement shall prevail

4. THE term of this Agreement shall be   years from the date hereof except that

(1) if the Council shall decide that the land has ceased to be an area of special scientific interest they may determine this Agreement upon giving not less than   months notice in writing to the 'Occupier/ Owner'

(2) if there shall be any breach or non-observance of any of the obligations or agreements on the part of the Occupier/Owner herein contained the Council may (without prejudice to any other remedy) give the 'Occupier/Owner' notice in writing determining this Agreement forthwith

5. IN any matters as to which the approval of or consultation with the Council is required under the Agreed Management Policy the 'Occupier/Owner' shall apply for that purpose to the Nature Conservancy Council at 19/20 Belgrave Square, London SW1X 8PY or such other address as the Council may notify to the 'Occupier/ Owner'.

AS WITNESS the hands of the 'Occuper/Owner' and of   for and on behalf of the Council the day and year first before written

SIGNED by the said   )
in the presence of:–   )

SIGNED by the said   )
for and on behalf of the   )
NATURE CONSERVANCY)
COUNCIL in the presence of)

"MODEL" AGREED MANAGEMENT POLICY

(Note: This precedent will need to be varied as required to meet the particular management "intentions".)

1. As from the commencement of the Agreement the land shall be managed in accordance with the policy hereafter set out subject to any variations or amendments of such policy or of any parts or items thereof as may from time to time be agreed between the parties. Any such agreed variations or amendments shall be recorded by way of addenda at the foot hereof which shall be signed on behalf of the parties and deemed to form part hereof.

2. The parties agree to consult with each other annually, and on such additional occasions as circumstances may require, in order to promote to the utmost practicable extent the fulfilment of this Policy.

(Note: see note against 5(c) below)

[3. The land shall permanently remain so far as practicable in its present uncultivated state]

[3. The land shall be managed silviculturally in accordance with the Silvicultural Plan annexed hereto (Annex 3)]

4. The land shall so far as practicable be safeguarded against:–

   (a) harmful and uncontrolled fires;

   (b) ploughing or other form of land reclamation or cultivation (except where otherwise agreed and provided that the
   shall be free to graze cattle or sheep as required);

   (c) afforestation or planting of trees, shrubs or other vegetation except as may be agreed from time to time;

   (d) mining or extraction of minerals (including gravel);

   (e) introduction deliberately from elsewhere of any species or variety of animal or plant;

   (f) infestation by any of the species for the time being listed in Annex   ;

   (g) building or other development except the erection of huts and hides for scientific or administrative purposes by agreement between the parties.

5. The land being thus safeguarded shall be managed permanently for the purposes of:–

    (a) maintaining a varied and numerous population of fauna and flora and especially of certain species which are scarce or whose survival is threatened in unprotected areas;

    (b) facilitating scientific research and the making of observations and experiments and keeping of detailed records for scientific purposes;

    (c) the growing of such trees as are natural to the area and such others as may be mutually agreed on existing afforested areas and other areas which may from time to time be agreed.

(Note: In a woodland area there may be a Silvicultural Plan which will be annexed to the Agreed Management Policy and referred to therein)

6. The   shall determine what maintenance operations, repairs or new works from time to time appear necessary or desirable and shall notify the Council of details of such (i) in cases where it considers that under the Agreement the whole or part of the cost should fall to be met by the Council, or (ii) in other cases where the interests of the Council will or may be thereby affected whether on account of risk of disturbance to animal or plant life or otherwise and shall not commence to carry out any such operations repairs or works unless and until the Council shall have signified its assent to the execution thereof. The Council shall signify either its assent or objection thereto without undue delay.

7. Where works by statutory undertakers or other outside agencies prove necessary the   will make with such agencies such arrangements as may be agreed by the Council.

8. The   shall promptly and adequately inform the Council of any communications concerning the land received by the   and affecting (a) the relations with central or local government authorities (b) the drainage of the land or (c) the animal or plant life therein.

9. The Council shall give advance notification to the   of any projected scientific work which may affect the estate management or other of the   interests in the land and shall also inform the   of any scientific findings relevant to the above interests.

10. The Council shall consult the
before erecting on the land any notice fence hide tent or
other construction.

(Note: This small paragraph
will require drafting to fit
particular circumstances)
11.

12. The   shall not on the land shoot or permit
its employees wardens or other agents to shoot (otherwise
than by inadvertence) any birds or mammals except those
listed in Annex   (subject to any amendments therein
that may be made subsequently to mutual consent) and
shall keep and furnish to the Council on or before the 1st
March each year full and complete lists of numbers of
each species shot or otherwise destroyed on the land
during the year preceding. The
shall use his/its best endeavours to control the species
listed in Annex   (subject to any amendment therein
made as aforesaid) to such extent as they may be
requested in writing so to do by the Council but shall
secure the approval of the Council for all types of traps
proposed to be employed and for the use of poisons or any
other methods proposed to be used except shooting.
Shooting shall be carried out with full regard to the
importance of avoiding unnecessary disturbance to wildlife
or to scientific observations.

13. The   shall not introduce new species or varieties
of animals or plants without the consent of the Council.

14. The   shall instruct its employees and any
other person or persons exercising on his/its behalf all or
any of the functions of a keeper or engaged in pest control
to carry out and observe strictly the obligations under the
Agreement and under this policy and also to co-operate
with the Council and its representatives in all matters
affecting the Council's interests. The   shall
from time to time consult with the Council in regard to
the instructions to be given by the   to
such persons for the furtherance and implementation of
this Agreed Management Policy and shall use his/its best
endeavours to ensure that such instructions are observed
and carried out.

15. The   agrees to take all reasonable steps to prevent fire and to control outbreaks of fire and not to start fires on the land for any purpose except at such times and in such places as may have been agreed with the Council.

16. The   agrees not to use on the land without prior consent of the Council any chemical spray herbicide insecticide or similar preparation or to pollute or knowingly and avoidably permit the pollution of water.

17. When cattle and sheep graze on the land or produce is extracted from it by agreement the   shall keep an annual record of numbers of beasts grazing and of any produce which may have been extracted or removed and will supply a copy of each such record to the Council. No produce shall be extracted without the prior consent of the Council.

(Note: There may be one or two or three Annexes as indicated according to the particular circumstances)

ANNEX 1

Species permitted to be killed as game

ANNEX 2

Species to be killed as pests

ANNEX 3

Silvicultural Plan

WILDLIFE AND COUNTRYSIDE ACT 1981—FINANCIAL GUIDELINES FOR MANAGEMENT AGREEMENTS

Scope of Guidance

1. Section 50 of the Wildlife and Countryside Act 1981 provides that where management agreements are offered, in specified circumstances, by either the Nature Conservancy Council or a "relevant authority"[1] for the purposes of conservation or amenity, payments under such agreements shall be determined by the body concerned (the offeror) in accordance with guidance given by Ministers.

2. These provisions have statutory application in the following circumstances:—

(i) *Sites of Special Scientific Interest* (SSSI)

—If the *Nature Conservancy Council* (NCC) has been notified[2] by an owner or occupier of a proposal to undertake an operation specified as likely to damage an SSSI and,

—in consequence offers to enter into a management agreement with him.

(ii) *Sites of Special Scientific Interest, National Parks and other specified areas*

—if, in respect of land within an SSSI, National Park, or other specified area[3], an owner or occupier proposes to undertake an operation on which *farm capital grant* will be claimed under Section 29 of the Agriculture Act 1970 and,

—either the *NCC* or the *relevant authority* objects,[4] in consequence of which the grant application is refused with effect that the objecting body *is obliged* to offer a management agreement.

3. The financial terms of these agreements must be proposed by the offeror in accordance with guidance by Ministers, and such guidance is given in these notes. However, an individual owner or occupier (the offeree) may wish to make his personal contribution to conservation of the land concerned within the terms of the agreement by offering to accept a lesser payment, or alternative arrangements (including payments in kind).

4. The Nature Conservancy Council has further stated that it will voluntarily apply the provisions of Section 32(2) of the Act to applications made for *all* types of farm capital grant (including grants under the Crofting Counties Agricultural Grants Scheme) and, normally, for grants or felling permission under *forestry* legislation; and that agreements so offered will accord with the terms of the guidelines (subject, as above, to any abatement proposed by the owner or occupier himself).

---

[1] In *England and Wales* the *"relevant authority"* means:
    (a) as respects land in a National Park, the county planning authority;
    (b) as respects land in Greater London, the Greater London Council or the London borough council; and
    (c) as respects any other land, the local planning authority;
    in *Scotland* it means the authority exercising district planning functions.
[2] Under Section 28(5) or 29(4) of the Wildlife and Countryside Act 1981.
[3] Specified by Ministers under section 41(3) of the 1981 Act.
[4] Under Section 32(1)(b) or 41(3)(b) of the 1981 Act.

Wider aspects of agreements

5. The immediate purpose of a management agreement offered under these provisions is to conserve the countryside by providing for agreed *restrictions* on operations which would damage the conservation value of the land and to ensure that all necessary steps are taken to *maintain* the land in its present state. However, the parties may also agree to include other requirements, whereby an owner or occupier undertakes to implement measures aimed, as appropriate, at *enhancing* the natural beauty or amenity of the land: eg creating or improving public access where appropriate, or specific land management works. Any payment in respect of such further requirements should in general be determined in accordance with the merits of the individual case.[1]

"Dual responsibility"

6. Where a Site of Special Scientific Interest falls within a National Park or other specified area, proposed agricultural operations on that site should first be considered by the Nature Conservancy Council, who will consult the relevant authority and agree with it which body or bodies should lodge objection, if any, to the payment of farm capital grant and which of them should subsequently take the lead role in negotiations with the owner or occupier. Subsequently the bodies concerned should agree between themselves an appropriate apportionment of payments due under any agreements thus concluded.

Landlords and Tenants

7. Where land is let and a tenant proposes to accept an offer of a management agreement, the terms of the agreement may have implications for his tenancy agreement[2] and for his landlord. The offeror should therefore require a tenant's written assurance that his landlord has been informed:

—of the proposed operation where this is required;

—that the offer of a management agreement is likely to be accepted by the tenant;

—of the area and the location to be covered by the agreement and the parties to that agreement.

8. *Complementary agreements:* A tenant's interest will be limited and any management agreement with that tenant cannot bind a future occupier. In view of this, it may best serve to ensure the long-term protection of a site if the offeror seeks to include the landlord's interests in the principal agreement, or otherwise seeks a complementary agreement with him. Normally there should be no need to make more than a nominal payment, to encourage the making of such agreements, as the landlord's interest will be secured by the Agricultural Holdings legislation. As part of an agreement of this type the landlord should normally undertake not to serve a notice to remedy contrary to the intentions of the management agreement.

9. *End of tenancy:* The agreement with the landlord should provide that, where he plans to take the land in hand at the termination of the tenancy,[2] he should give *6 months'* advance notice to the NCC or relevant authority of his wish to terminate the agreement. Where this happens or where the landlord leases the land to a new tenant,[3] a management agreement should be offered on terms similar to those enjoyed by the previous occupier.

---

(1) Statutory provisions govern compensation for *access*.
(2) Or in Scotland, lease.
(3) In Scotland, where a lease is acquired by a successor.

Mortgagees and Other Interested Parties

10. Mortgagees, and other parties having interests in the property (eg fishing rights), should also be consulted, as appropriate, by the offeree before he enters into a management agreement.

First Steps Towards Agreement

Minimising loss

11. From the date of initial notification of his proposed operation, an owner or occupier should not take any action which may increase the sum eventually payable to him under these guidelines, eg entering into any contract or commitment with third parties relating to the proposed work. *If he enters into such a contract or commitment during that period he will have no claim on the offeror if it is inconsistent with restrictions which are contained in a management agreement subsequently completed, and involves him in financial loss.*

Short-term agreement

12. Detailed negotiations to conclude the terms of a proposed management agreement may extend over a period of some months, and the negotiating parties are recommended to take early action (ie within the period of 3 months following notification) to enter into a short-term agreement. Such an agreement would be for a fixed term (between 6 and 12 months, as appropriate) and would include a commitment by the owner or occupier not to undertake the proposed operation while discussions on the subsequent long-term agreement continue. A nominal sum should be payable to the offeree on entering into a short-term agreement of this type and the right of the owner or occupier to arbitration on the payment proposed under the subsequent agreement (see paragraph 33 below) would be retained.

Long-term agreement; methods of payments. [1]

13. For the purposes of the long-term agreement, owners or owner-occupiers may choose *either* lump sum payment *or* annual payments, as described below, and should be encouraged to state their preference as early as possible. Only annual payments are available to *tenants* and, in general, *landlords* would be expected only to enter into an agreement of the type described in paragraph 8 above.

(a) Lump sum payment: (owners or owner-occupiers)

14. Payment, at the commencement of the agreement, of a single *lump sum* for a management agreement over a 20-year period (or such other period, possibly operating in perpetuity, as may be agreed between the parties). *The amount should be equal to the difference between the restricted and unrestricted value of the owner or owner-occupier's interest,* calculated having regard to the rules for assessment in respect of the compulsory acquisition of an interest in land, as set out in Section 5 of the Land Compensation Act 1961[2] so far as applicable and subject to any necessary modifications; and in so far as there is no statutory eligibility for compensation in this respect under Section 30(2) of the 1981 Act.

15. *Offerees choosing this method should be requested to provide the information listed at Annex B.*

---

[1] Different considerations apply in forestry cases—see Annex A.
[2] In Scotland, Section 12 of the Land Compensation (Scotland) Act 1963.

(*b*) *Annual payments: (owners or owner-occupiers)*

16. Payment of *annual sums* for an agreement over a 20-year period, or such other period as may be agreed between the parties. *The payments should reflect net profits forgone because of the agreement* (or, in the case of payments to landlords, be nominal—see paragraph 8), the last payment to fall due 12 months before expiry.

(*c*) *Annual payments: (tenants/occupiers)*

17. Annual payments as above while the offeree is in continued occupancy. Lump sum payment is *not* available.

Assessment of annual payments

18. *Individual assessment* will be appropriate in most cases to calculate the sums payable. *The offeree should provide the information listed at Annex C* and indicate the amount he seeks. However, *by agreement of both parties,* provision of more limited information may be sufficient in certain cases. In some cases, eg involving non-agricultural operations, different information will be required; this should be as agreed between the parties.

19. *'Standard' payments:* Where well-defined categories of land and restrictions on farming operation are involved the offeror may wish to determine[1] and periodically revise,[2] *standard annual payments* as an alternative option. Such payments would be offered as a tariff, with uniform payments per hectare for particular categories of agreement. The use of standard sums in this way may be found convenient by both parties, since the need for detailed assessment of a proposed operation is eliminated, and agreement can therefore be reached more quickly.

20. If standard payments are available, the offeror should ask the offeree whether he wishes to choose that option. Where the offeree opts for individual assessment he will be unable subsequently to change to a standard payment.

The draft agreement[3]

21. Where the Minister has refused an application for farm capital grant,[4] in consequence of an objection by the Nature Conservancy Council or relevant authority, the Act requires that body to submit a *draft agreement* to the applicant within *3 months* of its receiving notice of the Minister's decision.

22. Such an agreement should be as complete as possible, drawn up in the light of progress in the negotiations between the parties at that stage. In particular the draft agreement should record:

—the main heads of agreement including the proposed restrictions and the period;

—the method of payment where this has been decided;

—if appropriate, the relevant standard payment (where this option is available);

---

(1) In consultation with representative bodies of farmers and landowners.
(2) Not less frequently than each five years, in consultation as above.
(3) Under Section 32(2) or 41(4) of the 1981 Act.
(4) Grant under Section 29 of the Agriculture Act 1970.

—the sum or sums payable or, if not yet determined, that payment will
be determined in accordance with this guidance by further negotiation,
or following arbitration (see paragraph 33 below);

—if agreement is not complete, a date (not more than 6 months ahead)
by which a formal offer will be made (see paragraph 32 below).

Other Factors Determining Payment

(i) *Deemed eligibility for grant*

23. For the purpose of calculating payment under a management
agreement it should be assumed that, but for the conservation
considerations, farm capital grant *would* have been payable on a proposed
agricultural operation which the offeree undertakes in the agreement not to
carry out.

24. *Exceptions:* However, if:

(a) the proposed operation is ineligible[1] for such grant; *or*

(b) the business is not an agricultural business, or is an agricultural
business which does not satisfy[1] the sufficient employment test, where
that applies in respect of the proposed investment; *or*

(c) if the operation is begun before the appropriate Agriculture
Minister determines the grant application;

neither the Nature Conservancy Council nor relevant authority is under a
statutory obligation to offer an agreement; and agreements offered
voluntarily[2] by the Nature Conservancy Council in such circumstances
(which by virtue of Section 50(1)(a)(i) of the Act are also subject to this
guidance) should assume that farm capital grant would not have been paid.
(Advice to the offeror on items (a) and (b) above will be given on request by
the local office of MAFF.[3] As regards (c), the Headquarters of the Agriculture Department concerned will inform the offeror and offeree of the date
of the Minister's decision.)

25. *Investment limits:* The farm capital grant schemes prescribe limits on
the overall level of investments on which a farmer may claim grant. If
expenditure on a proposal would in whole or in part exceed the relevant
limit, the excess would not be eligible for grant until such time as it could
be accommodated within that limit. The offeror should invite the offeree to
consent that MAFF[3] notify the former whether the proposed expenditure is
within the offeree's investment limit and, if not, when (in the absence of
other claims) it would become eligible for grant. *If the offeree refuses
consent to such disclosure, payment under the agreement should be
calculated without allowance for grant.*

26. If the offeree consents, the local office of MAFF[3] will notify the offeror
of the amount of investment eligible for grant on the effective date of the
agreement (see paragraph 38 below). Where the cost of the proposed
operation exceeds the amount so notified, the offeree should be asked
whether he would still be prepared to accept from the effective date an

(1) Under the published criteria of the Agriculture Departments.
(2) Following notification under Section 28(5) or 29(4) of the 1981 Act.
(3) In Scotland DAFS; in Wales WOAD.

agreement with abatement in respect of that part of the cost which would not be eligible for grant until a later date. If the offeree declines, he should be invited to withdraw his notification on the understanding that he may represent it at a time when the whole cost of the operation would be within his eligible investment limit. Once an agreement has become effective it should not be amended to take account of investments claimed subsequent to the effective date and during the life of the agreement.

27.   *Rate of grant:* The local office of MAFF[1] will also advise the offeror on the *rate of grant* for which a proposed operation would have qualified on the effective date of the agreement (see paragraph 38 below) and under which grant scheme the application was made.

(ii) *Phasing in of proposed operations*

28.   The offeror should have regard to the practical limit on the amount of work which can be undertaken by the offeree in a given period of time and that a development may take a number of years to implement or give a full return. In such cases it will be appropriate for lump sum payments to be correspondingly smaller, or for payments on an annual basis to be phased in during the early years of the agreement.

(iii) *Professional fees and other expenditure incurred*

29.   *Fees:* On completion of a management agreement the offeror should pay the reasonable costs of the offeree incurred in retaining professional advisers to assist him in connexion with the agreement. (VAT on such fees should be met only where the offeree is not registered for VAT purposes.)

30.   *Other costs:* A management agreement may also provide for payment:—

> (a) for expenditure reasonably incurred within the previous 12 months of the date of notification which has been rendered abortive or in undertaking work rendered abortive by the agreement (subject to minimising loss—see paragraph 11 above);

> (b) for any loss or damage directly attributable to the agreement;

in so far as there is no statutory eligibility for compensation in this respect under Section 30(3) of the 1981 Act, and no relevant payment is available under other provisions of these guidelines.

31.   *Abortive negotiations:* Where the offeror withdraws from negotiations it should defray costs incurred by the offeree, unless the latter has acted in an unreasonable manner: eg if the offeree carries out operations which would render the agreement abortive.

The Formal Offer

32.   The formal offer should record full details of the financial and other terms of agreement proposed, *the offeror appending thereto the following statement:*

> "These terms constitute the formal offer of a management agreement. Under Section 50(3) of the Wildlife and Countryside Act 1981 you have the right to dispute the offer, within one month of receipt, and to require that determination of the payment offered shall be referred to arbitration."

---

[1] In Scotland DAFS; in Wales WOAD.

Arbitration

33.   Where an offeree disputes the financial terms of the agreement he may, within *one month*[1] of receiving the formal offer, require determination by an arbitrator[2] of the amounts payable.

34.   In default of agreement on the appointment of an arbitrator[2] he will be appointed by the appropriate Secretary of State[1] on the recommendation of relevant professional bodies.

35.   If the making of the offer was *mandatory*—ie made in the circumstances described at paragraph 2(ii) above—and the amounts payable determined by the arbitrator[2] exceed those determined by the offeror, the latter must amend its offer accordingly.[1]

36.   If the making of the offer was *non-mandatory*—ie made in the circumstances described at paragraph 2(i) above—the offeror may choose *either* to amend the offer to give effect to the arbitrator's[2] determination, *or* to withdraw that offer.[1]

37.   *Costs of arbitration:* Costs will be awarded by the arbitrator.[2]

Commencement of Agreement

38.   For the purpose of this guidance the *effective date* of the management agreement should be the date of the agreement or *3 months* after the date of receipt by the authority of the owner's or occupier's notification of details of the proposed operations, whichever is the earlier.

39.   Where a *lump sum payment* has been chosen the date of valuation should be as at the effective date. Payment should fall due on the completion of the agreement and interest[3] should be payable in respect of the period between the effective date and completion. Where *annual payments* have been chosen the first payment should be backdated to the effective date and paid with interest[3] on completion; thereafter payments should be on regular dates specified in the agreement.

40.   The lump sum payment or the first annual payment under the management agreement should be abated by the nominal sum paid to the offeree under the short-term management agreement where applicable (see paragraph 12 above).

Adjusting Payments (Annual Payments Only)

41.   Agreements providing for annual payments should include provision for making adjustments in such payments to reflect *annual* changes in farm productivity and profitability, using *indices* which will be provided for this purpose (except that, by the consent of both parties, other bases of adjustment may be employed, eg: where the agreement is non-agricultural).

---

[1] Under Section 50(3) of the 1981 Act.
[2] In Scotland, arbiter.
[3] *Interest* should be assessed at a rate prescribed by regulations under Section 32 of the Land Compensation Act 1961 or, in Scotland, under Section 40 of the Land Compensation (Scotland) Act 1963.

42. In addition, where the management agreement is based upon individual assessment, it should be open to either party at intervals of not less than *five years* to require full reassessment of further annual payments due, and to refer any consequent dispute to arbitration.

Breach, or Voiding, of Agreement

43. If an agreement is breached by deliberate action of the owner or occupier, the offeror should, by the terms of that agreement, be entitled:—

(a) in the case of *lump sum*s: to require *proportionate repayment* by the offeree, ie of a sum which *at the time of breach* would represent the value of a notional agreement offered for the unexpired period (subject in the case of a 20 year agreement to a minimum recoupment of 1/20 of the original payment for each year remaining of the terminated agreement or, in the case of an agreement made for a different period,[1] a corresponding fraction). Repayment should be net of any liability to capital gains tax[2] attracted by the original payment;

(b) in the case of *annual payments:* to cease further payments, *but there should be no provision for recoupment of those paid over before the breach of the agreement.*

44. An agreement may be terminated in the event that it is no longer possible to achieve its purposes by virtue of the action of a third party or by natural or accidental causes. In such circumstances:

(a) in the case of *lump sums:* the offeror should be entitled similarly to require proportionate repayment as above but may at its discretion abandon its claim or seek a reduced sum. If a claim is made it should be open to the offeree to require an arbitrator[3] to determine whether repayment should be waived or reduced after consideration of the full circumstances of the case including any hardship likely to arise from enforcement of a requirement to repay;

(b) in the case of *annual payments:* the offeror should be required to honour the next payment due under the agreement, after which further payments should cease.

Partial damage

45. The agreement should also provide for the possibility that partial damage to the land may occur. In such cases it should be open to the offeror to terminate the agreement on terms as in paragraphs 43 and 44 above suitably modified; and to offer to enter into a new management agreement in respect of the changed situation.

Renewal of Agreement

46. *Two years* before an agreement with a fixed termination date is due to expire, the offeror should initiate negotiations about possible renewal, *and should in all cases inform the offeree at least one year before expiry whether the offeror wishes, in principle, to renew the agreement.*

---

[1] An agreement operating in perpetuity should be treated as if it were for a period of 60 years for this purpose.
[2] Or corporation tax in respect of a capital gain.
[3] In Scotland, arbiter.

Capital Taxation

47. Various fiscal reliefs are available to owners of heritage land. These are explained in detail in the explanatory memorandum "Capital Taxation and the National Heritage" (issued by the Treasury in December 1980 and soon to be revised). In particular conditional exemption from capital transfer tax may be given in respect of land of outstanding scenic, historic or scientific interest; and such land may be designated if a maintenance fund is set up to provide for its upkeep and the provision of public access. If land is conditionally exempted or designated the owner is statutorily required to give undertakings that reasonable steps will be taken for the maintenance of the land and the preservation of its character and for securing reasonable public access. These undertakings will normally impose broadly the same restrictions on land use as a management agreement because both are designed to secure the same general heritage objectives.

48. Accordingly, management agreements should require the offeree to notify the authority with which the agreement was concluded of the granting of conditional exemption or designation in respect of land which is subject to a management agreement, and such agreements (whether made with an owner, a tenant or both) should provide for their termination on the date from which conditional exemption or designation is granted: *annual payment* under the agreement should thereby cease from that date; in the case of an agreement based on *lump sum* payment partial recoupment of the sum expended should be effected in accordance with the provisions of paragraph 43 above. If conditional exemption or designation relates to only part of an area of land which is the subject of a management agreement, or if the conditions of the management agreement were more onerous than the statutory undertakings, fresh agreements should be negotiated accordingly, with recourse to arbitration in the event of dispute. Agreements should also provide for renegotiation in the case of conditional exemption or designation being withdrawn since in that event the statutory undertakings will no longer apply.

49. *Position of tenants:* Where a landlord gains conditional exemption or designation in respect of his land it will clearly be necessary for him to secure the undertakings he is required to give in return by an agreement or arrangement with his tenant. Such an agreement or arrangement will no doubt take account of the financial implications of the restrictions imposed on the tenant's use of the land by the undertakings given for conditional exemption or designation. This applies equally whether the land has been subject to a management agreement or not.

FORESTRY OPERATIONS

1. Conditions which may be sought on forestry operations are likely to fall into the following main categories:

    (a) *Outright prohibition*
        —Planting of bare land
        —Felling of woodland

    The prohibition should be for a stated number of years.

    (b) *Modification of management practices*
        —New planting and restocking (eg choice of species)
        —Maintenance operations (eg application of fertiliser)
        —Clearfelling (eg design of coups)

    Modifications may apply throughout the whole crop rotation or only to part of it.

2. The Forestry Commission will advise the offeror whether forestry grant would have been payable in the circumstances of the application and, if so, the rate of grant for which the proposed operation would have qualified. This information should be taken into account in assessing the financial terms of the management agreement.

3. *Lump sums* should be determined by individual assessments of net revenue forgone based generally on a comparison of *discounted streams of expenditure and income over the appropriate period* and calculated (a) with, and (b) without, the constraints imposed by the management agreement. The rate of discount should be set in real terms and be that generally used by woodland owners in calculating present worth as agreed between the representative body for private forestry and the Nature Conservancy Council.

4. Alternatively the offeree may elect to receive payment based on the *depreciation in value* of the land or woodlands concerned. Payment should be calculated having regard to the rules for assessment in respect of the compulsory acquisition of an interest in land, as set out in Section 5 of the Land Compensation Act 1961[1] so far as applicable and subject to any necessary modifications.

5. Where *annual payments* are required, these should be derived from the lump sum (calculated as in paragraph 3 above) rentalised (amortised) to produce a flow of annual payments based on an estimate of current market rates of interest over the period of the management agreement.

6. Because of the wide variability in circumstances, payment based on a *standard sum* is not appropriate for conditions placed on forestry operations.

7. Forms will be available from the Nature Conservancy Council.

8. The general provisions of the guidance in relation to wider agreements, landlords and tenants, mortgagees, minimising loss, short-term agreements, phasing in of proposed operations, professional fees and other costs, abortive negotiations, the formal offer, arbitration, commencement of agreement, breach or voiding of agreement, renewal of agreement and capital taxation, apply equally to forestry as they do to agricultural operations.

---

[1] In Scotland, Section 12 of the Land Compensation (Scotland) Act 1963.

ANNEX B

LUMP SUM PAYMENT

The owner should provide full details of the land over which restrictions are proposed (including its area) and should state the sum which he wishes to claim as payment for the agreement. Information should, if possible, be supplied to the offeror within one month of being requested and should include the following:—

(a) Interest in the land—whether freehold[1] or leased; the terms of any tenancy agreement; rent passing; and date of the last rent review;

(b) details of restrictions, easements[2] or rights of way affecting the land; and of any land charges and mineral rights;

(c) Names and addresses of professional advisers acting for the offeree.

Brief details should also be given of any adjoining land which the offeree holds (including a plan of the total holding). The offeror may, in addition, request such other relevant information as considered necessary.

---

[1] In Scotland, dominium utile.
[2] In Scotland, servitudes.

ANNUAL PAYMENTS FOR NET PROFITS FORGONE

1.   If the owner or occupier chooses individual assessment, then he should provide the offeror, if possible within one month of being requested, with the required information as set out in the following forms. In addition, he should supply:

— A plan showing the total area farmed by him, including the area proposed for improvement;

— If requested by the offeror, confirmation of his financial ability to carry out the proposed operation: eg a bank manager's letter;

— Any other relevant information that the offeror may request.

2.   The offeror will either accept the sum claimed or enter into negotiations with the offeree.

3.   The information given in the forms should be as complete as possible because it will form the basis for negotiations. Nevertheless, other factors may emerge which will need to be included.

IN CONFIDENCE

Information submitted in support of a claim for annual payments based on an individual assessment of net profits forgone.

I claim the sum of £ .... as detailed in Part 5 of this form

Signed... Date..............................

Information on the claimant

Full name...

Address:.. Postcode.......................

If the address of your farm is different, please enter it here ....

.... Postcode.......................

Please give the name(s) and address(es) of your professional adviser(s)...................................

....

.... Postcode(s)....................

Is your interest in the land freehold* ☐ or leasehold ☐ ? *(Please tick the appropriate box).*

If you lease the land, state the name and address of your landlord, the terms of tenancy, rent passing and date of last review; and confirm that the landlord has been notified as required by paragraph 7 of the guidance...

....

....

....

Please detail any restrictions, easements† or rights of way affecting the land

....

Please detail any land charges or mineral rights ....

....

In Scotland:* = dominium utile. † = servitudes.

County (in Scotland, Region)..

1—Information on current crops, livestock and labour

Please complete these summaries of the cropping area, number of livestock and labour engaged for the whole farm.

Crops, etc	Hectares*
Wheat	
Barley	
Oats	
Other cash crops (please specify)	
Permanent grass	
Temporary grass	
Fodder crops	
Total crops and grass	
Rough grazing	
Buildings, Roads, Woodlands etc.	
Total farm area	

Stock	Number
Dairy cows	
Beef cows	
Beef heifers	
Fattening/rearing cattle	
Ewes	
Sows	
Fattening pigs (over 20kg)	
Laying hens	
Broilers	
Other stock (please specify)	

Labour	Number
Farmers and partners	
Farmers' and partners' spouses doing farmwork	
Regular full-time workers	
Regular part-time workers	
Seasonal and casual workers	

*1 acre = 0.40 hectares

2—Description of the current situation and the proposed improvement

---

What is the extent of the area you propose to improve?

| 10 | hectares* |

1 acre = 0.40 hectares

Please describe:

—The current situation (*eg "The area is mainly rough grazing (mostly heather), supporting about 50 ewes and lambs throughout the summer. Lambs are sold as stores"*)

> Low lying permanent pasture at present supporting about 13 Spring calving suckler cows.

—The proposed improvement (*eg "The area is to be drained, limed, fertilised and reseeded"*)

> Area to be drained, ploughed and sown to winter wheat.

—The proposed practice after improvement (*eg "the stocking rate would be raised to 200 ewes during the summer. Lambs would still be sold as stores"*)

> Cereal growing, other arable crops, rotational grass as deemed necessary.

3—Annual financial effect of the proposed improvement.

Include all revenue and cost changes (variable and fixed) which would be expected as a result of the improvement. Use current values and costs.

If there are substantial year by year differences (eg because of phasing of improvements) **use a fresh sheet for each year.** The final sheet should reflect the full effects.

Budget for 19...................

Extra Variable and Operating Costs

Number and type of Units eg 2 tonnes compound fertilizer	Cost/Unit £	Total Cost £
1.6t seed	230/t	368
1500 kg N	0.32/ha	480
400 kg P$_2$O$_5$	0.33/ha	132
400 kg K$_2$O	0.17/ha	68
Herbicide and fungicide sprays	34/ha	340
Extra fuel and repairs	15/ha	150*
Total		1538 **(a)**

Extra Revenue

Number and type of Units eg 10 heifers	Value/Unit £	Total Revenue £
54t wheat	109/tonne	5886
Total		5886 **(c)**

*In this example it is assumed that extra labour and machinery costs are minimal. These costs could be substantially greater, particularly if these resources cannot be provided from the existing farm system.

Revenue Forgone

Number and type of Units eg 10 lambs	Value/Unit £	Total Revenue £
12.5 calves	290/head	3625
Brucellosis incentive (13)	5/head	65
Suckler cow premium (13)	12.37/head	161
2 cull cows	260/head	520
Total		4371 **(b)**

Variable and Operating Costs Saved

Number and type of Units eg 200 kg N	Value/Unit £	Total Cost £
2 repl. heifers	500/head	1000
2t feed (cows)	142/t	284
1.4t creepfeed	108/t	151
11t straw	16/t	176
Vet etc	17/head	221
Forage (fert)	57/ha	570
Total		2402 **(d)**

Annual Benefit from Proposed Improvements (before fixed cost adjustment)

$(c + d) - (a + b) = £\underline{\quad 2379 \quad}$ **(A)**

4—Capital requirements of the improvement *(if any)*

Please give details of any additional capital expenditure for buildings, drainage, fencing, machinery etc.

No	Description	Gross unit Cost (£)	Total Cost £ Gross	Total Cost £ Net of Grant	*Annual Charge Factor	Annual Charge Net of Grant £
10ha	Land drainage	750/ha	7500	4688	0.163	764
	Interest on Extra Tenant-type Capital					
13	Suckler cows sold (capital released)	350/head		-4550		
	Working capital released: ie the difference between 2402 (Box 3d) and 1538 (Box 3a) (A cash flow would provide more precise figures).			- 864		
				-5414	0.10	-541
	Total					223 **(B)**

5—Amount claimed

Estimated Net Annual Profits Forgone

A – B = £_____2156_____ **(C)**

*The multiplying factor used should reflect the economic life of the item and the appropriate interest rate: eg the factor is 0.163 for an item with a 10 year life at 10% interest.

INDEX

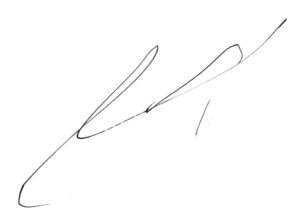

B P D Denyer-Green
LL.M., FRICS,
Barrister

Barry Denyer-Green is a member of the Land Agency and Agriculture Division of the Institution (Percy Wilkinson and Beadle Prizeman); he has the LL.B. (Hons) and LL.M. degrees of the University of London. His experience includes professional practice and teaching and lecturing for Kingston Polytechnic, the College of Estate Management and CALUS.

He has written two other books: *Compulsory Purchase and Compensation* (1980) and *Development and Planning Law* (1982), both published by the Estates Gazette Ltd.